Number 124
Winter 2009

New Directions for Evaluation

Sandra Mathison
Editor-in-Chief

Knowledge Utilization, Diffusion, Implementation, Transfer, and Translation: Implications for Evaluation

Judith M. Ottoson
Penelope Hawe
Editors

KNOWLEDGE UTILIZATION, DIFFUSION, IMPLEMENTATION, TRANSFER, AND
TRANSLATION: IMPLICATIONS FOR EVALUATION
Judith M. Ottoson, Penelope Hawe (eds.)
New Directions for Evaluation, no. 124
Sandra Mathison, Editor-in-Chief

Microfilm copies of issues and articles are available in 16mm and 35mm,
as well as microfiche in 105mm, through University Microfilms Inc., 300
North Zeeb Road, Ann Arbor, Michigan 48106-1346.

New Directions for Evaluation is indexed in Cambridge Scientific Abstracts
(CSA/CIG), Contents Pages in Education (T & F), Educational Research
Abstracts Online (T & F), ERIC Database (Education Resources
Information Center), Higher Education Abstracts (Claremont Graduate
University), Social Services Abstracts (CSA/CIG), Sociological Abstracts
(CSA/CIG), and Worldwide Political Sciences Abstracts (CSA/CIG).

NEW DIRECTIONS FOR EVALUATION (ISSN 1097-6736, electronic ISSN
1534-875X) is part of The Jossey-Bass Education Series and is published
quarterly by Wiley Subscription Services, Inc., A Wiley Company, at
Jossey-Bass, 989 Market Street, San Francisco, California 94103-1741.

SUBSCRIPTIONS cost $85 for U.S./Canada/Mexico; $109 international.
For institutions, agencies, and libraries, $256 U.S.; $296 Canada/Mexico;
$330 international. Prices subject to change.

EDITORIAL CORRESPONDENCE should be addressed to the Editor-in-Chief,
Sandra Mathison, University of British Columbia, 2125 Main Mall,
Vancouver, BC V6T 1Z4, Canada.

www.josseybass.com

Editorial Policy and Procedures

New Directions for Evaluation, a quarterly sourcebook, is an official publication of the American Evaluation Association. The journal publishes empirical, methodological, and theoretical works on all aspects of evaluation. A reflective approach to evaluation is an essential strand to be woven through every issue. The editors encourage issues that have one of three foci: (1) craft issues that present approaches, methods, or techniques that can be applied in evaluation practice, such as the use of templates, case studies, or survey research; (2) professional issues that present topics of import for the field of evaluation, such as utilization of evaluation or locus of evaluation capacity; (3) societal issues that draw out the implications of intellectual, social, or cultural developments for the field of evaluation, such as the women's movement, communitarianism, or multiculturalism. A wide range of substantive domains is appropriate for *New Directions for Evaluation;* however, the domains must be of interest to a large audience within the field of evaluation. We encourage a diversity of perspectives and experiences within each issue, as well as creative bridges between evaluation and other sectors of our collective lives.

The editors do not consider or publish unsolicited single manuscripts. Each issue of the journal is devoted to a single topic, with contributions solicited, organized, reviewed, and edited by a guest editor. Issues may take any of several forms, such as a series of related chapters, a debate, or a long article followed by brief critical commentaries. In all cases, the proposals must follow a specific format, which can be obtained from the editor-in-chief. These proposals are sent to members of the editorial board and to relevant substantive experts for peer review. The process may result in acceptance, a recommendation to revise and resubmit, or rejection. However, the editors are committed to working constructively with potential guest editors to help them develop acceptable proposals.

Sandra Mathison, Editor-in-Chief
University of British Columbia
2125 Main Mall
Vancouver, BC V6T 1Z4
CANADA
e-mail: nde@eval.org

CONTENTS

FOREWORD

Judith M. Ottoson and Penelope Hawe, the editors of this issue of *New Directions for Evaluation*, provide an informative, content-rich introduction that sets the direction for the issue. As author of this Foreword, I am probably well advised just to get out of its way. But having been invited to the banquet, I feel duty bound to offer a few observations.

It is no longer original to say that evaluators should consider the potential use of their study when they design and conduct it. The design of the evaluation is likely to have a big influence on who pays attention to its findings and what, if anything, they will do with them. The evaluator can help to shape the audience and the audience's responsiveness to the study through the attention she gives to alternative designs, measures, duration of study, controls, contextual variables, and so on. If she wants the study to impress a government sponsor, she may put a lot of emphasis on randomized design. If she wants to help a struggling agency attract community support, her priorities will probably be elsewhere.

We know that. What this issue does is team up knowledge utilization with related theories of diffusion, transfer, implementation, and translation to provide multiple lenses on the processes of change and extract implications for evaluation practice. Scattered across the literature and often used interchangeably in discourse, these theories have different roots, assumptions, change levers, and implied paths and criteria of success. Beyond digging into the individual theories, the authors work to integrate them. To be even more relevant, they apply insights to the evaluation of the same program or case study. These discussions illustrate the ways that multiple concepts about change can affect the way that evaluations are formulated, implemented, and judged.

Judith M. Ottoson was a student of mine longer ago than either of us cares to say. It is exciting for any teacher to see the fine work that a former student performs. In this case, students of my one-time student are major contributors. I look on them as my grandstudents. In this issue they have formed a partnership with coeditor Penelope Hawe and her student and colleagues and collectively fashioned a provocative and useful discussion.

Carol Hirschon Weiss

CAROL HIRSCHON WEISS is emerita professor of education at Harvard University.

NEW DIRECTIONS FOR EVALUATION, no. 124, Winter 2009 © Wiley Periodicals, Inc., and the American Evaluation Association.

EDITORS' NOTES

This issue of *New Directions for Evaluation* explores the role of selected change theories in evaluation—knowledge utilization, diffusion, implementation, transfer, and translation—and applies them to complex interventions in both theory and practice using a case study. The ideas for this comparative study were initially presented at the American Evaluation Association in Atlanta, Georgia, in November 2004. Subsequently a theory of translation was added and the ideas developed into what you will read in this issue. To the best of our knowledge, this is the first time these five knowledge-for-action theories have shared the same table of contents and been explored together for their evaluation implications.

It is important to make our rationale clear. Our purpose is not to do better evaluation of knowledge translation, or utilization, or any of the theories contained here. Rather our purpose is to ask *what can be learned from each of these theories that would benefit any evaluation*? How does, say, a diffusion lens or an implementation lens sensitize evaluators to the mechanisms and impacts of change processes?

Chapter 1 sets forth the case for studying these selected theories, and then summarizes and compares them. Chapters 2 through 6 offer literature reviews of the selected theories. Each chapter identifies key models, variables, and concepts of that theory and applies those ideas to a single case study. Although many underlying concepts in these theories overlap, the chapters highlight the value added that is unique to each theory. Chapter 7 adds a complexity lens to the mix. This new frontier invites evaluators to think differently—in particular, to consider how the dynamics of the preexisting context amplify or stifle change processes.

The chapter authors took a tiered approach to understanding the theories in this issue. First, the authors of Chapters 2 through 6 researched one of five knowledge-for-action theories introduced in Chapter 1. A jointly developed and evolving framework guided each chapter's literature search over time. Common areas of exploration included disciplinary roots, constructs, definitions, stakeholders, context, and "what" moves and "how." The international perspectives brought by authors, albeit from selected

An award from the Canadian Institutes of Health Research, Institute of Population and Public Health to establish the International Collaboration on Complex Interventions, enabled Judith M. Ottoson and Penelope Hawe to work on this issue of *New Directions for Evaluation*.

Western countries, offered an additional dimension to the review and case study application. Each chapter was reviewed externally by an expert in that knowledge-for-action theory.

A second analytical tier, cross-process reviews by chapter authors and editors, inevitably led to invidious comparisons among the theories. Included among these were perceived misunderstandings and stereotyping among theories. These debatable comparisons were allowed to stand. For example, we did not "correct" a translation theory perspective on how it differs from transfer theory. This allowed within-theory assumptions to be transparent and contribute to a broader discussion among these theories.

A third analytical tier was the use of a case study to emphasize the lessons authors drew from each theory. The Gatehouse Project (see the box) was a whole-school organizational development intervention targeting adolescent social inclusion and well-being. Each chapter author was asked to illustrate a unique or prominent feature of the theory she reviewed by demonstrating what it would add if she used that theory to guide evaluation design of the Gatehouse Project. To that end, Chapter 2 explores how a knowledge utilization lens sharpens the focus on what counts as use; Chapter 3 uses diffusion theory to describe three selective uptakes of an innovation; Chapter 4 uses implementation theory to illuminate evaluation approaches to networked structures; Chapter 5 analyzes program replication as a transfer process; and Chapter 6 explores the use of a knowledge translation to inform evaluation.

We thank Carole Estabrooks, Lawrence W. Green, Trisha Greenhalgh, Ken McLeroy, Mary Ann Scheirer, and Alan Shiell for their review of individual chapters. We thank Sandra Mathison for her wise counsel and patience. We could not have completed this without the keen eye, skill, and support of Lindsay Bradshaw. Our journey on completing this issue itself has been a statement of the complexities of process. To that end, we acknowledge the relocations, graduations, and promotions encountered; the spouses and partners who have joined us; and the children who multiplied our team. Thank you all.

A School-Based Evaluation Case Study: The Gatehouse Project

The Gatehouse Project was a multilevel school-based project to improve the emotional well-being of adolescents by increasing their connectedness to school. The project was a cluster randomized trial conducted in Victoria, Australia. Twenty-six schools were allocated to the intervention or the control group (the usual practice).

The intervention focused on increasing students' skills and knowledge for dealing with everyday life challenges through all aspects of the curriculum, alongside a whole-school component, which sought to make

changes to the schools' social and learning environment. The central
idea was to make all students feel safe, connected, and valued. The
intervention adopted a survey-feedback-action-survey sequence.
A full-time facilitator was shared among every three schools. Within
each school, a school-based action team (made up of students, teachers, and parents) used the local data to review the school environment
and drive change. This might include, for example, improved practices to orient and welcome new students, more activities to draw parents into the school, and teaching and talking about emotions and
feelings and how to handle them through the discussion of plots
and characters in English literature texts (as an alternative to teaching this subject matter directly in health classes).

After 2 years, the project showed an unprecedented effect: reductions in drug use, tobacco use, and alcohol intake. This was achieved
by focusing entirely on social inclusion; no extra lessons on tobacco,
alcohol, or drugs were given (Glover & Butler, 2004; Patton, Bond,
Butler, & Glover, 2003; Patton et al., 2006).

References

Glover, S., & Butler, H. (2004). Facilitating health promotion within school communities. In R. Moodie & A. Hulme (Eds.), *Hands-on health promotion*. Melbourne: IP Communications.

Patton, G. C., Bond, L., Butler, H., & Glover, S. (2003). Changing schools, changing
health? The design and implementation of the Gatehouse Project. *Journal of Adolescent Health, 33*, 231–239.

Patton, G. C., Bond, L., Carlin, J. B., Thomas, L., Butler, H., & Glover, S., et al. (2006).
Promoting social inclusion in schools: A group randomized trial of effects on student
risk behaviors. *American Journal of Public Health, 96*(9), 1582–1588.

Judith M. Ottoson
Penelope Hawe
Editors

*JUDITH M. OTTOSON is an independent evaluation consultant and an adjunct
lecturer at San Francisco State University. She initiated this project when
she was an associate professor at the Andrew Young School of Policy Studies,
Georgia State University, Atlanta.*

*PENELOPE HAWE is the Markin Chair in Health and Society at the University of
Calgary and director of the Population Health Intervention Research Centre.
She holds a health scientist award from the Alberta Heritage Foundation for
Medical Research.*

Ottoson, J. M. (2009). Knowledge-for-action theories in evaluation: Knowledge utilization, diffusion, implementation, transfer, and translation. In J. M. Ottoson & P. Hawe (Eds.), *Knowledge utilization, diffusion, implementation, transfer, and translation: Implications for evaluation. New Directions for Evaluation, 124,* 7–20.

1

Knowledge-for-Action Theories in Evaluation: Knowledge Utilization, Diffusion, Implementation, Transfer, and Translation

Judith M. Ottoson

Abstract

Five knowledge-for-action theories are summarized and compared in this chapter for their evaluation implications: knowledge utilization, diffusion, implementation, transfer, and translation. Usually dispersed across multiple fields and disciplines, these theories are gathered here for a common focus on knowledge and change. Knowledge in some form (ideas, innovation, skills, or policy) moves in some direction (laterally, hierarchically, spreads, or exchanges) among various stakeholders (knowledge producers, end users, or intermediaries) and contexts (national, community, or organizational) to achieve some outcomes (intended benefits, unanticipated outcomes, or hijacked effects). Although rooted in different disciplines, sensitive to different key indicators, and following different process paths, these theories individually and collectively provide multiple lenses on the evaluation of complex interventions. A table compares key theory points of disciplinary roots, type of knowledge, movement of knowledge, contextual influences, and the added lens of each theory. These lenses are used to analyze the set of theories for evaluation implications. © Wiley Periodicals, Inc., and the American Evaluation Association.

NEW DIRECTIONS FOR EVALUATION, no. 124, Winter 2009 © Wiley Periodicals, Inc., and the American Evaluation Association. Published online in Wiley InterScience (www.interscience.wiley.com) • DOI: 10.1002/ev.310

This chapter begins with a practice-based evaluation dilemma: how to assess the outcomes of a nationwide public health intervention. Although the intended outcome of this intervention was substance abuse reduction, the dilemma will be familiar to many evaluators. The intervention consisted of 31 types of training programs, conducted at 249 separate sites, by multiple providers, with approximately 9,500 participants, over a 5-year period. There was no one outcome or stakeholder to answer questions about intended effects of this complex intervention. What was to count as success? Who would decide?

Hunting down objectives for individual programs did little to answer broader questions about intervention effects. Somewhere in the process, however, it became clear that a number of overlying theories about change (some explicit, others implicit) not only shaped where outcomes were sought, but whether stakeholders valued those outcomes. For example, funders wanted to know whether intended beneficiaries used knowledge gained from program participation. Knowledge utilization theory offered guidance on understanding the parameters of use, but other theories were needed to understand issues of fidelity, power, language, and knowledge movement. Did learning move as intended from the training site to the community context, or did it morph into alternative, adapted skills (transfer theory)? Did intended beneficiaries have the authority or opportunity to use a new skill (implementation theory)? Were ideas translated into actionable messages for intended beneficiaries (translation theory)? If intended beneficiaries shared but did not use their program experience, does that spread of knowledge count as nonuse or success (diffusion theory)?

To answer these questions, this chapter offers a summary review of individual theories and applies that knowledge to comparisons among and between theories and their implications for program evaluation.

Knowledge-for-Action Theories

Five knowledge-for-action theories or processes are the focus of this chapter: knowledge utilization, diffusion, implementation, transfer, and translation. Each of these theories offers evaluators an added lens to view program and policy process and outcomes (Ottoson, 1997). But, first, a few more questions: Are these theories? Why these five? Why the knowledge-for-action moniker? How can they benefit evaluation?

Theory is used here with a small "t" as "a set of beliefs that underlie action" (Weiss, 1998a, p. 55). The five selected theories all focus on knowledge and change. Knowledge in some form (ideas, innovation, skills, or policy) moves in some direction (laterally, hierarchically, spreads, or exchanges) among various stakeholders (knowledge producers, end users, or intermediaries) and contexts (national, community, or organizational) to achieve some outcomes (intended benefits, unanticipated outcomes, or hijacked effects). These theories are collectively referred to here by their intent and movement of knowledge as *knowledge-for-action*. Others have used this label and multiple other terms to describe the movement of knowledge into action (Argyis, 1993; Graham et al., 2006). Limited by space, these five theories were picked because they have history, literature, practical applications, disciplinary support, and, in some cases, legal or professional requirements. They stand in contrast to other kinds of processes, such as "application," which is a commonly used term but a poorly studied process (Ottoson, 1995).

It is time these various understandings of change met as subheadings in the same chapter. While many of these processes acknowledge roots in knowledge utilization, it is not clear that knowledge utilization reciprocates awareness of its extended family. The intent in this effort is not to promote or improve the evaluation of any individual knowledge-for-action theory, such as doing better transfer evaluation; rather, the intent is to understand these theories, individually and collectively, in ways that would benefit any evaluation. For example, what can be learned from transfer theory that would benefit any evaluation? These theories have commonalities and differences that can widen the peripheral vision and perspective of those involved in the evaluation of complex systems and processes. Taken individually or together, they explain "what the outcomes are outcomes of" (Weiss, 1998a, p. 10).

Knowledge-for-Action Theories: A Summary Review

The following summaries of individual knowledge-for-action theories identify the roots, key variables, processes, and evaluation implications that are compared in Table 1.1. These summaries set the stage for the intertheoretical exchanges that follow. The summaries draw on, but are not limited to, the in-depth discussion of knowledge utilization, diffusion, implementation, transfer, or translation theories in Chapters 2 through 6, respectively, in this issue.

Knowledge Utilization. Knowledge utilization embeds itself in both evaluation theory (Shadish, Cook, & Leviton, 1991) and program evaluation standards (Joint Committee on Standards of Educational Evaluation, 1994). Its roots lay at the intersection of science and philosophy and subsequent waves of knowledge utilization research (Backer, 1991). Early on, Weiss (1979) described multiple models of use, Patton (1997) focused on process as use, and Henry and Mark (2003) suggested a shift to focus to influence. Research knowledge is the *what* that moves in knowledge utilization theory (see Table 1.1). Models of knowledge use have been grouped by field (public policy or business), type of end user (researcher, consumer), or context (organization, society; Edwards, 1991). Key contextual influences on knowledge utilization include the roles of end users, timing, resources, social conditions, leadership, politics, and communication (Beyer & Trice, 1982; Kingdon, 2003; Landry, Amara, & Lamari, 2001; Yin & Gwaltney, 1981).

Table 1.1. Comparing Knowledge-for-Action Theories

Theory	Roots	What Moves?	How?	Key Influences on Process	Added Lens	Evaluation Implications
Knowledge utilization	Intersection of science and philosophy	Research knowledge	Instrumentally Conceptually Symbolically As process	Time Resources Support Leadership Politics	Many meanings of use, nonuse, and misuse	Value linked to meaning of use by intent, stakeholder, and context
Diffusion	Rural sociology and communication	Innovation	Innovation is communicated through channels over time among members of a social system	Innovation characteristics Social system Time Communication channels	Spread	Outcomes link to adoption curve Innovation may be adapted
Implementation	Political science and public administration	Policy Program	Top down Bottom up Contingency Democratic Networked	Policy Context Stakeholders Politics, power Values Administration	Sociopolitical factors Feasibility	System influences Value transparency Contribution Process matters
Transfer	Science and technology	Learning Technology Policy	Mechanisms such as training, implementing, diffusing, or marketing	What moves Mechanism Context	Direction of movement Comparability of contexts	Initial and final *what* are comparable
Translation	Linguistics and communication	Research products or syntheses	Communication Ongoing interaction and exchange	Stakeholders Politics, power Commitment Capacity Communication	Language	Sustain stakeholders Informed decisions Outcome link

To engage the knowledge utilization lens effectively, evaluators need to understand the parameters of use in context and to be savvy about how knowledge engages in practice. "Did they use it?" is too simplistic a question.

Diffusion. In contrast to knowledge utilization, diffusion evolved toward a more unified theory and definition (Tornatzky & Fleischer, 1990) across multiple disciplines (Green & Johnson, 1996). Rooted in communications theory, diffusion is understood to be "the process by which an *innovation* is *communicated* through certain *channels* over *time* among the members of a *social system*" (Rogers, 2003, p. 7). In the unifying work of Rogers (2003), the *what* that moves in diffusion is an innovation (see Table 1.1); its shape can be as diverse as a product, practice, program, policy, or idea. An S-shaped (cumulative) curve represents the uptake, acceleration, and decline of innovation adoption in a population. Innovation characteristics that influence adoption include its perceived relative advantage, compatibility, complexity, trialability, and observability. Other broad influences on diffusion are the social system, time, and communication channels. Evaluation implications emerging from diffusion theory include the concept of spread, differences in adopters over time, and innovation adaptation.

Implementation. "Implementation is an iterative process, in which ideas expressed as policy, are transformed into behavior, expressed as social action" (Ottoson & Green, 1987, p. 362). Rooted in political science and public administration, implementation reflects a stage in the policy process sandwiched between policy development and policy impact. The *what* that moves in implementation is a policy or program (see Table 1.1). Implementation models and theories have variously described this process as bottom up, top down, contingency, democratic, or networked (Goggin, Bowman, Lester, & O'Toole, 1990; O'Toole, 2000). In their classic tale of implementation, Pressman & Wildavsky (1984) describe how policy changes as it engages multiple contexts, organizations, and stakeholders reflecting varied agendas, value differences, administrative practices, and politics. Continuing and contemporary challenges to macrolevel policy implementation include economic downturns, political shifts, and networked governance. Implementation adds a sociopolitical lens to evaluation, with special attention to power differentials among stakeholders and its implication for negotiating value in a transparent and democratic process.

Transfer. The diverse transfer literature spans multiple disciplines, fields, professions, and contexts. Transfer is both a ubiquitous and ambiguous concept. Evaluators using this lens need to consider three components central to any transfer process: the *what*, the context, and the mechanisms of transfer (see Table 1.1). The *what* that transfers might be a product, process, idea, skill, know-how, best practice, regulation, research, or policy (Bozeman, 1988; Haskell, 2001; Mossberger & Harold, 2003). The context of origin shapes *what* transfers and the context of application whether and how what is transferred engages in a new setting. For example, in learning transfer, key contextual variables include learner characteristics, the work site, and pedagogy (Baldwin & Ford, 1988); in technology transfer, key variables are location, economics, and mission (Bozeman, 2000). Transfer movement is most often described as unidirectional, but the direction also might be lateral or hierarchical. The movement or mechanism of transfer may involve other change processes; for example, learning may transfer by the mechanism of training, or policy may transfer by the mechanism of implementation.

Translation. With roots in applied linguistics and communication, knowledge translation is a transdisciplinary, multilevel knowledge-for-action theory. In the recent explosion of knowledge translation literature (Tugwell, Robinson, Grimshaw, & Santesso, 2006), translation has been conceptualized as the practice, science, and art of bridging the "know-do gap" between knowledge accumulation and use (World Health Organization, 2006). The *what* that moves in knowledge translation is research products or synthesis (see Table 1.1). Knowledge translation assumes a path that has been variously described as multidirectional, circular, or iterative; however, its stages or situations are described by some as unidirectional, for example, knowledge translation from basic to applied research (Hiss, 2004). The research-initiated messages of this communications-driven process are translated with stakeholders through a complex set of interactions, including synthesizing research, developing actionable messages, improving practitioner or public awareness, and adapting and reporting findings to multiple audiences and contexts. Fidelity is not a key determinant of translation success.

Added Lenses and Implications for Evaluation

From individual theory summaries, this chapter now turns to cross-theory comparisons using the added lenses introduced in Table 1.1. By virtue of their emphasis, uniqueness, research, or roots, these lenses add in-depth understandings of selected components of the change process. The following discussion explores common and disparate ground among theories and the evaluation implications for the set of theories.

Translation Theory Adds the Lens of Language. In practice, these various terms, such as *transfer* or *use,* are tossed around continuously, informally, and often lightly. Translation theory reminds us that language matters. For example, one stakeholder's "transfer" might be another stakeholder's "implementation." These terms mean something, and evaluations benefit when that meaning is understood and shared in context.

All of these knowledge-for-action theories evolved over time. Such evolution includes adding, expanding, or sharpening theoretical constructs. Examples include the movement from instrumental to conceptual understandings of use (Weiss, 1998b), the addition of an implementation phase to the innovation adoption process of diffusion, and the increasing role of context in transfer theory. For some theories, such as implementation, evolution has meant waxing, waning, and morphing over time in levels of interest, disciplinary commitment, and focus. While some theories evolved, new ones, such as translation, were born. To know a theory at one point in time and use that experience and language to embrace or to stereotype it henceforth is fallacy. Even if the language of theory remains the same, the concepts and constructs may not.

Could any one of these theories be the overarching theory to all others? While knowledge utilization may attempt to float off with the umbrella metaphor (Backer, 1991), it is not without challenges. The roots, the concepts, the language, and the culture around these theories show them to be related but not synonymous. Multiple theoretical umbrellas covering different aspects of a change process may be a more apt metaphor than one umbrella covering all.

Not only is an umbrella a problematic metaphor among theories, it is a problematic metaphor within theories. Diffusion, with its synthesizing work by Rogers (2003), probably comes closer to having a unified theory and common conceptual model than any of the other theories. The other four knowledge-for-action theories comprise multiple, even competing, theories that may be comprehensive, context driven, variable illuminating, or field specific. While some lament the lack of unifying theory, others reject or lament the idea of a single theory as antithetical to context-specific change (Estabrooks, Thompson, Lovely, & Hofmeyer, 2006).

Despite differences, commonalities exist among theories. For example, an instrumental understanding of knowledge utilization, early transfer theory, and top-down implementation all use fidelity as a criterion of success, that is, knowledge, technology, or policy is unchanged by context. In contrast, a symbolic understanding of knowledge utilization and a bottom-up view of implementation theory share a political understanding of change that includes knowledge and policy adaptation as part of a definition of success. Furthermore, bottom-up implementation and translation theory share a common interest in early stakeholder involvement in the change process and local relevance.

The commonalities, the differences, and the crossovers make the translation, interpretation, and retranslation of these theories a process in itself. The evolution of these theories can result in greater commonalities among the theories than within them. Language matters, and so does meaning in context.

Transfer and Diffusion Theories Add the Lens of Movement. The five selected theories all consider how knowledge moves among various stakeholders and contexts to achieve outcomes. Transfer theory adds multiple views on linear point A to point B movement, and diffusion adds the concept of spread. Together these theories sharpen the lenses on what moves, where it moves, the pattern of movement, the context of movement, and key influences on movement.

What Moves. Table 1.1 summarizes the *what* that moves in each of these theories that shapes the change process and outcomes. Understanding the *what* is consistent with evaluation theory about the need to understand the evaluand before marshaling value indicators and knowledge construction procedures. The evaluand shapes process and outcomes.

How It Moves. Movement of the *what* might be one-way, bidirectional, multidirectional, or some combination of these. Lateral and hierarchical concepts of movement may be as much about power as they are about structure. Early knowledge utilization, implementation, and transfer theories emphasized one-way, top-down movement. Researchers, politicians, or entrepreneurs created knowledge, policy, or technology that moved to intended beneficiaries. Later theories of bottom-up or evolutionary implementation and participatory research tended to keep the one-way focus, but turned the process on its head by moving the *what* from the community or consumers to researchers and politicians. Translation theory purports a bidirectional approach with knowledge created at multiple points. Diffusion and networked approaches to implementation go beyond the "from-to" movement to the concept of spread or the metaphor of a web. Keeping an eye on such dizzying movement requires that evaluators use more than one pair of lenses. For example, evaluating a bottom-up innovation that became a top-down policy before diffusing to other sites required a broader lens than any one theory could offer (Hubbard & Ottoson, 1997).

Context of Movement. In a contemporary understanding of all these theories, context matters. It shapes process and outcomes. General contextual variables that cut across these theories include timing, location, opportunity, resources, social support, leadership, organizational structures, politics, and communication. Transfer theory assumes that the comparability between starting and ending contexts aids transfer. Implementation and translation theories anticipate contextual differences and influences in shaping what moves. Diffusion theory considers how contextual factors, including social norms, affect decision making about innovation adoption. No matter how new the innovation, rigorous the knowledge production, or savvy the policy, context has the potential to shape it, sink it, or salvage it. Evaluators need to work with stakeholders to identify and account for contextual influences.

Key Stakeholders. Determination of the priority end users and intermediaries is shaped by theory. The priority end user for knowledge utilization is the decision maker; for diffusion, the priority end user is the adopter, which changes over time; for implementation, the priority end user is the intended beneficiary; for transfer, the priority end user is the consumer, organization, or country; and for translation, the priority end user might be one of the six P's: public, patient, press, practitioner, policymaker, or private sector (Tugwell et al., 2006). The felt need, motivation, and receptivity of end users shape whether and how knowledge, policy, or an innovation is adopted or received. To reach the end user, individual theories identify some type of intermediary or mechanism between the producers and users of knowledge. For example, diffusion has change agents and opinion leaders

(Rogers, 2003), translation suggests knowledge brokers (Lomas, 2000), and transfer describes various mechanisms. Whether and how the intermediary role is performed has the potential to shape process and outcomes.

In summary, the transfer and diffusion lenses add multiple perspectives on the complexity of change. It is not just *what* moves, how it moves, the context through which it moves, or the key stakeholders that influences the process and outcomes of programs, policies, and innovations. It is all of these combined.

Knowledge Utilization Adds the Lens of Use. All of these knowledge-for-action theories connect with use at some point. Although the *what* of knowledge utilization theory is research knowledge, this theory sharpens the lens on two key variables to consider in evaluation: timing and fidelity.

Time. The length of time it takes for the *what*—knowledge, innovation, or policy—to move from production to action has varying importance for these theories and evaluation. Timeliness or least delay (Hiss, 2004) generally is considered a good thing. Implementation theory might like quick results, but its practical side prepares for the effects of time and context on policy and program intent. As knowledge utilization theory evolved (Weiss, 1998b), the time dimension in its theories grew from a short gap into long and winding roads. Finding the link between research in one decade and informed policy change in another (Ottoson et al., 2009) changed the work of evaluation from attribution to contribution. In diffusion theory, adopters vary over time, with early adopters more likely to be social leaders, educated, and connected to an expansive network compared to late adopters, who tend to be more skeptical and have lower socioeconomic status, fewer resources, and smaller networks. In translation theory, the use or translation of ideas is conceived as an ongoing time line rather than an end-of-process event. The time dimension in these theories shapes evaluation methods, as well as key variables.

Fidelity and Valuing. How much can the *what*—knowledge, innovation, technology, or policy—change and still be considered successfully transferred, used, diffused, translated, or implemented? What counts as success from the perspective of these knowledge-for-action theories? This is a core evaluation question about valuing.

A contemporary understanding of all these theories allows for some level of change in the *what* as it moves across time, context, stakeholders, intents, and resources. These theories are awash with the realities of change. Knowledge utilization theory asks an array of value-related questions about how much of *what* is used over time, by whom, and how well. From an implementation perspective, the increasing involvement of networks ensures increasing numbers of stakeholders and competing agendas that challenge notions of fidelity and complicate valuing. Translation focuses less on changing knowledge than on changing the message, or the mode of message delivery, so that the research is accessible and understood by intended beneficiaries. Diffusion does not hold to the invariance of the innovation; rather, it anticipates adaptability to fit the context as an aid to adoption and maintenance over time. Even transfer theory, associated most closely with a fidelity stance, recognizes that change in the *what* may occur.

The extent to which fidelity is important in these various change processes depends on several factors. First, it depends on what is being moved. Fidelity concerns become increasingly anticipated as abstract ideas move toward more concrete representations of knowledge—for example, reformulated messages, packaged programs, or boxed innovations. Second, the importance of fidelity depends on stakeholder stance. The inventor, politician, or researcher who produced the innovation, policy, or knowledge may have a higher stake or expectation of fidelity than intended users, beneficiaries, or consumers, who have to figure out how to act in context. This leaves a critical role for evaluators to negotiate among stakeholders about expectations of fidelity and their role in determining success. Finally, when the time dimension is added to characteristics of what is moved and over which context, the *what* itself becomes increasingly challenging to find, let alone measure its fidelity.

Implementation Theory Adds the Social-Political Lens. With an exploration of social-political factors within each of these knowledge-for-action theories, the implementation lens sharpens a view of power, resources, and relationships within theories. No matter how strong the *what*, how well timed its arrival, how supportive the context, or how receptive the stakeholders, social-political factors can shape both the processes and outcomes of change. Who has the resources or political capital to benefit from research knowledge, the latest innovation, or changed policy? Who has the power to receive that *what* and break it, shape it, or share it? The implementation lens has particular relevance to valuing theory in evaluation. What is valued? Who decides?

While the initial impetus here was to use the implementation lens to look within knowledge-for-action theories, that lens instead is used to look at the whole set of theories themselves. What are visible through the implementation lens are not just theories; these are also movements, cultures, and institutions. The first observation is that these theories spring from different disciplines, issues, and contexts. Although they may share some common roots, these theories start with different assumptions, intent, and disciplinary perspective. Few professionals have an ecumenical education that spans all of these theories, credentialed competence in them, or the ability to break the tower of theoretical and methodological Babel down to a common language.

Added to this observation is a kind of referencing or dismissal among theories of each other. True enough, there is some intertheory referencing, particularly to use. It is the lack of references among theories, however, that exposes the gaps among them. For example, it is unclear how the knowledge brokers of the new millennium translation (Lomas, 2000) have benefited from the experiences of the linking agents who played an early role in dissemination and translation (Havelock, 1967). Unawareness is one thing, but disparaging remarks among the theories take the separation a step further. For example, diffusion theory explains that the adoption of an innovation is not necessarily "a passive role of just implementing a standard template of the new idea" (Rogers, 2003, p. 17). "Mere transfer" has been used to criticize the inadequacy of transfer theory to explain the complexities of moving learning into practice. It is hard to imagine that anyone who understood contemporary implementation or transfer theory would refer to such processes as "passive," "just," or "mere." What is going on here?

One explanation from an implementation perspective is that these theories have been institutionalized in various ways. For example, the National Institutes of Health has established the Office of Transfer Technology; the Centers for Disease Control and Prevention has established the Division of Diabetes Translation; the health administration field has launched the *Journal of Implementation Science;* Rogers's book *Diffusion of Innovations* (2003) is in its fifth edition; and the University of Alberta has established the Knowledge Utilization Studies Program. The institutionalization of these theories shows a commitment or generation of resources, legitimization, agenda setting, voice, and authority. The lens for viewing change gets set, at least for a time.

Turned on itself, the implementation lens shows the potential shelf life of these theories. The implementation boom of the 1970s dropped off by the mid-1990s when implementation was pronounced dead. By the early millennium, implementation was reborn in the health administration field. Will the current explosion of literature in translation theory follow a similar path?

Recommendations for Evaluators: Adjust the Lenses

For evaluators negotiating within and across the culture and context of the theories reviewed here, staying grounded in evaluation theory provides perspective. The additional theoretical lenses reviewed here complement evaluation theory by providing depth and perspective on the change process. Evaluations benefit when theories are exposed and understood, variables influencing change are clarified, use is revealed for all its complexities, and the context within and around change is made transparent.

Change theories inform evaluation theories of social programming, valuing, knowledge use, knowledge construction, and evaluation practice (Shadish et al., 1991). For example, "good" social program theory explains the evaluand, including the intended change process by which it proposes to contribute to social betterment. While some evaluators and stakeholders place emphasis on the outcomes of social program theory, "lenses" was deliberately chosen as a metaphor for the intent of this chapter. The change process needs to be seen, its workings visible, and the influence of process on outcomes transparent. Outcomes are not conceived in an immaculate process.

NEW DIRECTIONS FOR EVALUATION • DOI: 10.1002/ev

The values inherent in these über theories of knowledge-for-action offer what counts as success (or not) and why. They direct attention to different process indicators and outcomes. For example, success from a transfer perspective might be an intact skill moving from a training context to a work site. From a knowledge utilization perspective, this example represents instrumental use rather than conceptual use. Neither of these theories looks at knowledge spread, an indicator of success from a diffusion perspective. Together these theories help answer the difficult questions of evaluation: What will be valued? Who decides?

Evaluation practice and the use of evaluation findings are enhanced by an understanding of these not just as theories but also as supporting disciplines, professional cultures, and institutionalized perspectives. This acculturation of change shapes an understanding of key variables, stakeholders, values, and outcomes. For example, an evaluator working in a context shaped by diffusion and translation theories benefits from an understanding that use of evaluation findings is shaped by more than communication messages, language, and opinion leaders. Adding an implementation perspective sharpens an understanding of the role of context, power, and resources. Evaluators often cross multiple boundaries in their work. They are not bound to praise translation, push diffusion, or punish transfer as the only understanding of change. Our loyalties are not to any single process, but rather to understanding whether and how process unfolds and what its implications are for valuing.

Taken together, an understanding of change as theory and culture influences evaluators' understanding of process, flags key indicators, and explains use in context in ways that influence knowledge construction and evaluation practice.

References

Argyis, C. (1993). *Knowledge for action: A guide to overcoming barriers to organizational change*. Hoboken, NJ: Wiley.
Backer, T. E. (1991). Knowledge utilization: The third wave. *Knowledge: Creation, Diffusion, Utilization, 12*(3), 225–240.
Baldwin, T. T., & Ford, J. K. (1988). Transfer of training: A review and directions for further research. *Personnel Psychology, 41*(1), 63–105.
Beyer, J. M., & Trice, H. M. (1982). The utilization process: A conceptual framework and synthesis of empirical findings. *Administrative Science Quarterly, 27*, 591–622.
Bozeman, B. (1988). Evaluating technology transfer and diffusion. *Evaluation and Program Planning, 11*(1), 63–104.
Bozeman, B. (2000). Technology transfer and public policy: A review of research and theory. *Research Policy, 29*(4–5), 627–655.
Edwards, L. A. (1991). *Using knowledge and technology to improve the quality of life of people who have disabilities*. Philadelphia: Knowledge Utilization Program, Pennsylvania College of Optometry.
Estabrooks, C., Thompson, D., Lovely, J., & Hofmeyer, A. (2006). A guide to knowledge translation theory. *Journal of Continuing Education in the Health Professions, 26*, 25–36.
Goggin, M. L., Bowman, A. O., Lester, J. P., & O'Toole, L. J. (1990). *Implementation theory and practice: Toward a third generation*. Glenview, IL: Scott, Foresman.

Graham, I., Logan, J., Harrison, M., Straus, S., Tetroe, J., Caswell, W., et al. (2006). Lost in knowledge translation: Time for a map? *Journal of Continuing Education in the Health Professions, 26*, 13–24.

Green, L. W., & Johnson, J. L. (1996). Dissemination and utilization of health promotion and disease prevention knowledge: Theory, research and experience. *Canadian Journal of Public Health, 87*(Suppl. 2), 11–17.

Haskell, R. E. (2001). *Transfer of learning: Cognition, instruction, and reasoning.* Orlando, FL: Academic Press.

Havelock, R. G. (1967). *Dissemination and translation roles in education and other fields: A comparative analysis.* Ann Arbor: University of Michigan, Institute for Social Research. Retrieved October 3, 2009, from ERIC (ED015535).

Henry, G. T., & Mark, M. M. (2003). Beyond use: Understanding evaluation's influence on attitudes and actions. *American Journal of Evaluation, 24*(3), 203–314.

Hiss, R. (2004, January 12–13). *Fundamental issues in translational research.* Introductory session at the conference From Clinical Trials to Community: The Science of Translating Diabetes and Obesity Research, Bethesda, MD. Retrieved October 3, 2009, from http://www.niddk.nih.gov/fund/other/diabetes-translation/conf-publication.pdf

Hubbard, L., & Ottoson, J. M. (1997). When a bottom-up innovation meets itself as a top down policy: The AVID untracking program. *Science Communication, 19*(1), 41–55.

Joint Committee on Standards of Educational Evaluation. (1994). *The program evaluation standards* (2nd ed.). Thousand Oaks, CA: Sage.

Kingdon, J. W. (2003). *Agendas, alternatives, and public policies.* Reading, MA: Addison-Wesley.

Landry, R., Amara, N., & Lamari, M. (2001). Climbing the ladder of research utilization. *Science Communication, 122*(4), 396–422.

Lomas, J. (2000). Using "linkage and exchange" to move research into policy at a Canadian foundation. *Health Affairs, 19*(3), 236–240.

Mossberger, K., & Harold, W. (2003). Policy transfer as a form of prospective policy evaluation: Challenges and recommendations. *Public Administration Review, 63*(4), 428–440.

O'Toole, L. J. (2000). Research on policy implementation: Assessment and prospects. *Journal of Public Administration Research and Theory, 10*(2), 263–288.

Ottoson, J. M. (1995). Reclaiming the concept of application: From social to technological process and back again. *Adult Education Quarterly, 46*, 1–30.

Ottoson, J. M. (1997). Beyond transfer of training: Using multiple lenses to assess community education programs. In A. D. Rose, & M. A. Leahy (Eds.), *Assessing Adult Learning in Diverse Settings: Current Issues and Approaches* (pp. 87–96). New Directions for Adult and Continuing Education, no. 75. San Francisco: Jossey-Bass.

Ottoson, J. M., & Green, L. W. (1987). Reconciling concept and context: Theory of implementation. *Advances in Health Education and Promotion, 2*, 353–382.

Ottoson, J. M., Green, L. W., Beery, W. L., Senter, S. K., Cahill, C. L., Pearson, D. C., et al. (2009). Policy-contribution assessment and field-building analysis of the Robert Wood Johnson Foundation's Active Living Research Program. *American Journal of Preventive Medicine, 36*(2, Supplement 1), S34–S43.

Patton, M. Q. (1997). *Utilization-focused evaluation* (3rd ed.). Thousand Oaks, CA: Sage.

Pressman, J. L., & Wildavsky, A. (1984). *Implementation* (3rd ed.). Berkeley: University of California Press.

Rogers, E. (2003). *Diffusion of innovations* (5th ed.). New York: Free Press.

Shadish, W. R., Cook, T. D., & Leviton, L. C. (1991). *Foundations of program evaluation: Theories of practice.* Thousand Oaks, CA: Sage.

Tornatzky, L. G., & Fleischer, M. (1990). *The process of technological innovation.* Lanham, MD: Lexington Books.

Tugwell, P., Robinson, V., Grimshaw, J., & Santesso, N. (2006). Systematic reviews and knowledge translation. *Bulletin of the World Health Organisation, 84*, 643–651.

Weiss, C. H. (1979). The many meanings of research utilization. *Public Administration Review, 39*(5), 426–431.

Weiss, C. H. (1998a). *Evaluation* (2nd ed.). Upper Saddle River, NJ: Prentice Hall.

Weiss, C. H. (1998b). Have we learned from anything new about the use of evaluation? *American Journal of Evaluation, 19*(1), 21–33.

World Health Organization. (2006). *Bridging the "know-do" gap: Meeting on knowledge translation in global health.* Geneva: World Health Organisation.

Yin, R. K., & Gwaltney, M. K. (1981). Knowledge utilization as a networking process. *Knowledge: Creation, Diffusion, and Utilization, 2*(4), 555–580.

JUDITH M. OTTOSON is an independent evaluation consultant and an adjunct lecturer at San Francisco State University. She initiated this project when she was an associate professor at the Andrew Young School of Policy Studies, Georgia State University, Atlanta.

Blake, S. C., & Ottoson, J. M. (2009). Knowledge utilization: Implications for evaluation. In J. M. Ottoson & P. Hawe (Eds.), *Knowledge utilization, diffusion, implementation, transfer, and translation: Implications for evaluation. New Directions for Evaluation, 124*, 21–34.

2

Knowledge Utilization: Implications for Evaluation

Sarah C. Blake, Judith M. Ottoson

Abstract

Knowledge utilization is a field crossing many sectors, from agriculture, since the 1920s, to health care today. Evaluators have made long-standing contributions to understanding knowledge utilization. Different models or ways to think about knowledge utilization have evolved to reflect different perspectives, contexts, and stages of the process, from knowledge creation to the use of effectiveness results in policymaking. The rich interdisciplinary history of this field challenges evaluators to interrogate what knowledge (really) means within a policy or program—whether knowledge is being used more symbolically, rhetorically, or tactically, for example. Differences in program or policy effectiveness across different program sites might result from different types of knowledge use in those sites. © Wiley Periodicals, Inc., and the American Evaluation Association.

E valuators have a long-standing interest in knowledge utilization, and they have contributed significantly to an understanding of its process and value (Weiss, 1972; Weiss, 1998; Patton, 2008). Use is not only fundamental to a theoretical understanding of evaluation (Shadish, Cook, & Leviton, 1991); it is core to the standards that guide evaluation practice

(Joint Committee on Standards for Educational Evaluation, 1994). This chapter begins with a summary review of metaphorical waves of knowledge utilization history. Next, components of the knowledge utilization process are explored, including the many meanings of *use*, key theories and models, and influential contextual variables. Then we analyze knowledge utilization comparatively in its self-proclaimed umbrella role related to processes of diffusion, knowledge transfer, knowledge translation, and implementation. The chapter concludes with implications of a knowledge utilization lens for evaluation.

Literature Search

The following online resources were used to locate articles for this chapter: PAIS, Medline, JSTOR (including the subfields of public administration/ political science, sociology, education, psychology, and sociology), Academic Premier, PROQUEST, and ERIC. In addition, Google was employed to explore non-peer-reviewed literature in the field. The search was narrowed to articles published from 1970 to 2007 using the key words *knowledge utilization, information utilization, use of knowledge, research utilization*, and *knowledge use*.

Numerous theoretical and empirical articles related to knowledge utilization emerged. In most circumstances, knowledge utilization was not a stand-alone subject, but rather a point of inquiry along with related processes, such as dissemination, diffusion, translation, or transfer of knowledge. Interest in knowledge utilization spreads over a number of disciplines and fields, including education, health care, political science, social work, sociology, and psychology. In almost every article, a common theme is found regarding knowledge utilization: that it is a complex concept, without solid consensus in its meaning or definition, but of inherent value to the worlds of research, policy, and practice.

A Brief History. Knowledge utilization finds roots in ancient and early European societies interested in knowledge as the intersection of philosophy and science and concerned with how this junction served population needs (Backer, 1991; Beal, Dissanayake, & Konoshima, 1986). Rogers (2003) suggests that knowledge utilization, as a specific field of inquiry, dates back to the beginnings of social science, specifically to the work of British and German anthropologists whom he terms the first diffusionists. During these early years, a diverse population of scientists and philosophers contributed to a new understanding that the advancement of civilization runs parallel with the advancement of knowledge and its uses (Edwards, 1991).

Backer (1991) uses a wave analogy to classify his interpretation of a mostly U.S. history of knowledge utilization. In the first wave (1920–1960), knowledge utilization activities began with diffusion studies of agricultural innovations to farmers, including the seminal 1943 hybrid seed corn study by Ryan and Gross (Rogers, 2003). The post–World War II information explosion and development efforts increased the international transfer of resources, knowledge, technology, personnel, and skills (Beal et al., 1986), with increasing attention given to knowledge production, dissemination, and application (Backer, 1991).

In Backer's second wave (1960–1980), most studies of knowledge utilization emphasized the adoption of technological innovation by organizations, not just by individuals. Federal health, education, and human service agencies funded the adoption of innovations emerging from research and demonstrations. This second wave coincided with a time of great optimism about social betterment. Programs such as Lyndon Johnson's Great Society brought substantial expense and subsequent measures of accountability in the federal government (Weiss, 1972). Program evaluation was born as a new field of scientific inquiry and professional practice. New sources of U.S. federal funding became available for research utilization studies intended to assess whether research results affiliated with these new programs produced measurable outcomes and had practical benefits.

The third wave (1990s–present) centers largely on how knowledge utilization can achieve improvements in health, education, and human services (Backer, 1991; Edwards, 1991). Many U.S. federal agencies that created or revitalized their knowledge utilization programs in the early part of this wave, such as the National Cancer Institute, seem to be moving now toward translational research (http://www.cancer.gov/trwg.). Despite its varying definitions within the National Institutes of Health, translational research shares "the idea that the goal of translation is to ensure that results of scientific research will be used to directly benefit human health" (http://www. niehs.nih.gov/about/od/otr/). Evident international attention has also been placed on knowledge utilization. Organizations such as the United Nations and the World Health Organization have invested resources into the exploration of knowledge use and knowledge management. The United Nations instituted the Knowledge System for Development, explicitly tied to strategies to promote economic growth. The World Health Organization (2004) supports knowledge sharing among countries in a global effort to improve population-based health and health systems.

Whether we are in a fourth wave of knowledge utilization is unclear. However, in certain fields, such as health care and public health, the emergence of systematic reviews leading to guidelines for evidence-based practice in the early 1990s and 2000s has imposed a new demand on knowledge utilization. Evidence-based practice is concerned with how scientific research is applied to or used in the medical or community setting and whether this application of research can be ensured from previous research to lead to improved health outcomes. Sackett, Rosenberg, Gray, Haynes, and Richardson (1996) characterize evidence-based medicine as a practice that integrates individual clinical expertise with the best available external clinical evidence from systematic reviews of research.

NEW DIRECTIONS FOR EVALUATION • DOI: 10.1002/ev

Evaluators can thus play a significant role in helping deliver the knowledge useful to evidence-based practice within and outside clinical or other settings. Indeed, a major limitation of evidence-based practice guidelines that have been derived from most systematic reviews is that the controlled trials on which they are based are largely conducted under academically controlled circumstances that do not reflect the usual circumstances in which the practice would be implemented (Green, 2001; Green & Glasgow, 2006). This has led to a growing recognition that if we want more evidence-based practice, we need more practice-based evidence (Green & Ottoson, 2004). This is precisely what evaluation can offer.

The Knowledge Utilization Process. The following discussion highlights the many influences that shape the parameters of knowledge use and compares several models of knowledge utilization.

What Counts as Knowledge. Multiple types of knowledge exist in the literature, including practical, intellectual, spiritual, and unwanted knowledge (Machlup, 1993). Knowledge has been classified also as explicit or tacit (implicit). Explicit knowledge is formal in character and can be easily communicated. Tacit knowledge has been described as unorganized (Hayek, 1945) and personal, context driven, and difficult to communicate (Hood, 2002). Despite these varieties of knowledge, the primary focus of knowledge utilization has been on "knowledge that derives from systematic research and analysis" (Weiss, 1980, p. 381).

Multiple parameters influence what counts as knowledge. For example, the meaning of knowledge can be influenced by both the type of research being conducted and the limitations that a particular type of research may inherently possess (Neilson, 2001). Some suggest that knowledge is not a static or inert object (Farkas, Jette, Tennstedt, Haley, & Quinn, 2003); rather, it is shaped by those who send and receive it into a set of understandings (Hutchinson & Huberman, 1993). In early research, Hayek (1945) asserted that knowledge in the market-based system disperses among many users, not just a few. If these multiple end users take up knowledge and try to make meaning of it in their own context, evaluators are challenged to even find adapted or transformed knowledge, let alone assess its use.

What Counts as Use. To find "use," evaluators need to make assumptions about use explicit, including assumptions by stakeholders and the evaluator. Unlike the field of diffusion with its synthesizing work by Rogers (2003), knowledge utilization has been variously conceptualized and modeled by the fields of public policymaking, business, medicine, and technology. Some models are grouped according to the end user, such as researcher, policymaker, or consumer, while others have been classified by context, such as organizations or societies (Edwards, 1991). From extensive knowledge utilization reviews elsewhere (Caplan, 1979; Conner, 1980; Logan & Graham, 1998; Stetler, 2001), four popular and diverse conceptualizations of knowledge utilization are reviewed here.

Many Meanings of Research Utilization. Among Weiss's evolving contributions to knowledge utilization (Weiss, 1998) is an early and frequently cited one that offers six conceptualizations of research utilization: knowledge driven, problem solving, interactive, political, tactical, and enlightenment (Weiss, 1979). For example, in the problem-solving model, the assumption is that knowledge use follows a linear path between researcher and user. The interactive model, in contrast, suggests that the use of research is not straightforward in purpose or process. Other factors, such as politics and multiple stakeholders, meld into the process of use. Weiss suggests that the enlightenment model, in which research indirectly shapes ideas about social issues, portrays the way in which social science research most frequently enters the policy arena.

Push, Pull, Dissemination, and Interactive Models of Knowledge Utilization. Landry, Amara, and Lamari (2001a) summarize four models of knowledge utilization that complement Weiss's work. The technological or science push model follows a linear sequence in which knowledge utilization rests on research supply to decision makers and practitioners. The economic or demand pull model emphasizes a similar linear knowledge sequence; however, in this model, knowledge users define the problems and ask researchers to find the solutions. In the institutional dissemination model, the transfer of knowledge to users is not assumed to be automatic, and two other steps are involved: adaptation of research products and dissemination to intended users. Finally, the social interaction model posits a nonlinear sequence in which knowledge utilization is explained by sustained and intense interaction between researchers and users. The simple reception of knowledge by a user does not imply its "use"; rather, other factors must be considered, such as research outputs and the organizational interest of potential users.

Metamodel of Evaluation Utilization. Johnson (1998) presents a metamodel of utilization that suggests that evaluation use occurs in an internal environment set in an external context. Variables associated with use are grouped into three major categories: background, interactional or social-psychological, and evaluation use. The feedback loops of this model suggest that evaluation use is continual, it evolves and changes shape over time, and it is an iterative, multistakeholder process of reflection and program adaptation (Johnson, 1998). Johnson contends that ideas from complexity theory, organizational learning, and organization design improve evaluation use and effectiveness. (Chapter 7 in this issue follows up on these ideas.)

ACE Star Model of Knowledge Transformation. Stevens (2004) developed a five-stage model of knowledge transformation: knowledge discovery, evidence summary, translation, integration, and evaluation. With primary application to evidence-based practice, this model depicts various forms of knowledge moving through cycles, combining with other knowledge, and integrating into clinical practice. The underlying premises of this model of knowledge transformation are that knowledge transformation is necessary before research results are usable in clinical decision making; although knowledge derives from a variety of sources, sources of knowledge in health care include research evidence, experience, authority, trial and error, and theoretical principles; the most stable and generalizable knowledge is discovered through systematic processes that control bias; and the form in which knowledge exists can be referenced to its use.

Other Parameters of Use. As both a challenge and complement to the preceding models, other issues surface, including stages of use, process use, misuse, nonuse, and influence. Landry, Amara, and Lamari (2001b) identify a ladder of utilization on which intended users can progress: reception, cognition, discussion, reference, adoption, and influence. These stages reflect on utilization as internal learning, not an external event. Process use involves behavioral and cognitive changes in people as a result of their participation in the knowledge utilization process (Patton, 2008; Henry & Mark, 2003; Johnson, 1998). Beyer and Trice (1982) concur; they found that people do something differently as a result of research utilization. As use increases, however, so does the potential for misuse, intentional or unintentional (Patton, 2008). While Patton believes that misuse is often political and that evaluators can feel they have no control over misuse, Cousins (2004) believes that evaluators are responsible for understanding what users choose to do with evaluation findings. He suggests a four-part taxonomy that describes use, nonuse, misuse, and legitimate use. Among his conclusions is the finding that nonuse is justified when the findings are flawed or the evaluator is incompetent (Cousins, 2004). Finally, Henry (2005) switches the focus from use to influence on the end goal of social betterment.

Summary of Use Parameters. Evaluators are blessed and beleaguered with multiple understandings of use. Nevertheless, a common ground has been laid among the models reviewed. A one shot, one-way, one-meaning view of knowledge use has given way to a process that is understood to be interactive, iterative, and interpretive.

Contextual Influences on Use. Numerous influences on the use of knowledge have been identified (Huberman, 1996; Landry, Lamari, & Amara, 2003), elaborated (Green, Ottoson, Garcia, & Hiatt, 2009), and grouped elsewhere according to the knowledge source, content, medium, user, and context. We highlight key contextual variables to consider when evaluating use from a knowledge utilization lens.

Along with the user or users (individual versus organization), contextual influences on the knowledge utilization process include timing, resources, supportive social conditions, leadership, politics, and communication (Kingdon, 2003; Beyer & Trice, 1982; Landry, Amara, & Lamari, 2001b; Weiss, 1998; Yin & Gwaltney, 1981). For example, knowledge use may be influenced by timing if the intended user needs to postpone decision making; by resources if an organization lacks funding to purchase new technology or make required contextual changes; by social or professional conditions if an intended user lacks the authority to act on new knowledge;

by leadership if there is no one to champion knowledge use; by a political environment in which power trumps knowledge; and by a miscommunication between both the producers and users of knowledge. These are some of the key variables for evaluators to consider in utilization assessment (Ottoson & Patterson, 2000).

Knowledge Utilization as an Umbrella

Knowledge utilization covers a lot of territory, but how extensive is its coverage? What does this mean for evaluation? According to Backer (1991), knowledge utilization is a metaphorical umbrella arching over a number of subfields, including technology transfer, information dissemination and utilization, research utilization, innovation diffusion, sociology of knowledge, organizational change, policy research, and interpersonal and mass communication. Others suggest that each subfield offers some variation on when, where, and how ideas expressed in different forms are moved into policy or practice. These differences have important implications for what and how utilization is evaluated (Ottoson, 1997).

Dissemination and Diffusion. Dissemination or diffusion of knowledge emphasizes the process of moving information from one place to another, most often to a user of knowledge. According to the National Center for the Dissemination of Disability Research (1996), utilization should be the goal of all dissemination. This includes getting the word out, as well as navigating new knowledge or information from creation through implementation by intended users. Knott and Wildavsky (1980) point out that dissemination or the diffusion of knowledge can be a solution to the problem of underutilization of knowledge. Weiss states that "the diffuse process of research use that we are calling enlightenment is highly compatible with the diffuse process of policymaking" (Weiss, 1982, p. 635). The use of knowledge in its movement or spread links diffusion and knowledge utilization.

Transfer. Dunn, Holzener, and Zaltman (1985) identify knowledge use as the conceptual premise for the transfer of technology: "Knowledge use is transactive. Although one may use the analogy of 'transfer,' knowledge is never truly marketed, transferred or exchanged. Knowledge is really negotiated between the parties involved" (p. 120). Also, knowledge is not transferred to the intended user without proximity and accessibility (Martinez-Brawley, 1995). Lavis, Robertson, Woodside, McLeod, and the Knowledge Transfer Study Group (2003) found that transfer occurred only when organizations understood what was being transferred, by whom, to whom, and for what purpose. In essence, effective transfer has knowledge utilization at its core.

Implementation. Implementation systematically analyzes how the ideas of policy move into practice and explores the roles of multiples users in that process (Lester & Goggin, 1998; O'Toole, 2000). Implementation activities are designed to increase the use of knowledge or change attitudes or behavior of organizations or individuals (National Center for the Dissemination of Disability Research, 1996). Lester and Goggin (1998) suggest that useful policy research and guidance is sought by those charged with policy implementation. The user of knowledge is a key consideration in the purpose, planning, and completion of implementation research (deLeon & deLeon, 2002).

Translation. Knowledge translation encompasses both the creation of knowledge and its application, in which knowledge is turned into action (Graham et al., 2006). Knowledge translation is an ongoing and iterative process that requires engaged participation by researchers and intended users (International Development Research Centre, 2007). In order for knowledge to be used as policy or programs, there must be a process of translation or conversion.

Comparison Summary. Knowledge utilization connects with core concepts of all of these related understandings of process, but does not replace them. For evaluators this means that an understanding of knowledge utilization is necessary but not sufficient to explore and place value on process.

Implications for Evaluation

Knowledge utilization serves as the natural starting point for evaluation. Indeed "evaluation starts out with use in mind" (Weiss, 1972, p. 6). According to Shadish et al. (1991), the use component of evaluation theory should have three elements: "a description of possible kinds of use; a depiction of time frames in which use occurs; and an explanation of what the evaluator can do to facilitate use" (p. 52). From a knowledge utilization lens, we concur with these criteria and add others that tie use broadly to evaluation theory.

Understanding the Evaluand. Using a knowledge utilization lens, the evaluator needs to understand the evaluand (What is being evaluated?), the process intended to achieve outcomes (How does it work?), and contextual influences on use (When is it used? Where is it used? Who uses it?). Embedded in the evaluand are both the kind of knowledge to be used and its form. As noted earlier, the knowledge utilization literature has focused on research-derived knowledge, and this literature in evaluation focuses on the use of knowledge derived from evaluation. These are not the only two kinds of knowledge that evaluators confront. Do evaluators accept practice-based evidence as knowledge? What are the boundaries, both existing and expanding, of what counts as knowledge? These questions are pushed in the following chapters, where the forms of knowledge may be expressed not as an idea but as an innovation, technology, or policy. What kinds and forms of knowledge count?

The process by which knowledge is produced, moved, and used varies with the utilization theory, model, or understanding applied. Just the few models reviewed here show that utilization is a multiphenomenal concept. Although it can take a dizzying array of directions among users, producers, and intermediaries, the idea that knowledge travels the path of the silver bullet has been left behind. In a more iterative understanding of use, contextual influences matter. We concur with Shadish et al. (1991) that the time frame of use matters in evaluation—for example, in knowledge construction (finding knowledge over time), valuing (applying ideas sooner rather than later), or practice (stakeholder expectations or requirements). From a knowledge utilization lens, our review suggests other key factors that evaluators need to consider in assessing use, such as resources and social support. Use may take more than a good idea; it also may take money and social support. If evaluation starts with use in mind, then understanding the evaluand starts an understanding of use.

Valuing Use. What are key criteria in valuing the utilization of knowledge? In the previous section, timing was one of many criteria to assess utilization. For example, stakeholders may agree that the faster that knowledge is used, the better. Other criteria of use might include amount (How much is used?), kind of intended user (By whom?), process of use (How was it used?), or outcomes of use (What happened as a result of use?). Added to these questions is another that dogs utilization and all the related processes explored in this issue: With what fidelity does knowledge need to be used (transferred, implemented, diffused, or translated) to be considered successful? That is, how much can knowledge change, adapt, adopt, morph, recede, sustain, multiply, or couple in the utilization process? With all the complexities of the knowledge utilization process and the lack of common agreement on models or criteria, it is critical that stakeholders be engaged in the process of valuing. What will count as knowledge? What will count as use?

Knowledge Construction. The potential for knowledge to change substantially during utilization makes it not only difficult to assess use, but to find knowledge in the first place—or the second, third, and fourth place to which it diffuses. Knowledge utilization calls for methods that can track change over time, across contexts, among multiple stakeholders, and through possible multiple forms of the evaluand (knowledge). Time series designs enable the long view of knowledge utilization; interviews, observations, and focus groups offer the potential of in-depth explorations of knowledge in action. Such qualitative methods allow an understanding of knowledge adaptation that invariant survey items do not.

Facilitating Use. What evaluators have learned about the use of evaluation knowledge can be applied to the use of other kinds and forms of knowledge. For example, did trainees use the knowledge learned on the job? To begin, use needs to be a forethought, not an afterthought. Engaging stakeholders in identifying the potential uses of knowledge as both a process and outcome increases the opportunities for knowledge use. Tied to stakeholder engagement is the emergent understanding of knowledge and use in context. To go back to the training example, evaluators would engage training stakeholders in identifying the parameters of use in a given context and the potential uses of evaluation process and outcome findings. Furthermore, the understandings of knowledge utilization can inform other process-related theories and models, and vice versa. Despite its umbrella ambitions, knowledge utilization does not have to cover all process understanding to be relevant. Finally, knowledge utilization, in all its complexity, makes it clear that it is too simplistic to ask, Did they use it? without a broader understanding of evaluation theory.

Case Study Application: Evaluating the Gatehouse Project With a Knowledge Utilization Lens

The Gatehouse Project was a successful, multilevel school-based intervention aimed at promoting the emotional well-being of young people by increasing students' connectedness to school (Patton et al., 2000, 2006; Patton, Bond, Butler, & Glover, 2003).

The intervention included a curriculum component focused on increasing students' skills and knowledge for dealing with everyday life challenges, and a whole-school component that sought to make changes to the schools' social and learning environment to enhance security, communication, and positive regard through valued participation. A member of the research team facilitated the project implementation process. Key elements were the establishment of a school-based health action team, the use of local data to review the school environment and drive change, targeted professional development, and opportunities for reflective practice (Glover & Butler, 2004; Patton et al., 2003; Patton et al., 2006). This process resulted in schools' identifying and implementing activities and strategies appropriate to their local context; thus, what was done varied from school to school.

With an understanding of the different definitions and concepts of use, an evaluator can approach the Gatehouse Project in various ways. Knowledge of the difference between symbolic use and process use would alert the evaluators to look at the differences in the schools that evoked the language and images of the project (symbolic use) but made no substantive changes to their practices from those that made instrumental use of the training and guidance they received and made observable changes to such practices, such as orientation procedures or classroom seating practices (process use). After the main findings were released, instrumental use of the findings might be evident if the government mandated that all schools reform their bullying policies in specific ways. Conceptual use of the Gatehouse Project findings might also be observed by how policymakers view the overall value of the intervention. These views, captured through an "enlightened" knowledge of Gatehouse, might influence future decisions by policymakers about funding similar interventions. Tactical use might be to link the findings to a concession to the teachers' union request to build more communication training into government-funded teacher professional development. From an evaluation perspective, one might hypothesize that the effects of the intervention might be different in localities according to which type of use predominated.

References

Backer, T. E. (1991). Knowledge utilization: The third wave. *Knowledge: Creation, Diffusion, Utilization, 12*(3), 225–240.

Beal, G. M., Dissanayake, W., & Konoshima, S. (1986). *Knowledge generation, exchange, and utilization.* Boulder, CO: Westview Press.

Beyer, J. M., & Trice, H. M. (1982). The utilization process: A conceptual framework and synthesis of empirical findings. *Administrative Science Quarterly, 27,* 591–622.

Caplan, N. (1979). The two-communities theory and knowledge utilization. *American Behavioral Scientist, 22,* 459–470.

Conner, R. F. (1980). The evaluation of research utilization. In M. W. Klein & K. S. Teilmann (Eds.), *Handbook of criminal justice evaluation* (pp. 629–653). Thousand Oaks, CA: Sage.

Cousins, J. B. (2004). Commentary: Minimizing evaluation misuse as principled practice. *American Journal of Evaluation, 25*(3), 391–397.

deLeon, P., & deLeon, L.(2002). Whatever happened to policy implementation? An alternative approach. *Journal of Public Administration Research and Theory, 4,* 467–492.

Dunn, W., Holzener, B., & Zaltman, G. (1985). Knowledge utilization. In T. Husen & T. N. Postlethwaite (Eds.), *The international encyclopedia of education* (Vol. 1, pp. 2831–2839). New York: Pergamon Press.

Edwards, L. A. (1991). *Using knowledge and technology to improve the quality of life of people who have disabilities.* Philadelphia: Knowledge Utilization Program, Pennsylvania College of Optometry.

Farkas, M., Jette, A. M., Tennstedt, S., Haley, S. M., & Quinn, V. (2003). Knowledge dissemination and utilization in gerontology: An organizing framework. *Gerontologist, 43*(1), 47–56.

Glover, S., & Butler, H. (2004). Facilitating health promotion within school communities. In R. Moodie & A. Hulme (Eds.), *Hands-on health promotion.* Melbourne: IP Communications.

Graham, I. D., Logan, J., Harrison, M. B., Straus, S. E., Tetroe, J., Caswell, W., et al. (2006). Lost in knowledge translation: Time for a map? *Journal of Continuing Education, 26,* 13–24.

Green, L. W. (2001). From research to "best practices" in other settings and populations. *American Journal of Health Behavior, 25,* 165–178.

Green, L. W., & Glasgow, R. (2006). Evaluating the relevance, generalization, and applicability of research: Issues in external validation and translation methodology. *Evaluation and the Health Professions, 29*(1), 126–153.

Green, L. W., & Ottoson, J. M. (2004). From efficacy to effectiveness to community and back: Evidence-based practice vs. practice-based evidence. In L. Green, R. Hiss, R. Glasgow, et al. (Eds.), *From clinical trials to community: The science of translating diabetes and obesity research* (pp. 15–18). Bethesda, MD: National Institutes of Health.

Green, L. W., Ottoson, J. M., Garcia, G., & Hiatt, R. A. (2009). Diffusion theory, and knowledge dissemination, utilization, and integration in public health. *Annual Review of Public Health, 30,* 27–41.

Hayek, F. (1945). The use of knowledge in society. *American Economic Review, 34*(4), 519–530.

Henry, G. T. (2005). Questions and answers: A conversation with Gary Henry. *Evaluation Exchange, 11*(2), 10–11.

Henry, G. T., & Mark, M. M. (2003). Beyond use: Understanding evaluation's influence on attitudes and actions. *American Journal of Evaluation, 24*(3), 203–314.

Hood, P. (2002). *Perspectives on knowledge utilization in education.* San Francisco: WestEd.

Huberman, M. (1996). *A review of the literature on dissemination and knowledge utilization.* National Center for the Dissemination of Disability Research, Southwest Educational Development Laboratory. Retrieved October 3, 2009, from http://www.researchutilization.org/matrix/resources/review

Hutchinson, J., & Huberman, M. (1993). *Knowledge dissemination and utilization in science and mathematics education: A literature review.* Washington, DC: National Science Foundation.

International Development Research Centre. (2007). *Knowledge translation: Basic theories, approaches and application.* Retrieved October 2, 2009, from http://www.idrc.ca/en/ev-125826–201-1-DO_TOPIC.html

Johnson, R. B. (1998). Toward a theoretical model of evaluation utilization. *Evaluation and Program Planning, 21,* 93–110.

Joint Committee on Standards of Educational Evaluation. (1994). *The program evaluation standards* (2nd ed.). Thousand Oaks, CA: Sage.

Kingdon, J. W. (2003). *Agendas, alternatives, and public policies.* Reading, MA: Addison-Wesley.

Knott, J., & Wildavsky, A. (1980). If dissemination is the solution, What is the problem? *Knowledge: Creation, Diffusion, Utilization, 1*(4), 537–578.

Landry, R., Amara, N., & Lamari, M. (2001a). Climbing the ladder of research utilization. *Science Communication, 22*(4), 396–422.

Landry, R., Amara, N., & Lamari, M. (2001b). Utilization of social science research knowledge in Canada. *Research Policy, 30*(2), 333–349.

Landry, R., Lamari, M., & Amara, N. (2003). The extent and determinants of the utilization of university research in government agencies. *Public Administration Review, 63*(2), 192–205.

Lavis, J., Robertson, D., Woodside, J. M., McLeod, C. B., & the Knowledge Transfer Study Group. (2003). How can research organizations more effectively transfer research knowledge to decision makers? *Millbank Quarterly, 81*(2), 221–248.

Lester, J. P., & Goggin, M. L. (1998). Back to the future: The rediscovery of implementation studies. *Policy Currents, 8*(3), 1–9.

Logan, J., & Graham, I. D. (1998). Toward a comprehensive interdisciplinary model of health care research use. *Science Communication, 20,* 227–246.

Machlup, F. (1993). Uses, value, and benefits of knowledge. *Knowledge: Creation, Diffusion, Utilization, 14*(4), 448–466.

Martinez-Brawley, E. E. (1995). Knowledge diffusion and transfer of technology: Conceptual premise and concrete steps for human services innovators. *Social Work, 40*(5), 670–682.

National Center for the Dissemination of Disability Research. (1996). *A review of the literature on dissemination and knowledge utilization.* Retrieved December 11, 2008, from http://www.ncddr.org/du/products/review/

Neilson, S. (2001). *IDRC-supported research and its influence on public policy: Knowledge utilization and public policy processes: A literature review.* Retrieved October 2, 2009, from http://www.idrc.ca/en/ev-12186-201-1-DO_TOPIC.html

O'Toole, L. J. (2000). Research on policy implementation: Assessment and prospects. *Journal of Public Administration Research and Theory, 10*(2), 263–288.

Ottoson, J. M. (1997). Beyond transfer of training: Using multiple lenses to assess community education programs. In A. D. Rose & M. A. Leahy (Eds.), *Assessing Adult Learning in Diverse Settings: Current Issues and Approaches* (pp. 87–96). New Directions for Adult and Continuing Education, no. 75. San Francisco: Jossey-Bass.

Ottoson, J. M., & Patterson, I. M. (2000). Contextual influences on learning application in practice: An extended role for process evaluation. *Evaluation and the Health Professions, 23*(2), 194–211.

Patton, G., Bond, L., Butler, H., & Glover, S. (2003). Changing schools, changing health? The design and implementation of the Gatehouse Project. *Journal of Adolescent Health, 33*(4), 231–239.

Patton, G. C., Bond, L., Carlin, J. B., Thomas, L., Butler, H., Glover, S., et al. (2006). Promoting social inclusion in secondary schools: A group-randomized trial of effects on student health risk behavior and well-being. *American Journal of Public Health, 96,* 1582–1587.

Patton, G. C., Glover, S., Bond, L., Butler, H., Godfrey, C., DiPietro, G., et al. (2000). The Gatehouse Project: A systematic approach to mental health promotion in secondary schools. *Australian and New Zealand Journal of Psychiatry, 34,* 586–593.

Patton, M. Q. (2008). *Utilization-focused evaluation* (4th ed.). Thousand Oaks, CA: Sage.

Rogers, E. M. (2003). *Diffusion of innovations* (5th ed.). New York: Free Press.

Sackett, D. L., Rosenberg, W.M.C., Gray, J.A.M., Haynes, R. B., & Richardson, W. S. (1996). Evidence-based medicine: What it is and what it isn't. *British Medical Journal, 212,* 71–72.

Shadish, W. R., Cook, T. D., & Leviton, L. C. (1991). *Foundations of program evaluation: Theories of practice.* Thousand Oaks, CA: Sage.

Stetler, C. B. (2001). Updating the Stetler model of research utilization to facilitate evidence-based practice. *Nursing Outlook, 49,* 272–278.

Stevens, K. R. (2004). *ACE star model of EBP: Knowledge transformation.* San Antonio: Academic Center for Evidence-Based Practice, University of Texas Health Science Center at San Antonio. Retrieved October 2, 2009, from http://www.acestar.uthscsa.edu/Learn_model.htm

Weiss, C. H. (1972; 1998). *Evaluation research: Methods of assessing program effectiveness.* Upper Saddle River, NJ: Prentice-Hall.

Weiss, C. H. (1979, September/October). The many meanings of research utilization. *Public Administration Review,* 426–431.

Weiss, C. H. (1980). Knowledge creep and decision accretion. *Knowledge: Creation, Diffusion, Utilization, 1*(3), 381–404.

Weiss, C. H. (1982). Policy research in the context of diffuse decision making. *Journal of Higher Education, 53*(6), 619–639.

Weiss, C. H. (1998). Have we learned from anything new about the use of evaluation? *American Journal of Evaluation, 19*(1), 21–33.

World Health Organization. (2004). *World report on knowledge for better health: Strengthening health systems.* Geneva: World Health Organization. Retrieved December 11,

2008, from http://www.who.int/rpc/meetings/en/world_report_on_knowledge_for_
better_health2.pdf

Yin, R. K., & Gwaltney, M. K. (1981). Knowledge utilization as a networking process. *Knowledge: Creation, Diffusion, and Utilization, 2*(4), 555–580.

SARAH C. BLAKE is senior associate faculty in the Department of Health Policy and Management at Emory University's Rollins School of Public Health.

JUDITH M. OTTOSON is an independent evaluation consultant and an adjunct lecturer at San Francisco State University. She initiated this project when she was an associate professor at the Andrew Young School of Policy Studies, Georgia State University, Atlanta.

NEW DIRECTIONS FOR EVALUATION • DOI: 10.1002/ev

Ashley, S. R. (2009). Innovation diffusion: Implications for evaluation. In J. M. Ottoson &
P. Hawe (Eds.), *Knowledge utilization, diffusion, implementation, transfer, and translation:
Implications for evaluation. New Directions for Evaluation, 124,* 35–45.

3

Innovation Diffusion: Implications for Evaluation

Shena R. Ashley

Abstract

Whether looking at the spread and adoption of an intervention across a community, across multiple units, or within a single unit, an understanding of diffusion theory can help evaluators uncover patterns and impacts that might otherwise be overlooked. The theory alerts evaluators to examine why uptake of an intervention appeared different in different sites, according to the characteristics of the people involved, the social systems involved (for example, neighborhoods, states, or organizations), or the communications channels used. Insights might explain intervention intensity across sites and consequent differential effects. It also yields useful information to assist with subsequent replication of the intervention by practitioners and policymakers. © Wiley Periodicals, Inc., and the American Evaluation Association.

D iffusion theory can be value-added to evaluators. An understanding of the diffusion process can deepen and broaden the scope of an evaluation to reveal the factors determining the adoption of an intervention, the patterns underlying the spread of an intervention, and the determinants influencing the adaptation of an intervention to a local context. This broadened perspective has the potential to influence the evaluation process and the ultimate determination of the merit or worth of an

intervention. This is especially true when specific groups within the target population selectively adopt the intervention. An example is a poverty alleviation program that is mainly adopted by the transient poor rather than the long-term poor. Such selective uptake may render different conclusions about the program's success.

The diffusion process is not an unfamiliar concept in the evaluation field. In numerous cases, evaluators have used diffusion theory to guide the formulation of research questions and the design of measurement instruments (Guba, 1967; Bozeman, 1988). Pankratz, Hallfors, and Cho (2002) applied diffusion theory in the evaluation of the U.S. Department of Education's principle of effectiveness by school districts. Hubbard, Huang, and Mulvey (2003) used diffusion theory to evaluate the spread of treatment improvement protocols throughout the substance abuse treatment system. In each case, the theory drew attention to how attributes of the intervention and factors in the environment influenced intervention effects.

For the evaluator, the diffusion process provides a unique set of focal points for an understanding of change. The components of the diffusion process are described in this chapter with particular attention to the applicability of the process to evaluation practice.

The Diffusion Process: Defined and Dissected

Since Ryan and Gross's hybrid corn study in 1943, the diffusion process has been the focus of scholarly research in a wide range of disciplines, including agriculture, sociology, psychology, communications, anthropology, marketing, epidemiology, systems analysis, public policy, education, public health, geography, economics, and organization science (Wolfe, 1994). The result is tens of thousands of articles on the topic (Nutley, Davies, & Walter, 2002) and a complex model of change that explains and predicts the spread of innovations.

Like other theories of change processes (knowledge utilization, transfer, implementation, and knowledge translation), diffusion draws from a wide range of fields. Unlike these theories, however, it has had both a synthesizer and a champion to meld the ideas into a coherent, evolving, and sustainable model. Everett Rogers played this central role in diffusion theory, which resulted in his seminal text, now in its fifth edition, *Diffusion of Innovations* (2003). While other diffusion models exist (Mahajan & Peterson, 1985), the dominance and comprehensiveness of Roger's efforts legitimate using his work as a basis for understanding and critiquing diffusion theory as applied to evaluation.

Diffusion is defined as "the process by which an *innovation* is *communicated* through certain *channels* over *time* among the members of a *social system*" (Rogers, 2003, p. 7). This is the standard definition of diffusion in the field (Tornatzky & Fleischer, 1990). Diffusion is a model of change that focuses on individual decision making, although it has been applied to organizations. Simply stated, diffusion is concerned with the spread and adoption (or rejection) of products, practices, programs, policies, or ideas. The key lever of change in the diffusion process is the adoption of an innovation. The major components of the diffusion process are the innovation, the social system through which the innovation moves, the communication channels of that system, the time it takes for an innovation to spread through the social system, and the adoption of the innovation by the intended recipients. Each component is described next with particular focus on its relevance and implications for evaluation practice.

The Innovation. The innovation (or *intervention* in evaluation terminology) is central to the diffusion process. As defined in diffusion theory, innovation is a slight variant of the general concept of innovation. In general, an innovation is any new idea, method, or object. In diffusion theory, an innovation is "an idea, practice, or object *perceived as new* by an individual or other unit of adoption" (Rogers, 2003, p. 43). The focus on the perception of newness in diffusion theory signifies the relevance of the diffusion process not only when an idea, practice, or object moves from invention to first use, but also in the movement of that idea, practice, or object through different contexts over time. For example, a middle school reform with a long history of practice would be an innovation to the school district considering adopting it for the first time.

Adaptability is a quality of the innovation that differentiates diffusion theory from other theories of change processes. In early diffusion studies, adoption was recognized only as the exact replication of an innovation. That was later changed. The current accepted wisdom is that an innovation that has been changed or modified can still be recognized as having been adopted (Charters & Pellegrin, 1972). Describing the importance of allowing adaptation in the diffusion process, Rogers (2003, p. 115) states, "We should remember that an innovation is not necessarily invariant and adopting an innovation is not necessarily a passive role of just implementing a standard template of the new idea." Diffusion theory anticipates modifications to interventions and purports that adaptability of the intervention to fit the context is critical to its adoption and maintenance over time. In evaluation, adaptability makes valuing challenging, especially when fidelity to the program model is a priority.

In addition to adaptability, the perceived characteristics of an innovation can influence adoption. Diffusion theory highlights five innovation characteristics that determine whether an innovation is appealing to the potential adopter (Rogers, 2003):

- *Relative advantage* is the extent to which the innovation is perceived to have significant advantages over current alternatives. Adoption is more prevalent when the innovation is considered superior to current practice.
- *Compatibility* refers to the degree to which the innovation is seen as being consistent with past practices, current values, and existing needs. Innovations that fit within the current context are more likely to be adopted.

- *Complexity* expresses the level at which the innovation can be readily understood and implemented. The more complex the innovation is, the less likely it is to be adopted.
- *Trialability* refers to the extent to which portions of the innovation can be tried out before full adoption. This allows potential adopters to have early exposure to the innovation and increases the likelihood of adoption.
- *Observability* of the innovation is the degree to which its use and benefits are visible to others. Adoption is more prevalent when the benefits of adoption are exposed.

Diffusion theory's focus on understanding the innovation is consistent with the component of the Shadish, Cook, and Leviton (1991) framework that calls for a thorough understanding of the evaluand. Diffusion theory emphasizes the important role of understanding the evaluand since characteristics of the evaluand can have a direct impact on its adoption. The five characteristics of innovations in diffusion theory can be helpful to evaluators who are looking to understand the selective uptake of an intervention. Furthermore, an evaluation of the diffusion of a program, product, or idea should be aware that the evaluand may have been adapted to fit the local context when adopted and a strict focus on fidelity to the original model may limit the scope of adopting units.

Social System. The social system is the contextual space within which the innovation is diffused—for example, organizations, neighborhoods, and states. Within the social system are individual, institutional, political, and environmental factors that determine how and if an innovation reaches its intended audience (Damanpour, 1991; Kimberly & Evanisko, 1981; Tornatzky & Fleischer, 1990). Factors highlighted in diffusion theory include prior conditions, characteristics of the adopter, and the influence of change agents and opinion leaders in promoting the innovation (Wolfe, 1994). Prior conditions of adopters include previous practice, the felt needs or problems experienced by the potential adopter, the potential adopter's level of innovativeness, and the norms of the social system in which the potential adopter is embedded. When the potential adopter is an individual, the characteristics that influence adoption include socioeconomic characteristics, especially the ability to afford an innovation, personality variables, and the individual's communication behavior (Brown, 1981). When the adopting unit is an organization, structural characteristics tend to influence the adoption process. Structural characteristics of the organization that affect the rate of adoption include the degree to which power and control in an organization are concentrated in the hands of a few individuals, the availability of persons in the organization with a high degree of knowledge and expertise, the degree to which an organization stresses following rules and procedures, the interconnectedness of the organization in a social system, and the availability of slack resources to invest in the innovation (Mohr, 1969; Moch & Morse, 1977; Kimberly & Evanisko, 1981; Abrahamson, 1991).

In addition to the influence of prior and current conditions, intermediaries can influence adoption. Diffusion theory emphasizes two types of intermediaries: the change agent and the opinion leader. The change agent creates or enhances demand for an innovation by reducing barriers and convincing potential adopters that the innovation is a sufficient fit. In this role, the change agent serves as the bridge between the technical experts or group that created the innovation and the target audience. Opinion leaders are early adopters of an innovation who, by their own adoption, improve the likelihood of adoption among their peers and work in the process to persuade the middle and late adopters of an innovation. Identification of the conditions of the intended adopters, the broader contextual factors, and the role of intermediaries can direct the evaluator to the types of variables that shape the adoption of the intervention (Gray & Scheirer, 1988). This type of analysis is consistent with the systems approach to evaluation (Cabrera & Trochim, 2006).

Communication Channel. The communication channel refers to the process by which messages move from one individual to another. Drawing heavily on communications theory, diffusion theory highlights mass media channels and interpersonal networks as effective types of communication channels (Brown, 1968). The process of diffusion is complex, sequential, and interactive (Van de Ven, Polley, Garud, & Venkatarum, 1999). In general, an innovation enters a social setting from an external source; it is then spread throughout that setting by interpersonal contact networks and either adopted or rejected by the target population (Wejnert, 2002). Interpersonal networks facilitate exposure to the innovation. Early perceptions of the innovation, shared within an interpersonal network, can influence whether an innovation is adopted (Valente, 1995). Diffusion theory draws the evaluator's attention to network effects and their potential impact on intervention adoption. The theory also proposes an examination of the media used to communicate the intervention since media design can also influence adoption (Brink et al., 1995).

Time. Time is central to the diffusion process. According to diffusion theory, immediate take-up of a program is not to be expected. Rogers (2003) theorized that the rate of adoption of innovations would spread in the shape of an S curve as the cumulative number of adopters increases over time. This S-shaped pattern has been confirmed in studies across a variety of innovations (Damanpour, 1991; Wright & Charlett, 1995; Backer & Rogers, 1998; Scheirer, 1990). The shape of the curve is significant; it holds that a small set of the intended audience will adopt early in the diffusion process and that adoption will continue at a faster pace as more individuals are exposed to the innovation until the saturation point is met.

Diffusion theory also classifies adopters according to the time of adoption. The five categories, with the proportion estimated to fall into each category, are innovators (2.5%), early adopters (the next 13.5%), early majority (34%), late majority (34%), and laggards (16%) (Mahajan & Peterson, 1985; Nutley et al., 2002; Rogers, 2003). This has direct implications for the timing of an evaluation. An evaluation of an intervention in its early stages of adoption might yield different results than an evaluation that includes both early and late adopters. Individuals adopting early are more likely to be social leaders, educated, and connected to an expansive network compared to individuals who adopt at later stages, tend to be more skeptical, have a lower socioeconomic status, and have a smaller network. To assess the appropriate time to evaluate a program, an evaluator might examine the diversity of adopters prior to conducting the evaluation. Diversity of adopters is an indicator of a highly developed diffusion process.

Adoption. Change in the diffusion process occurs through the adoption of an innovation. Diffusion theory anticipates different responses to the innovation. Some people adopt an idea or practice right away, some wait to see how successful it is before deciding to adopt, and others never adopt the innovation at all. Those who adopt the innovation might also adapt the intervention to fit their context, such that the innovation might not look the same from one place to the next.

Diffusion theory focuses on adoption as a process. It holds that each individual passes through a five-stage process when deciding whether to adopt an innovation (Davies, 1979; Brown, 1981; Rogers, 2003). First stage is the knowledge stage, when the individual or organization is first exposed to the innovation's existence. Next is the persuasion stage, when the individual or organization forms a favorable or unfavorable attitude toward the innovation. The third stage is about making the decision to adopt or reject the innovation. The fourth stage is implementation: the individual or organization puts the adopted innovation to use. And the final stage is confirmation, where the individual or organization seeks reinforcement for the decision made and may reverse the decision if exposed to conflicted messages about the innovation.

This stage model is similar to the transtheoretical model of change (Prochaska & Velicer, 1997) made popular in health behavior research. The stages in the diffusion process highlight for the evaluator the decision-making process that individuals experience when adopting an innovation. The distinction between the implementation and confirmation stages is especially important in the evaluation context, since judgments of success that end at implementation could overstate the level of adoption given that individuals may reverse their adoption decision during confirmation.

Distinguishing Diffusion From Dissemination

Dissemination and *diffusion* are terms often used synonymously in the evaluation literature, although there are no agreed-on boundaries for delineating the two concepts. Greenhalgh, Robert, MacFarlane, Bate, and Kyriakidou (2004) distinguish between diffusion and dissemination based on the level of intention behind the spread. They suggest that diffusion refers to passive spread, while dissemination is relevant to active and planned efforts to persuade target groups to adopt an innovation. This distinction is not supported by the diffusion literature, which recognizes planned efforts to spread innovations as part of the diffusion process and identifies the change agents and opinion leaders as individuals in the process responsible for persuasion toward adoption (Brown, 1981; Rogers, 2003).

Graham and others (2006) offer another perspective on the distinctions between diffusion and dissemination—one where the focus is the type of innovation being spread as the delineating factor. They consider diffusion to be a broad category representing the spread of a range of innovations; however, when that innovation is knowledge or research, the spread process for them becomes dissemination.

An alternative view proposed here is that the distinction between diffusion and dissemination be based on the continuum from distribution to receipt. Dissemination is conceptually preoccupied with the process of sending out innovations; by contrast, diffusion begins with the initial sending out of innovations and then continues to examine the spread and adoption of the innovation.

In evaluation literature, the term *dissemination* is often used when fidelity is important. Dissemination is prevalent in the literature regarding the spread of evidence-based interventions from the testing space to the public space (Langberg & Smith, 2006). The issue of fidelity to the original design is of primary concern in this setting (Henggeler, Melton, Brondino, Scherer, & Hanley, 1997), which might explain the focus on the term *dissemination* rather than diffusion. Evaluators might look to dissemination instead of diffusion theory when the evaluation context requires fidelity throughout the spreading process.

Summary of Implications for Evaluation. For the evaluator, the components of the diffusion process—the innovation, social system, communication channel, time, and adoption—provide focal points for an understanding of change. The focus of the evaluation is not only an idea or object, but also one that is perceived as an innovation. Newness counts as a value. The innovativeness is determined by a social system, which means that context shapes innovation value. Fundamental to the theory is that the diffusion of an innovation takes place over an extended period of time. Characteristics of time, especially speed, shape value from a diffusion perspective. The message most clearly relevant from diffusion theory to the evaluator is that selective uptake is inevitable. The theory challenges the evaluator to explore factors associated with selectivity and suggests a set of factors to explore: the nature of the intervention itself, the interpersonal communication networks, the media used in communication of the intervention, and the social, cultural, and institutional factors that impact adoption. Evaluators might use these questions when applying perspectives from diffusion theory in evaluation:

1. Who are the opinion leaders among the intended audience, and what role do they play in diffusing the intervention?
2. How are the actors in the social system interconnected?

3. Which communication channels were most effective at different times in the diffusion process or with different categories of potential adopters?
4. What were the attributes of the intervention that facilitated or impeded adoption?
5. In what ways do the adopters of the innovation differ from the non-adopters?
6. What contextual factors contributed to adoption of the intervention?
7. Were potential adopters given enough time to process their decision to adopt the intervention?

Methods Used in Tracing Diffusion

In the diffusion literature, methods for understanding and tracing the spread of innovations include surveys, experiments, network analysis, and episodic communication channels in organization (ECCO) analysis. Of these methods, evaluators may be least familiar with ECCO analysis. ECCO analysis is a technique for mapping exchange relationships where questionnaires are used that ask respondents to indicate whether they have been informed about a message, the source of their information, and the channel through which they heard it (Downs & Adrian, 2004). Logistic regression is often used in diffusion studies to analyze the factors associated with the variations in the adoption of innovations (Kimberly & Evanisko, 1981).

Case Study Application: Evaluating the Gatehouse Project With a Diffusion Lens

The Gatehouse Project was a successful multilevel, school-based intervention aimed at promoting the emotional well-being of young people by increasing students' connectedness to school (Patton et al., 2000, 2006; Patton, Bond, Butler, & Glover, 2003).

The intervention included a curriculum component focused on increasing students' skills and knowledge for dealing with everyday life challenges and a whole-school component that sought to make changes to the schools' social and learning environment to enhance security, communication, and positive regard through valued participation. A member of the research team facilitated the project implementation process. Key elements were the establishment of a school-based health action team, the use of local data to review the school environment and drive change, targeted professional development, and opportunities for reflective practice (Glover & Butler, 2004; Patton et al., 2003; Patton et al., 2006). This process resulted in schools' identifying and implementing activities and strategies appropriate to their local context; thus, what was done varied from school to school.

A diffusion perspective could help an evaluator understand the factors associated with the varied uptake of strategies by the different schools. These might be factors associated with the intervention itself, the adopting individuals, communication effects, and contextual effects. To describe the spread and distribution of the intervention strategies, the evaluator would first have to compile a list of the intervention elements he or she wished to trace, such as adherence to and delivery of all curriculum recommendations, adoption of policies to welcome new students, or new activities to connect parents with the school. A survey tool could then be used to trace the uptake and distribution of these elements across time and across sites quantitatively (and prospectively if possible). A series of qualitative interviews could then be conducted to help explain the spread. This would be an opportunity to explore, for example, whether the presence of prior existing programs made it easier for some sites to develop Gatehouse activities faster than others or whether high teacher turnover in some sites mitigated against sustained activities. These data would be important not simply for illuminating the intensity of effects in the Gatehouse trial; they would help others who are seeking to replicate the project elsewhere to appreciate adjustment to context.

References

Abrahamson, E. (1991). Managerial fads and fashions: The diffusion and rejection of innovations. *Academy of Management Review, 16*(3), 586–612.

Backer, T., & Rogers, E. (1998). Diffusion of innovations theory and work-site AIDS programs. *Journal of Health Communication, 3*(1), 17–29.

Bozeman, B. (1988). Evaluating technology transfer and diffusion. *Evaluation and Program Planning, 11*(1), 63–104.

Brink, S., Basen-Engquist, K., O'Hara-Tompkins, N., Parcel, G., Gottlieb, N., & Lovato, C. (1995). Diffusion of an effective tobacco prevention program. Part I: Evaluation of the dissemination phase. *Health Education Research, 10*(3), 283–295.

Brown, L. (1968). *Diffusion dynamics: A review and revision of the quantitative theory of the spatial diffusion of innovation.* Lund: Royal University of Lund.

Brown, L. (1981). *Innovation diffusion: A new perspective.* New York: Methuen.

Bryce, R., & Gross, N. C. (1943). The diffusion of hybrid seed in two Iowa communities. *Rural Sociology, 8*(6), 815–824.

Cabrera, D., & Trochim, W. (2006). A theory of systems evaluation. In D. Cabrera (Ed.), *Systems evaluation and evaluation systems whitepaper series.* Ithaca, NY: Cornell University National Science Foundation Systems Evaluation Grant No. EREC-0535492. Dspace Open Access Repository.

Charters, W. W., & Pellegrin, R. S. (1972). Barriers to the innovation process: Four case studies of differentiated staffing. *Educational Agricultural Quarterly, 9*, 3–4.

Damanpour, F. (1991). Organizational innovations: A meta-analysis of effects of determinants and moderators. *Academy of Management Journal, 34*, 555–590.

Davies, S. (1979). *The diffusion of process innovations.* Cambridge: Cambridge University Press.

Downs, C., & Adrian, A. (2004). *Assessing organizational communication: Strategic communication audits.* New York: Guilford Press.

Glover, S., & Butler, H. (2004) Facilitating health promotion within school communities. In R. Moodie & A. Hulme (Eds.), *Hands-on health promotion.* Melbourne: IP Communications.

Graham, I., Logan, J., Harrison, M., Straus, S., Tetroe, J., Caswell, W., et al. (2006). Lost in knowledge translation: Time for a map? *Journal of Continuing Education in the Health Professions, 26,* 13–24.

Gray, C. R., & Scheirer, M. A. (1988). Checking the congruence between a program and its organizational environment. *New Directions for Program Evaluation, 40,* 63–81.

Greenhalgh, T., Robert, G., MacFarlane, F., Bate, P., & Kyriakidou, O. (2004). Diffusion of innovation in service organizations: Systematic review and recommendation. *Milbank Quarterly, 82*(4), 581–629.

Guba, E. (1967). *Development, diffusion, evaluation.* Paper presented at the University Council for Educational Administration Career Development Seminar, Portland, OR.

Henggeler, S. W., Melton, G. B., Brondino, M. J., Scherer, D. G., & Hanley, J. H. (1997). Multisystemic therapy with chronic and violent juvenile offenders and their families: The role of treatment fidelity in successful dissemination. *Journal of Consulting and Clinical Psychology, 65,* 821–833.

Hubbard, S., Huang, J., & Mulvey, K. (2003). Application of diffusion of innovations theory to the TIPs evaluation project results and beyond. *Evaluation and Program Planning, 26*(1), 99–107.

Kimberly, J. R., & Evanisko, M. J. (1981). Organizational innovation: The influence of individual, organizational, and contextual factors on hospital adoption of technological and administrative innovations. *Academy of Management Journal, 24,* 689–713.

Langberg, J., & Smith, B. (2006). Developing evidence-based interventions for deployment into school settings: A case example highlighting key issues of efficacy and effectiveness. *Evaluation and Program Planning, 29,* 323–334.

Mahajan, V., & Peterson, R. A. (1985). *Models for innovation diffusion.* Thousand Oaks, CA: Sage.

Moch, M. K., & Morse, E. V. (1977). Size, centralization, and organizational adoption of innovations. *American Sociological Review, 42,* 716–725.

Mohr, L. B. (1969). Determinants of innovation in organizations. *American Political Science Review, 63,* 111–126.

Nutley, S., Davies, H., & Walter, I. (2002). *Conceptual synthesis 1: Learning from the diffusion of innovations.* Unpublished manuscript.

Pankratz, M., Hallfors, D., & Cho, H. (2002). Measuring perceptions of innovation adoption: The diffusion of federal drug prevention policy. *Health Education Research, 17*(3), 315–326.

Patton, G., Bond, L., Butler, H., & Glover, S. (2003). Changing schools, changing health? Design and implementation of the Gatehouse Project. *Journal of Adolescent Health, 33*(4), 231–239.

Patton, G. C., Bond, L., Carlin, J. B., Thomas, L., Butler, H., Glover, S., et al. (2006). Promoting social inclusion in schools: A group-randomized trial of effects on student health risk behaviour and well-being. *American Journal of Public Health, 96,* 1582–1587.

Patton, G. C., Glover, S., Bond, L., Butler, H., Godfrey, C., Bowes, G., et al. (2000). The Gatehouse Project: A systematic approach to mental health promotion in secondary schools. *Australian and New Zealand Journal of Psychiatry, 34,* 586.

Prochaska, J. O., & Velicer, W. F. (1997). The transtheoretical model of health behavior change. *American Journal of Health Promotion, 12,* 38–48.

Rogers, E. (2003). *Diffusion of innovations* (5th ed.). New York: Free Press.

Scheirer, M. A. (1990). The life cycle of an innovation: Adoption vs. discontinuation of the fluoride mouth rinse programs in schools. *Journal of Health and Social Behavior, 331*, 203–215.

Shadish, W., Cook, T., & Leviton, L. (1991). *Foundations of program evaluation: Theories of practice.* Thousand Oaks, CA: Sage.

Tornatzky, L. G., & Fleischer, M. (1990). *The process of technological innovation.* Lanham, MD: Lexington Books.

Valente, T. W. (1995). *Network models of the diffusion of innovations.* Cresskill, NJ: Hampton Press.

Van de Ven, A. H., Polley, D. E., Garud, R., & Venkatarum, S. (1999). *The innovation journey.* New York: Oxford University Press.

Wejnert, B. (2002). Integrating models of diffusion of innovations: A conceptual framework. *Annual Review of Sociology, 28*, 297–326.

Wolfe, R. (1994). Organizational innovation: Review, critique, and suggested research directions. *Journal of Management Studies, 31*(3), 405–431.

Wright, M., & Charlett, D. (1995). New product diffusion models in marketing: An assessment of two approaches. *Marketing Bulletin, 6*, 32–41.

SHENA R. ASHLEY *is an assistant professor in the Maxwell School of Citizenship and Public Affairs at Syracuse University.*

DeGroff, A., & Cargo, M. (2009). Policy implementation: Implications for evaluation. In
J. M. Ottoson & P. Hawe (Eds.), *Knowledge utilization, diffusion, implementation, transfer,
and translation: Implications for evaluation. New Directions for Evaluation, 124,* 47–60.

4

Policy Implementation: Implications for Evaluation

Amy DeGroff, Margaret Cargo

Abstract

*Policy implementation reflects a complex change process where government deci-
sions are transformed into programs, procedures, regulations, or practices aimed
at social betterment. Three factors affecting contemporary implementation
processes are explored: networked governance, sociopolitical context and the democratic turn, and new public management. This frame of reference invites evaluators to consider challenges present when evaluating macrolevel change processes,
such as the inherent complexity of health and social problems, multiple actors with
variable degrees of power and influence, and a political environment that emphasizes accountability. The evaluator requires a deep and cogent understanding of
the health or social issues involved; strong analysis and facilitation skills to deal
with a multiplicity of values, interests, and agendas; and a comprehensive toolbox
of evaluation approaches and methods, including network analysis to assess
and track the interconnectedness of key champions (and saboteurs) who might
affect intervention effects and sustainability.* © Wiley Periodicals, Inc., and the
American Evaluation Association.

The findings and conclusions in this chapter are those of the authors and do not necessarily represent the views of the Centers for Disease Control. They do not represent and
should not be construed to represent any agency determination of policy.

I mplementation has long been recognized as a distinct stage in the policy process, unique for representing the transformation of a policy idea or expectation to action aimed at remedying social problems (Lester & Goggin, 1998). Reflecting a process involving change over time, implementation is characterized by the actions of multiple levels of agencies, institutions, organizations, and their actors and is influenced by context throughout. As Parsons (1995) suggests, "A study of implementation is a study of change: how change occurs, possibly how it may be induced" (p. 461).

It is important for evaluators to understand the policy implementation process in part because many social programs are publicly funded, and they are initiated and influenced by public policy. In addition, evaluators frequently assess policy or program implementation to inform ongoing programmatic decision making and to explore how and why outcomes were or were not achieved. Consequently, the policy sciences and, in particular, literature pertaining to policy implementation provide an important lens to inform our understanding of implementation as a change process.

Based on a review of the literature, this chapter presents a brief history of the related theory building and then introduces three factors affecting the contemporary implementation processes and discusses their implications for its evaluation: networked governance, the sociopolitical context and the democratic turn, and new public management. In closing, we apply the policy implementation lens to the Gatehouse Project case study .

A broad view of federal-level policy implementation is adopted—one that recognizes the macropolicy process and implementation chain within which programs implemented in community or organizational settings are embedded. This is distinct from an equally significant literature on program implementation, which focuses on microlevel implementation processes occurring within organizations and is influenced by factors such as organizational culture, capacity, and internal champions (Scheirer, 1981).

Literature Search: Situating Implementation in the Policy Process

A literature review led to the identification of classic works in the field of policy implementation and other contemporary articles related to theory development. JSTOR, PAIS, MEDLINE, PROQUEST, and EBSCO Academic Premier indexes were searched using the key words *implementation theory, implementation research,* and *policy implementation.* Articles were searched for the time period 1990 forward; references for important works, including textbooks, conducted before 1990 were also identified.

The study of policy implementation is grounded in the disciplines of public administration and the policy sciences. The policy process represents a heuristic for policy studies and has generally been conceptualized as including the following steps: (1) agenda setting, (2) issue definition, (3) policy formulation, (4) policy decision, (5) policy implementation, (6) evaluation, and

(7) maintenance, succession, or termination (Brewer, 1974; Jenkins, 1978; Laswell, 1956). Implementation and evaluation, characterized as two separate stages in this process, have been called two sides of the same coin with "implementation providing the experience that evaluation interrogates and evaluation providing the intelligence to make sense out of what is happening" (Pressman & Wildavsky, 1984, p. xv).

What Is Policy Implementation? In general, policy implementation can be considered the process of carrying out a government decision (Berman, 1978). In defining policy implementation, it is useful to make the conceptual distinction between the policy implementation process and policy outcomes, even though these are interactive in practice (O'Toole, 2000). The process involves action on the behalf of the policy, whereas policy outcomes refer to the ultimate effect on the policy problem. Ottoson and Green (1987) suggest that "implementation is an iterative process in which ideas, expressed as policy, are transformed into behavior, expressed as social action" (p. 362). The social action transformed from the policy is typically aimed at social betterment and most frequently manifests as programs, procedures, regulations, or practices.

Theory Development: A Brief History. Parsimonious theoretical frameworks describing the process of public policy implementation continue to evade policy theorists (Salamon, 2002). Although generations of implementation theory have been described (Goggin, Bowman, Lester, & O'Toole, 1990), theoretical consensus remains elusive, and none of these frameworks offers the predictive capacity characteristic of formal theory.

The history of theory development begins with the landmark case studies of the early 1970s (Derthick, 1972; Pressman & Wildavsky, 1973), which documented the challenges and complexities of bringing a policy to fruition in real-world circumstances. Pressman and Wildavsky's (1973) classic case study of the implementation of an economic development agency policy in Oakland, California, illustrated the extensive interagency interactions and political bargaining involved in that process.

Efforts to adopt an empirical approach followed, with a divide emerging between those viewing implementation as a top-down process and those advocating a bottom-up approach. A rational management perspective dominates the top-down model, where implementation is viewed as a product of strong bureaucratic management involving control, coercion, and compliance to ensure fidelity with the policy objectives (Mazmanian & Sabatier, 1989). In contrast, the bottom-up model suggests that successful implementation occurs only when those affected are involved earlier in the policy process—that is, in stages such as issue definition and policy formulation, as well as during the implementation stage (Berman, 1978).

In the 1990s, the debate between the top-downers and bottom-uppers was essentially put to rest, and integrated, contingency-based models (Goggin et al., 1990; Matland, 1995) were proposed that gave increased attention to the role that intergovernmental relationships, the political context, and conflict play in shaping the implementation process. At the same time, some leaders in the policy field (deLeon, 1997; Dryzek, 2000; Fischer, 2003) began promoting more democratic approaches to public policy, including policy implementation and evaluation, recognizing the broader purposes of enlightenment, citizen participation, and social consensus.

Factors Affecting Contemporary Implementation Processes

This theoretical account underscores policy implementation as a change process characterized by multiple organizations and shaped to some extent by administrative practice but also influenced by politics and value differences. Our review, particularly of more recent contributions to the literature, led us to examine three factors, consistent with these characteristics, that we propose play an important role in today's policy implementation process and its evaluation: networked governance, sociopolitical context and the democratic turn, and new public management. Although these factors clearly overlap, each is distinguished to facilitate our analysis and advance the related discourse.

Networked Governance.   Policy theorists recognize that implementation involves coordinating action across multiple organizational actors and implementers (O'Toole, 2000). The relationships and interaction among agencies across the implementation chain are growing more complex as newer networked approaches to policy implementation are adopted. Of interest, then, are the networked organizational structures that allow policy ideas to take their shape as real-world actions. This aspect of policy implementation requires the evaluator to confront a "world of multiple institutional actors whose cooperation and perhaps coordination are needed for implementation success" (O'Toole, 2000, p. 266).

Emerging literatures in the policy sciences around networked governance offer insights into the organizational structures and relationships involved in contemporary policy implementation (O'Toole, 2000). Beginning in the 1990s, governance was proposed as a newer organizing concept for public administration and management. Within a governance framework, network structures, rather than the formal institutions of government, dominate public policy and are increasingly responsible for policy implementation (Peters & Pierre, 1998). Networks can vary in structure, size, and complexity and are referred to by various terms, including *partnerships, coalitions,* and *consortiums,* among others (Agranoff, 2003). In networked governance, horizontal relationships aimed at improving service integration, often with nongovernmental partners, are typically joined with vertical or hierarchical ones reflecting traditional, intergovernmental relationships (Heinrich, Hill, & Lynn, 2004). These networked organizational structures are presumed to offer a collaborative advantage with the potential to achieve what no single program or agency could accomplish on its own (Lasker,

Weiss, & Miller, 2002). At the same time, networks introduce new challenges to implementation as a greater number of agency representatives come to the table, each with multiple interests and unique constituencies.

Implications for Evaluation. Evaluating policy implementation in a networked governance context poses several challenges given that complex social problems are usually addressed, accountability becomes fragmented, and the performance of the network itself is important to implementation success.

The prominence of network approaches to policy implementation has emerged in part owing to the complexity of today's social problems that require transdisciplinary and intersectoral responses (Stokols, 2006). Through collaboration among networked agencies, multiple interventions and strategies can be coordinated to address the host of factors contributing to the problem. Although many early evaluation approaches were developed by psychologists and educational researchers who applied an individual unit of analysis, networked approaches require different methods and tools that consider the larger social system. Network analysis and case studies may help evaluators better understand who is involved in policy implementation, their incentives for participation, and the nature and strength of the relationships. Finally, that evaluators are confronting more complex social problems and different implementation structures suggests that they possess not only strong methodological competencies but a cogent understanding of the particular social problem as well.

Although networks increasingly represent more appropriate structures to effectively and synergistically implement public policy, the implementation process itself becomes more complicated given the interdependencies among organizations (Keast, Mandell, Brown, & Woolcock, 2004). In particular, accountability becomes a central challenge of networked governance as policy implementation is decentralized, traditional hierarchical authority is compromised, political resources are shared, and monitoring channels are diffused and made unreliable (Peters, 2001). Consequently, when policy implementation involves networks, issues of accountability are likely to emerge as a challenge to evaluation. In particular, when longer-term outcomes reflect the actions of several interventions or activities, it becomes difficult to tease apart the unique contribution of individual programs and make claims of attribution.

For evaluators, elaborating program theory through the use of logic models or evaluability assessment may help clarify the causal relationships or mechanisms of change between specific activities and outcomes and may potentially delineate the unique, intended contributions of specific programs (Weiss, 1997; Wholey, 1987). But even with the use of theory-based approaches, when one is evaluating a multifaceted policy initiative, the ability to attribute specific long-term outcomes to individual programs may never be possible or may require evaluation designs that are cost prohibitive. Mayne (2001) describes contribution analysis as a means to build credible stories of attribution and reduce uncertainty about contributions that programs make. This analysis begins with developing a results chain delineating plausible associations between program activities and outcomes and then identifying alternate explanations and external factors affecting outcomes, examining weaknesses in the proposed associations, and building evidence over time to strengthen claims of contribution.

Policy implementation and other change processes involving interorganizational structures raise questions regarding the evaluation of the network itself. In public health, for example, the implicit assumption is that collaborative planning and priority setting among partners lead to more appropriate and integrated service delivery and, ultimately, better health outcomes than would be produced independently. Evaluation can be used to examine these assumptions. Similarly, in conducting participatory forms of research or evaluation, the health of the coalition is itself perceived to be vital to the research or evaluation process (Minkler, 2005). Therefore, the effectiveness of the network would seem to be an important object for evaluation within these types of implementation settings.

Although there has been increasing attention to evaluating networks, assessing their effectiveness is complex. Partnership synergy (Weiss, Anderson, & Lasker, 2002) has been proposed as an outcome for effective partnership, as has increased organizational social capital (Cohen & Prusak, 2001). In public policy, Provan and Milward (2001) argue that networks must be evaluated at three distinct levels: the community, network, and participant. They have applied network analysis methods to evaluate collaborative performance. While challenges remain in assessing network outcomes, process evaluation that attends to network development and functioning is equally important and will help inform ongoing program management efforts (Butterfoss, 2006).

The Sociopolitical Context and the Democratic Turn. Sociopolitical factors play out at all levels of the policy implementation process. Implementers' decisions about whose needs will be served, how they will be served, and which outcomes will be valued are determined in part by social and political factors. The emphasis and understanding of the sociopolitical aspects set policy implementation analysis apart from other change processes discussed in this issue and provide evaluators with a valuable lens to view change processes more generally.

One consequence of networked implementation structures is the participation of a larger number of third-party organizational actors in the implementation process. Given that each actor comes to the table with her own values, interests, and goals and those of her organization, implementation is increasingly being defined through sociopolitical processes of negotiation, compromise, and bargaining (Frederickson & Smith, 2003). Power differentials are inevitable in these processes, and some actors will have greater influence than others owing to differences in status, resources, formal authority, access to information, and expertise (Wallerstein & Duran, 2006).

These power issues relate closely to the more recent democratic turn in the policy sciences. Leaders of this movement argue that the field of public policy has largely adopted technocratic approaches perceived as overly responsive to the political demands of the elite who affect public policy (for example, interest groups and politicians) rather than to the popular needs of those affected by it (deLeon, 1997; Dryzek, 2000). These authors suggest that policy analysis increasingly is characterized by prevailing political ideology, which favors economic analysis and experimental design. Fischer (2003), Dryzek (2000), and deLeon (1997) all advocate a "democratization of the policy sciences" (deLeon, 1997, p. x), a practice that embraces more deliberative approaches aimed at collaborative consensus building that contribute toward a democracy characterized by broader and more meaningful public participation.

Implications for Evaluation. The realities of the sociopolitical context suggest that evaluators must attend to political factors affecting the policy implementation process by considering who has a stake in shaping implementation and which stakeholders have the power to define both program details and their outcomes. These power differentials have important implications for evaluating implementation and for evaluation practice more broadly.

Evaluators must consider the relationships and interactions among organizational actors where conflicts between government actors at different levels, private sector organizations, and the grassroots community can play out as a tug-of-war (Bardach, 1977; Chung & Lounsbury, 2006). The multiplicity of stakeholder views can challenge both evaluators' and stakeholders' abilities to reach consensus in determining program goals, defining the evaluand, and identifying priority outcomes. Inattention to conflicts and differences arising from competing agendas, mandates, reward structures, and constituencies can compromise the mutual respect and trust needed to reach agreeable solutions to pressing health and social problems while potentially discounting some actors' values and priorities that are relevant to an evaluation.

The ability of the evaluator to facilitate effectively in this context, supporting meaningful dialogue and negotiation among diverse parties, is critical. In public health, for example, federal agencies in the United States and Canada frequently convene stakeholder groups to discuss program goals, identify priority outcomes, and discuss evaluation strategies for policy initiatives that are implemented nationally. In these situations, evaluators may temper power differentials through effective group facilitation and help identify evaluation priorities that are responsive to the varied needs of those involved. Values inquiry, an approach Henry (2002) described, may be a useful strategy to systematically extract relevant stakeholder values that inform the evaluation's purpose, choice of evaluation questions, and criteria for success. Similarly, an inclusive approach to evaluability assessment (Wholey, 2004), a means to explore the feasibility of evaluation approaches, may also facilitate agreement on program goals, outcomes, and the evaluation approach, and promote the use of findings.

The democratic turn in policy studies coincides with the introduction of more participatory evaluation approaches, whether qualitative, quantitative, or mixed-methods approaches are used. For instance, evaluation models

New Directions for Evaluation • DOI: 10.1002/ev

advocated by Guba and Lincoln (1989), House and Howe (1999), and Fetterman and Wandersman (2005) promote stakeholder participation and empowerment of stakeholders through methods consistent with constructionist and other interpretive paradigms. Similarly, the application of participatory research approaches to evaluation, such as action research (Stokols, 2006), participatory research (Green et al., 1995), and community-based participatory research (Israel, Schulz, Parker, & Becker, 1998), especially at the program level, is also consistent with this democratic turn in policy evaluation. When these approaches are applied to policy implementation, such tenets as ensuring stakeholder engagement may promote the increased use of evaluation results (Weiss, 1998). Wang, Morrel-Samuels, Hutchison, Bell, and Pestronk (2004) describe a participatory action research effort using PhotoVoice that involved local policymakers as well as youths and resulted in a leveling of experience and social power. PhotoVoice engages people who are affected by an issue in a participatory process of using photography to identify and express issues and concerns that are important to their community. PhotoVoice can be used for needs assessment, asset mapping, and evaluation and is often used as a means for reaching policymakers.

Greene (2001) also recognizes the importance of discursive practices in facilitating more democratic deliberation about social programs that embrace evaluators' civic responsibility to improve society and contribute toward democratic reform. She suggests, "It is time to acknowledge that the social practice of evaluation helps to shape and constitute the sociopolitical institutions and political discourse to which it is designed to contribute. That is, our work is neither scientifically nor politically neutral" (p. 400). Greene also advances a pluralistic approach as central to understanding, and she encourages evaluators to adopt a stance of value plurality in order to better advance the interests of a diversity of stakeholders.

Striving for a more democratic practice requires that evaluators challenge their philosophical assumptions and consider alternative paradigms that embrace contextually sensitive methods and approaches, experiential knowledge, and the multiple perspectives and values of participants. Given that policy implementation is significantly influenced by context and the multiple actors engaged in the process, employing methods insensitive to both would likely compromise an evaluation effort. Qualitative methods, particularly forms of case study and grounded theory, represent evaluation approaches that aim for contextual, pluralistic understanding. These methods are also valuable in facilitating understanding of policy implementation processes, especially when time-series or other longitudinal designs are employed. In addition, integrating qualitative methods into quantitative evaluation designs can help evaluators understand why and how intended policy outcomes were or were not achieved and identify potential unintended outcomes that manifest during the course of policy implementation.

New Public Management. New public management (NPM), a global, public management reform that emerged in the early 1990s, advocates, in part, outcome-based performance. In fact, performance is so central to NPM that it has been called "results-oriented government" (Osborne & Gaebler, 1992, p. 138). Performance, as measured through outcomes rather than outputs, is emphasized in NPM as a means to assess management and policy effectiveness, as well as a means of accountability (Peters, 2001). The best-known manifestation of NPM is the Government Performance and Results Act of 1993 (GPRA), which was followed by a similar policy, the Program Assessment Rating Tool (PART). PART was developed to assess federal programs based on program performance and evaluation information and brings even greater attention to outcomes and results than GPRA did (Brass, 2004).

In regard to policy implementation, GPRA and PART reflect to some extent traditional top-down approaches. Their emphasis on performance outcomes, which are typically defined by the statute or by federal-level administrators, often with input from state and local partners, has significant implications for programming. For instance, given requirements to meet specified indicators, program managers must stress implementation activities that ensure those targets are met. Consequently, performance measurement offers an important tool for federal managers to promote priority activities, monitor policy implementation, and influence implementation behavior in positive ways. At the same time, performance measurement may compromise activities and outcomes deemed important by program implementers, and it can produce unintended effects (for example, creaming, goal displacement) with troublesome implications (Perrin, 1998).

Implications for Evaluation. As federal policies, GPRA and PART have important implications for evaluation practice. A 2005 study by the U.S. Government Accountability Office found that the PART process stimulated agencies to build their evaluation capacity, although programs more typically designed evaluations to meet their own needs related to program improvement rather than broader evaluations. Given this, evaluators may be well positioned to direct how limited evaluation resources are allocated and advocate for evaluation efforts deemed most likely to promote social betterment.

GPRA's and PART's emphasis on outcomes over process or outputs to assess policy implementation also has implications for evaluation practice. Radin (2006) suggests that the focus on outcomes fundamentally entitles accountability as an evaluation purpose over other purposes such as program improvement. In fact, the influence of NPM, specifically GPRA and PART, has spurred what some have described as an accountability movement in government (Behn, 2003; Radin, 2006). However, the complexity of contemporary social problems, along with implementation structures increasingly defined by networks, often makes attributing longer-term outcomes and results to a particular program difficult, if not impossible.

Evaluators may have opportunities for improving the practice of performance measurement while also educating decision makers; promoting alternative evaluation approaches, values, and purposes; and advocating for additional evaluation resources. First, evaluators can offer needed expertise in the development and design of performance measurement systems—in particular, on issues of measurement (Scheirer & Newcomer, 2001). Second, given the methodological challenges of assessing accountability based solely on outcome-level performance measures, evaluators can help educate decision makers, including policymakers, about such constraints, especially in relation to long-term outcomes. Specifically, evaluators can help shift the dialogue from one focused on attribution and accountability to one centered more appropriately on notions of contribution and shared accountability. Third, evaluators can help construct theory-based logic models to identify short- and intermediate-level outcomes that may be attributable to specific program efforts. Ideally, such indicators will have been demonstrated through prior research to relate to the long-term outcomes of a policy initiative.

Next, evaluators can emphasize the importance of other evaluation purposes and methods, including process evaluation, to better understand why certain outcomes may or may not have been achieved and to inform ongoing implementation decisions. Because policy and program implementation are evolving processes that typically entail extensive adaptation, evaluation efforts must continue to attend to process issues. As Green (2001) suggested, there is a need to reconceptualize "best practices" as "best processes."

Conclusion

Policy implementation is a dynamic and evolving change process owing to a confluence of factors, including networked implementation structures, sociopolitical conflict, and administrative reforms that shape how policy ideas are translated into social betterment programs. As Majone and Wildavsky (1984) point out, "When we act to implement a policy, we change it" (p. 177). And although parsimonious theoretical frameworks describing the policy implementation process continue to evade the profession, theory sharpens how evaluators understand the policy implementation process, as well as the methodologies and approaches applied to its evaluation. Although theorists agree on the adaptive process characterizing implementation, this chapter highlights both top-down pressures (administrative reforms such as NPM) and bottom-up influences (network management) that support an integrated view of the implementation process—one that is enmeshed in a sociopolitical context throughout.

The policy implementation lens invites evaluators to consider a multifaceted set of challenges, especially when evaluating macrolevel change processes. Some of these include contending with multiple institutional actors with variable degrees of power and influence, contemporary health and social problems that are inherently complex, and a political environment emphasizing accountability and program outcomes. These challenges suggest that evaluators must come to their task equipped with a cogent understanding of the health or social issue, a deep toolbox of evaluation approaches and methods, and strong facilitation skills to contend with the multiplicity of agendas, interests, and values represented throughout the implementation chain. Finally, the importance of the sociopolitical context of implementation encourages evaluators to consider democratic practices and other methods that embrace a stance of value plurality and promote mutual respect and trust among stakeholders throughout the evaluation process.

Case Study Application: Evaluating the Gatehouse Project With an Implementation Lens

The Gatehouse Project was a successful multilevel, school-based intervention aimed at promoting the emotional well-being of young people by increasing students' connectedness to school (Patton et al., 2000, 2006; Patton, Bond, Butler, & Glover, 2003).

The intervention included a curriculum component focused on increasing students' skills and knowledge for dealing with everyday life challenges and a whole-school component that sought to make changes to the schools' social and learning environment to enhance security, communication, and positive regard through valued participation. A member of the research team facilitated the project implementation process. Key elements were the establishment of a school-based health action team, the use of local data to review the school environment and drive change, targeted professional development, and opportunities for reflective practice (Glover & Butler, 2004; Patton et al., 2003; Patton et al., 2006). This process resulted in schools' identifying and implementing activities and strategies appropriate to their local context; thus, what was done varied from school to school.

One unique area that the implementation literature invites the evaluator to explore is the sociopolitical context of project delivery. Who was on the school health action teams? What were their networks and connections, inside and outside the school? How were these resources enabled and drawn on to influence the way the intervention was delivered or sustained? This network perspective focuses on the people, or actors, and how different characteristics of the different actor networks in different schools might have influenced the change processes in diverse directions. Exploration could be quantitative, using network analysis, or qualitative, or both. Such insights might help evaluators appreciate why an intervention seems to have more sway in some contexts than others. It also might assist with identifying minimum or threshold levels of interconnectedness among key champions that might predict both intervention effectiveness and sustainability.

References

Agranoff, R. (2003). *Leveraging networks: A guide for public managers working across organizations.* Washington, DC: IBM Endowment for the Business of Government.

Bardach, E. (1977). The implementation game. In S. Z. Theodoulou & M. A. Cahn (Eds.), *Public policy: The essential readings.* Upper Saddle River, NJ: Prentice Hall.

Behn, R. D. (2003). Why measure performance? Different purposes require different measures. *Public Administration Review, 63,* 586–606.

Berman, P. (1978). The study of macro- and micro-implementation. *Public Policy, 26*(2), 155–184.

Brass, C. T. (2004). *The Bush administration's Program Assessment Rating Tool (PART).* Washington, DC: Congressional Research Service, Library of Congress.

Brewer, G. D. (1974). The policy sciences emerge: To nurture and structure a discipline. *Policy Sciences, 5*(3), 239–244.

Butterfoss, F. D. (2006). Process evaluation for community participation. *Annual Review of Public Health, 27,* 323–340.

Chung, K., & Lounsbury, D. W. (2006). The role of power, process, and relationships in participatory research for statewide HIV/AIDS programming. *Social Science and Medicine, 63*(8), 2129–2140.

Cohen, D., & Prusak, L. (2001). *In good company: How social capital makes organizations work.* Boston: Harvard Business School Press.

deLeon, P. (1997). *Democracy and the policy sciences.* Albany, NY: SUNY Press.

Derthick, M. (1972). *New towns in town: Why a federal program failed.* Washington, DC: Urban Institute.

Dryzek, J. S. (2000). *Deliberative democracy and beyond: Liberals, critics, contestations.* New York: Oxford University Press.

Fetterman, D. M., & Wandersman, A. (2005). *Empowerment evaluation principles in practice.* New York: Guilford Press.

Fischer, F. (2003). *Reframing public policy: Discursive politics and deliberative practices.* New York: Oxford University Press.

Frederickson, G. H., & Smith, K. B. (2003). *The public administration theory primer: Essentials of public policy and administration.* Boulder, CO: Westview Press.

Glover, S., & Butler, H. (2004). Facilitating health promotion within school communities. In R. Moodie & A. Hulme (Eds.), *Hands-on health promotion.* Melbourne: IP Communications.

Goggin, M. L., Bowman, A. O., Lester, J. P., & O'Toole, L. J. (1990). *Implementation theory and practice: Toward a third generation.* Glenview, IL: Scott, Foresman.

Green, L. W. (2001). From research to "best practices" in other settings and populations. *American Journal of Health Behavior, 25*(3), 165–178.

Green, L. W., George, M. A., Daniel, M., Frankish, C. J., Herbert, C. P., Bowie, W. R., et al. (1995). *Study of participatory research in health promotion: Review and recommendations for the development of participatory research in health promotion in Canada* (pp. 43–50). Ottawa: Royal Society of Canada.

Greene, J. C. (2001). Evaluation extrapolations. *American Journal of Evaluation, 22*(3), 397–402.

Guba, E. G., & Lincoln, Y. S. (1989). *Fourth generation evaluation.* Thousand Oaks, CA: Sage.

Heinrich, C. J., Hill, C. J., & Lynn, L. E., Jr. (2004). Governance as an organizing theme for empirical research. In P. A. Ingraham & L. Lynn (Eds.), *The art of governance: Analyzing management and administration.* Washington, DC: Georgetown University Press.

Henry, G. (2002). Choosing criteria to judge program success: A values inquiry. *Evaluation, 8*(2), 182–204.

House, E. R., & Howe, K. R. (1999). *Values in evaluation and social research.* Thousand Oaks, CA: Sage.

Israel, B. A., Schulz, A., Parker, E. A., & Becker, A. B. (1998). Review of community-based research: Assessing partnership approaches to improve public health. *Annual Review of Public Health, 19,* 173–202.

Jenkins, W. I. (1978). *Policy analysis.* London: Martin Robertson.

Keast, R., Mandell, M., Brown, K., & Woolcock, G. (2004). Network structures: Working differently and changing expectations. *Public Administration Review, 64*(3), 363–371.

Lasker, R. D., Weiss, E. S., & Miller, R. (2002). Partnership synergy: A practical framework for studying and strengthening the collaborative advantage. *Milbank Quarterly, 79*(2), 179–205.

Laswell, H. D. (1956). *The decision process: Seven categories of functional analysis.* College Park: University of Maryland.

Lester, J. P., & Goggin, M. L. (1998). Back to the future: The rediscovery of implementation studies. *Policy Currents, 8*(3), 1–9.

Majone, G., & Wildavsky, A. (1984). Implementation as evolution. In J. L. Pressman & A. Wildavsky (Eds.), *Implementation* (3rd ed.). Berkeley: University of California Press.

Matland, R. E. (1995). Synthesizing the implementation literature: The ambiguity-conflict model of policy implementation. *Journal of Public Administration Research and Theory, 5*(2), 145–174.

Mayne, J. (2001). Addressing attribution through contribution analysis: Using performance measures sensibly. *Canadian Journal of Program Evaluation, 16*(1), 1–24.

Mazmanian, D. A., & Sabatier, P. A. (1989). *Implementation and public policy.* Lanham, MD: University Press of America.

Minkler, M. (2005). Community-based research partnerships: Challenges and opportunities. *Journal of Urban Health, 82*(2, Suppl. 2), ii3–ii12.

Osborne, D., & Gaebler, T. (1992). *Reinventing government: How the entrepreneurial spirit is transforming the public sector.* New York: Penguin Books.

O'Toole, L. J. (2000). Research on policy implementation: Assessment and prospects. *Journal of Public Administration Research and Theory, 10*(2), 263–288.

Ottoson, J. M., & Green, L. W. (1987). Reconciling concept and context: Theory of implementation. *Health Education and Promotion, 2,* 353–382.

Parsons, W. (1995). *Public policy: An introduction to the theory and practice of policy analysis.* Northampton, MA: Edward Elgar.

Patton, G., Bond, L., Butler, H., & Glover, S. (2003). Changing schools, changing health? Design and implementation of the Gatehouse Project. *Journal of Adolescent Health, 33*(4), 231–239.

Patton, G. C., Bond, L., Carlin, J. B., Thomas, L., Butler, H., Glover, S., et al. (2006). Promoting social inclusion in schools: A group-randomized trial of effects on student health risk behaviour and well-being. *American Journal of Public Health, 96,* 1582–1587.

Patton, G. C., Glover, S., Bond, L., Butler, H., Godfrey, C., Bowes, G., et al. (2000). The Gatehouse Project: A systematic approach to mental health promotion in secondary schools. *Australian and New Zealand Journal of Psychiatry, 34,* 586–593.

Perrin, B. (1998). Effective use and misuse of performance measurement. *American Journal of Evaluation, 19*(3), 367–379.

Peters, B. G. (2001). *The future of governing* (2nd ed.). Lawrence: University Press of Kansas.

Peters, B. G., & Pierre, J. (1998). Governance without government? Rethinking public administration. *Journal of Public Administration Research and Theory, 8*(2), 223–243.

Pressman, J. L., & Wildavsky, A. (1973). *Implementation* (3rd ed.). Berkeley: University of California Press.

Pressman, J. L., & Wildavsky, A. (1984). *Implementation* (3rd ed. with new Foreword). Berkeley: University of California Press.

Provan, K. G., & Milward, H. B. (2001). Do networks really work? A framework for evaluating public-sector organizational networks. *Public Administration Review, 61*(4), 414–423.

Radin, B. A. (2006). *Challenging the performance movement*. Washington, DC: Georgetown University Press.

Salamon, L. M. (2002). The new governance and the tools of public action: An introduction. In L. M. Salamon (Ed.), *The tools of government: A guide to the new governance* (pp. 1–47). New York: Oxford University Press.

Scheirer, M. A. (1981). *Program implementation: The organizational context*. Thousand Oaks, CA: Sage.

Scheirer, M. A., & Newcomer, K. E. (2001). Opportunities for program evaluators to facilitate performance-based management. *Evaluation and Program Planning, 24*(1), 63–71.

Stokols, D. (2006). Toward a science of transdisciplinary action research. *American Journal of Community Psychology, 38*(1–2), 63–77.

U.S. Government Accountability Office. (2005). *OMB's PART reviews increased agencies' attention to improving evidence of program results*. Washington DC: U.S. Government Accountability Office.

Wallerstein, N. B., & Duran, B. (2006). Using community-based participatory research to address health disparities. *Health Promotion Practice, 7*(3), 312–323.

Wang, C. C., Morrel-Samuels, S., Hutchison, P. M., Bell, L., & Pestronk, R. M. (2004). Flint PhotoVoice: Community building among youths, adults, and policymakers. *American Journal of Public Health, 94*(6), 911–913.

Weiss, C. H. (1997). Theory-based evaluation: Past, present, and future. In D. J. Rog & D. Fournier (Eds.), *Progress and future directions in evaluation: Perspectives on theory, practice, and methods* (pp. 41–56). New Directions for Evaluation, no. 76. San Francisco: Jossey-Bass.

Weiss, C. H. (1998). *Evaluation* (2nd ed.). Upper Saddle River, NJ: Prentice Hall.

Weiss, E. S., Anderson, R. M., & Lasker, R. D. (2002). Making the most of collaboration: Exploring the relationship between partnership synergy and partnership functioning. *Health Education and Behavior, 29,* 683–698.

Wholey, J. S. (1987). Evaluability assessment: Developing program theory. In L. Bickman (Ed.), *Using program theory in evaluation* (pp. 77–92). New Directions for Evaluation, no. 33. San Francisco: Jossey-Bass.

Wholey, J. S. (2004). Evaluability assessment. In J. S. Wholey, H. P. Hatry, & K. E. Newcomer (Eds.), *Handbook of practical program evaluation* (2nd ed.). San Francisco: Jossey-Bass.

AMY DEGROFF is a researcher in the Division of Cancer Prevention and Control at the Centers for Disease Control and Prevention.

MARGARET CARGO is senior lecturer, School of Health Sciences, University of South Australia, and holds adjunct appointments with McGill University through the Douglas Hospital Research Centre and Department of Psychiatry.

NEW DIRECTIONS FOR EVALUATION • DOI: 10.1002/ev

Oliver, M. L. (2009). The transfer process: Implications for evaluation. In J. M. Ottoson &
P. Hawe (Eds.), *Knowledge utilization, diffusion, implementation, transfer, and translation:
Implications for evaluation. New Directions for Evaluation, 124,* 61–73.

The Transfer Process: Implications for Evaluation

Monica LaBelle Oliver

Abstract

*Transfer is a term used in many fields to describe a change process involving move-
ment of knowledge, skills, or policy from one place to another. The central components of transfer invite the evaluator to conceptualize the change process in terms of
a starting point, different understandings of what is being transferred, the medium
or mechanism, the concomitant agents, the purpose, and the ending point. Technological models of transfer can be contrasted with learning models of transfer. This
means that the educational technology of the intervention might be easily transferred,
for example, but not the organizational engagement and inquiry process associated
with it. Such scenarios are common in fields where capacity varies widely from place
to place. It is therefore crucial to surface what was actually implemented, especially
if programs have the same name in various sites, but in reality have replicated very
different forms of the program.* © Wiley Periodicals, Inc., and the American
Evaluation Association.

W hether determining the impact of a health intervention, calculating the commercial success of a product, or assessing the effectiveness of a teaching or training program, evaluators ultimately
look at a process of change for whether and how that change occurred.
Transfer as a term for a change process permeates many academic fields and

practical settings. Indeed, it seems ubiquitous: we read about transfer of training, transfer of learning, technology transfer, knowledge transfer, and policy transfer, for example. Depending on what is being transferred, to whom, and where, evaluating the process that is transferred requires identifying who is on the receiving end of the transfer, as well as clearly delineating what is transferring.

In this chapter, the operable metaphor for the transfer process is a suspension bridge that carries a product, idea, or policy across to a recipient and thereby links the context of its origination with the context of its destination. These basic components of the transfer process ultimately shape evaluation of whether the transfer is successful. This chapter seeks to flesh out the components of the transfer process and identify a set of useful criteria for evaluating process from a transfer perspective. The aim is not to review the transfer literature authoritatively across disciplines or to extol transfer as the ultimate conveyor of knowledge. Rather, the chapter endeavors to reveal the components of the transfer process as multiple disciplines delineate them for the purpose of looking critically at the implications for evaluation of transfer. Addressing the question of whether *transfer* is an adequate moniker for a complex process also points to the challenges of evaluating a poorly understood process with many facets.

The transfer process offers a tool for evaluating programs and processes; the evaluator can draw from the image of transfer as a suspension bridge to discern the logic of a program or a process from its beginning to its end. Whether what is being transferred is a training program, a technological innovation, or a policy, an understanding of the fundamentals of any transfer process can help evaluators shape the undergirding model. Consider, for example, an image from a well-known use of the word *transfer*—a token or pass from a public transportation system that allows the rider to take an additional bus or train ride in a limited amount of time without having to pay another fare. The transfer process shares similar components with this image: a starting point (the point of embarkment), an ending point (the destination of the journey), and the fact that the nature of the rider remains intact. An evaluator will find these components in any transfer context. For example, in transfer of training, the point of embarkment is the uninitiated trainee in the hands of the trainer; the destination is the workplace. Plumbing the details of the transfer process offers insight into evaluating any particular process or program.

Literature Search

Comprehending the scope of the transfer process involved an extensive electronic literature search of articles since 1965. These databases revealed a breadth of disciplines addressing the transfer process: the Academic Search Premier, PAIS International, JSTOR (including economics, education, political science, psychology, and sociology), Medline, ERIC, and ProQuest.

NEW DIRECTIONS FOR EVALUATION • DOI: 10.1002/ev

The specific search terms were *transfer, transfer of training, transfer of learning, knowledge transfer,* and *technology transfer.* That prompted articles on transfer from a variety of fields: education, economics, health, management and human resources, industrial psychology, the military, international development, science and technology, and international policy. Other terms explicitly associated with transfer emerged from the electronic searches: *policy transfer, occupational transfer, transfer of a good, transfer of information,* and *transfer of best practice,* for example. Adjectival relationships surfaced as well, specifically *positive* and *negative* transfer, *uninformed* or *spontaneous* transfer, and *vertical* and *lateral* transfer.

Transfer Across Disciplines. The transfer literature spans a multitude of disciplines, and the broad range of writings suggests that the term *transfer* incorporates or comprises countless other processes. Transfer may look different according to the evaluator's particular context. The management literature, for example, suggests that effective transfer (of knowledge, usually through a training program) depends on good organizational leadership, organizational culture, and the skills of the trainees—the supposed recipients of the transfer (Goh, 2002). The emphasis is on good management as the linchpin of successful technology transfer.

The technology transfer tradition, by contrast, is less oriented toward the individual trainee as the recipient of the transfer and more focused on the organization, a country, or even the public at large as the recipient of the transfer. In this tradition, "technology" could mean a skill, some kind of knowledge, or a product from a laboratory. Landry, Amara, and Ouimet (2006) contend that *knowledge transfer* and *technology transfer* are often used interchangeably, but that technology transfer is a narrower category limited to change tools, and not inclusive of the broad theories that characterize knowledge transfer. Transfer of technology is notoriously difficult to evaluate, in part because of the difficulty of neatly capturing the process in a meaningful framework (Bozeman, 1988). Similarly, health policy lists transfer among its types of change. The health literature mostly refers to a transfer of research or laboratory knowledge to practice (Grol & Grimshaw, 2003) or of information to the patient.

The literature of education and psychology is a close cousin to the management perspective on transfer. Baldwin and Ford, in their extensive 1988 literature review on transfer of training, identify several factors that affect transfer. *Identical elements* is their name for training settings that simulate transfer settings. Design of training, training material that is generalizable, and maintenance of learning over a period of time also affect how and whether knowledge or skill transfers.

Other transfer-related concepts coming from education and educational psychology identify transfer categorically. *Positive* and *negative transfer* (Analoui, 1993) are terms describing whether the acquired knowledge or skills are being applied as intended (positive) or not (negative). Gagné (1970) identifies vertical transfer, wherein a skill directly applies to a task,

NEW DIRECTIONS FOR EVALUATION • DOI: 10.1002/ev

and lateral transfer, where the knowledge is dispersed generally and applies to a number of situations. Bereiter (1995) theorizes a transfer of disposi- tions, wherein students or trainees might learn a behavior or an attitude that they will apply to similar situations, if not a specific task-related skill. Unin- formed or spontaneous transfer is transfer of knowledge that occurs despite not being planned or intended (Gick & Holyoak, 1987). The problem of transfer is that the effects or results of the transfer are not sustainable over time; Analoui (1993) uses the analogy of an organ transplant: the organ works in the new body for a short time, but then the receiving body begins to reject it.

A growing body of work discusses policy transfer—the idea that an entire policy that has proven effective in one area of jurisdiction can be replicated in another. Different levels of jurisdiction (city, region, country) are sometimes articulated as different levels of transfer. The level of trans- fer also sometimes refers to the extent to which the original policy is imple- mented in its original form in the new context (Dolowitz & Marsh, 1996; Mestre, 2005). Greenhalgh, Robert, Macfarlane, Bate, and Kyriakidou (2004) introduce the idea of transferability of methodology—the notion of employing methodology systematically from one study to another for reviewing health policy.

This array of different forms, contexts, and conceptions of the transfer process seems at first to daunt the search for evaluation components. How- ever, a closer look at several aspects of different disciplines' takes on trans- fer reveals a pattern in the components comprising each different understanding of the process. These patterns, delineated in Table 5.1, offer a menu from which evaluators can select the appropriate pieces for a model of the transfer process.

What Is Transfer? A remarkably broad set of meanings and contexts ascribes itself to the change process labeled as transfer. An evaluator explor- ing the commonalities in each of the disciplines using the term *transfer* will find some identifiable central components of the process. Transfer is a mech- anism for getting knowledge in the form of learning, research discoveries, technology, or policy to a point where it can be used. It is a bridge between where the knowledge originates and where it will be applied. To "transfer" is to move something from one place to another. The roots of the word, from Latin *trans* (across) and *ferre* (bear, carry), imply a lateral motion of shuttling something from a place of origin to a different place. Beach (2003) describes the process as "movement across boundaries of activity contexts" (p. 101), emphasizing the motion and the location but not specifying that something (the what) is being transferred. Comparatively, Roessner (2000), describing technology transfer, defines it as "the movement of know-how, technical knowledge, or technology from one organizational setting to another" (p. 1). This view conveys a motion as well, but with the distinct implication of transporting something. There is a point of origin, a point of destination, and a *what* that is being transferred (research knowledge in a health system,

Table 5.1. Menu of Transfer Process Components

Starting Point	What Is Being Transferred	Transfer Mechanism or Medium	Concomitant Agents	Ending Point	Purpose
Classroom	Classroom learning	Training	Ability	Workplace	Developing a competent employee
Laboratory	Skill	Marketing	Motivation	Country	Building a learning culture
University	Product	Translating	Resources	Nonprofit	Creating a marketable product
Country	Process	Implementing	Identical elements	Commercial market	Improving health care
Corporation or firm	Information	Disseminating	Design	Community	Strengthening a country
Think tank	Policy	Diffusing	Generalizability	Organization	Solving a problem
Nonprofit	Task	Replicating	Communication	Firm	Bettering society
Government	Disposition	Transforming	Political relationships	Agency	
Foundation	Knowledge	Granting	Supporting policies or institutions	Civil society	
	Resources				

knowledge of effective policy, or classroom knowledge transferring from teacher to student, for example).

These varying definitions reflect both the similarities and the differences of the disciplines using them. When transfer is a process for training, for imbuing a trainee with knowledge or a skill to apply in the workplace, context emerges as essential to the definition of transfer. When researchers transfer technology from the laboratory to a commercial application, that which is being transferred (the what) is prominent in the definition because the completion of the transfer depends on that item's transformation. Yet disciplines as diverse as laboratory science and industrial psychology use the same term to describe their process of "carrying across." The Latin roots bring together multiple perspectives: fundamentally, something (the what) is being carried across from one context *to* another by means of a mechanism. For the evaluator seeking to assess the effectiveness of a transfer process, this is critical: designating what is being transferred is the first step. Key variables include the context of the transfer (which includes the origin of the transfer and the point of destination) and the mechanism that facilitates the transfer.

What Is Being Transferred?   Clearly something is being transferred. But within the varying fields, delineations of what is being transferred are no sharper than their descriptions of the transfer action itself. An extensive body of literature addresses technology transfer. But technology might be a process or a product; it might be know-how; it might be resource sharing (Bozeman, 1988). A social worker sees technology as technical assistance (Martinez-Brawley, 1995). Educational psychology theorists refer to transfer of training, transfer of learning, and knowledge transfer (Haskell, 2001). The field of public administration sees and defines policy transfer as the replication of a policy from one country to another (see Mossberger & Wolman, 2003). The what can be as concrete as a specific laboratory-generated product such as a microchip or as vague as knowledge.

So what is being transferred? The answer to this question underscores the importance of the evaluator's understanding the evaluand, the object of the evaluation (Scriven, 1991).

Mechanism of Transfer.   The mechanism for transfer is the process or skill or other means by which the what that is being transferred gets from point A to point B. For example, in a classroom, the teacher is transferring knowledge (the what) using the mechanism of pedagogy. Similarly, if a company were to develop a technological innovation conceived in a laboratory for commercial appeal, the innovation is transferred to the public through the development and marketing processes. The mechanism for transfer will hinge on what is being transferred; one can train someone in a skill, thereby transferring the skill from the trainer to the trainee, so training is the mechanism for transfer. But transferring a policy from one country to another would require a different mechanism, such as diffusion. One might diffuse or implement a policy; one would not train the policy. One might train an employee (thereby transferring learning or a skill—the what) but not diffuse the employee. Identifying the mechanism of transfer is arguably the murkiest of the tasks in elaborating the transfer process. The evaluator will find that pinpointing the mechanism of transfer helps to anchor the logic model for any transfer process.

From a semantic perspective, there is an implication of fidelity to the original in labeling an action as a transfer. For example, thinking of a skill transferring from trainer to trainee is to think of the skill as being the same at the end of the process as at the beginning. If a product concocted in a laboratory is transferred, or literally carried across from the laboratory to the consumer, the suggestion is that the product is the same when it reaches the consumer as it was when it left the laboratory. The semantic origins binding *transfer* speak to its limitations as a description of a complex change process. This limitation is evident in the literature from these various disciplines, as it is clear that knowledge, skills, products, and so forth do not necessarily have to stay true to their origins from starting point to destination in order for the transfer to have been successful.

The Context of the Transfer. If transfer is "carrying across," then something is moving from one context to another. An understanding of the transfer process helps evaluators identify key variables effecting transfer. That could be from a classroom to a workplace, from a laboratory to a market, from an industrialized country to a less developed country. Whatever the thing being transferred and the mechanism of the transfer, the beginning and the end of the process have respective contexts. Baldwin and Ford (1988), in reviewing the literature on transfer of learning, mention favorable environmental characteristics that facilitate transfer, such as trainee motivation or skill and workplace supervisor support. A large-scale study of information technology employees (Egan, Yang, & Bartlett, 2004), approached through a human resource development perspective, finds that the motivation among employees to transfer learning greatly affects the organizational learning culture. Bozeman (2000), in his review of the literature on technology transfer, refers to such environmental elements as geographical location, economic character, mission, and political opportunity or constraints. Speaking from a health policy perspective, Lavis, Posada, Haines, and Osei (2004) advocate for a structured approach to determining what is necessary for making a transfer work and whether it is worthwhile given what it would take. Management researchers meta-analyzing organizational knowledge transfer found evidence to support the idea that larger organizations and firms may have more resources than smaller ones to encourage the transfer of knowledge (van Wijk, Jansen, & Lyles, 2008). Mossberger and Wolman (2003) and Stone (2000) allude to the need for supportive structures and comparable origin and end environments for effective policy transfer. The originating context of what is being transferred facilitates or hinders its transfer just as its receiving context favors or discourages the effective completion of the transfer action.

NEW DIRECTIONS FOR EVALUATION • DOI: 10.1002/ev

The Transfer Process: Comparative Models

Baldwin and Ford (1988) elaborate a model of the transfer of learning process that sets out three key elements: training input factors, trainee characteristics, and conditions of transfer. Training design, trainee characteristics, and work-environment characteristics comprise the training input factors. The amount of original learning and subsequent retention of material constitute the training outcomes. Constraints, opportunities, and supervisor and peer support are the relevant characteristics of the work environment.

Bozeman (1988, 2000) identifies several models for how transfer works. His "out-the-door" model moves the product out of the laboratory as efficiently as possible. The marketing model depends on ultimate commercialization as the goal of the transfer. The political model emphasizes political climate and relationships. Bozeman ultimately combines these into a contingency model of technology transfer that has five components: the transfer agent (the input environment), the transfer media (the transfer mechanism), the object, the recipient of the transfer, and the environment. These components facilitate ultimate use, whose effectiveness is characterized by facets of the respective models.

Bozeman, and Baldwin and Ford, present compelling models of the transfer process that are strikingly similar in basic form despite their remarkably different disciplines of origin. Each acknowledges what is to be transferred, the transfer action, and the recipient individual or institution. Each presents context characteristics that favor an ultimately successful transfer. These models, from the education and technology fields, respectively, offer two distinctive renderings of the transfer process. They are not the only models, of course. Williams and Gibson (1990), for example, identify four technology transfer models, each of which characterizes transfer with a different context and end user. But the Baldwin and Ford model and the Bozeman contingency model, as with other models not depicted here, share parallel evaluation-conducive variables. Each has a context important to the success of the transfer; with Baldwin and Ford, it is the classroom or workplace, and with Bozeman, it is the laboratory and the market. Similarly, each model has a *what* that is being transferred: for Baldwin and Ford, it is learning, and for Bozeman, it is new technology. Although there is no formal model depicted here, one might imagine that for a policy transfer, the context might be two countries, and the *what* being transferred in this case might be a policy.

Transfer as a Bridge

A suspension bridge is a helpful metaphor for evaluators to use in thinking about the transfer process. The context preceding the transfer might be a laboratory, a classroom, or a country. The context following the transfer—receiving that which is transferred—could be a workplace, the commercial market, or another country. The prior knowledge representing what was known about the transfer object before the transfer represents the road leading up to the bridge. Utilization of the skill, knowledge, technology, or policy is the road leading away from the bridge. The bridge itself, a suspension bridge with supporting cables that represent variables facilitating successful transfer, is held together by the concomitant agents that are ancillary to the process of transfer. These might be Baldwin and Ford's (1988) ability and motivation of the trainee in the case of transfer of training, design of the product or process in the case of technology transfer, or supporting policies and institutions in the case of policy transfer.

The transfer process bridge has a starting point, an object (what) to be transferred, a mechanism for the transfer, and an ending point. Both the starting points and ending points have contextual characteristics. Prior knowledge or history (Rose, 1993) can prime the transfer, and utilization can employ what has been transferred. The menu of transfer process components in Table 5.1 represents components of the transfer bridge. As with any other bridge, there is a starting point with any transfer. This might be a classroom or a laboratory; an evaluator would want to identify this starting point, as well as the goal or ending point of the transfer. The thing being transferred (what) is being transported across the bridge in a truck; this might be a skill, a product, or a policy. The mechanism for the transfer, represented by the truck itself, might be instruction, diffusion, implementation, utilization, or any other means for getting the what from the point of origin to the point of destination. In the transfer bridge model, then, implementation, diffusion, translation, and utilization are simply mechanisms for transferring something from one person or place to another.

The suspension bridge as a metaphor provides a heuristic for the evaluator who is attempting to conceive a logic model for a transfer process. The what—the skill, product, or policy—moves from one context to another, such as from a classroom to a workplace. The what crosses the bridge by means of a mechanism such as training or implementing. Concomitant agents such as resources or trainee motivation facilitate or impede the process. The evaluator can follow the logic of the process across the bridge.

What Is Successful Transfer?

Success looks different depending on how the transfer bridge is constructed. For the transfer of knowledge from the classroom to the workplace through training, a successful trainee for whom learning occurred will exhibit new skills at work (Analoui, 1993). Educators measure learning rate, retention, and accuracy, including immediate versus long-term learning (Cormier & Hagman, 1987). Successful transfer could require fidelity to the original situation (Baldwin & Ford, 1988) or encourage adaptability across situations, with flexibility the measure of success (Kerlin, Auer, & Reid, 2003).

NEW DIRECTIONS FOR EVALUATION • DOI: 10.1002/ev

For the transfer of technology, successful transfer could mean the ultimate commercialization of a product (Williams & Gibson, 1990). For the transfer of a policy, success might be the adoption of a proposed policy. For the transfer of research knowledge to society, success might be the use of research-generated knowledge. The components of the transfer bridge table represent a menu for choosing the appropriate set of variables as a starting point for evaluation.

Bearing in mind the semantic limitations of transfer as a description of complex change, evaluating transfer requires identifying each component of the transfer process bridge for each particular situation. This thorough identification of the evaluand will leave the evaluator equipped to name key variables that will indicate success of the transfer:

- Identify the origin of the transfer and its context, including prior knowledge.
- Identify what is to be transferred.
- Identify the transfer media or mechanism.
- Identify any linking agents that facilitate the transfer.
- Identify the end destination of the transfer.

Key process evaluation variables from a transfer perspective include the origin and destination of the transfer, what is being transferred, facilitating linking agents, and context. The key outcome variables are time; adaptability versus fidelity from the original to the end product; retention, maintenance, and utilization of the transfer object; and uninformed or spontaneous transfer effects. These variables deserve attention from a transfer perspective, but the actual criteria constituting a success will depend on what is being transferred and how.

One thing we learn from understanding the transfer process is that although the variables might be the same, different expectations might set different standards of success. For example, evaluating the successful transfer of a skill needed for a job might require the trainee to maintain absolute fidelity to the task he learned in order to do his job by effectively employing that skill in the workplace. In contrast, evaluating the successful transfer of a policy from the United States to Great Britain might require that the policy be adaptable enough to fit the British context. The first example values rigid fidelity to the transfer origin; the second requires flexibility.

The transfer process appears to be linear and unidirectional; the sender of the information or technology (the teacher, for example, or the researcher) is not the receiver of the change. Instead, the student or the patient or the retail market receives the change. The success of the transfer depends on its moving forward rather than on its coming full circle.

For the intended transfer to occur, the evaluator carefully identifies the evaluand and pays attention to the context surrounding the process. Examining contrasting models of transfer shows just how different the process can appear from varied perspectives. The transfer process bridge metaphor high-lights the fundamental elements of the transfer process itself and facilitates identification of key variables for evaluation purposes. The evaluator can use these foundational elements as a guide for bridging the seeming ubiquity of the transfer process with the uniqueness of a given situation.

Case Study Application: Evaluating the Gatehouse Project With a Transfer Lens

The Gatehouse Project was a successful multilevel, school-based inter-vention aimed at promoting the emotional well-being of young peo-ple by increasing students' connectedness to school (Patton et al., 2000, 2006; Patton, Bond, Butler, & Glover, 2003).

The intervention included a curriculum component focused on increasing students' skills and knowledge for dealing with everyday life challenges and a whole-school component that sought to make changes to the schools' social and learning environment to enhance security, communication, and positive regard through valued participa-tion. A member of the research team facilitated the project implemen-tation process. Key elements were the establishment of a school-based health action team, the use of local data to review the school environ-ment and drive change, targeted professional development, and opportunities for reflective practice (Glover & Butler, 2004; Patton et al., 2003; 2006). This process resulted in schools' identifying and implementing activities and strategies appropriate to their local con-text; thus, what was done varied from school to school.

One question raised by the transfer lens pertains to what is really being transferred in replication studies of demonstration projects. Organizations might successfully replicate the teacher training or the classroom-level curriculum but withhold the survey-feedback cycle, thinking perhaps that it is part of the "research" and not needed in a program of proven effectiveness (or affordable, possibly). Thus, the educational technology of the intervention might be easily transferred, but not the organizational engagement and enquiry process. This might completely mistake what the intervention was really about. Such scenarios are common in practice fields where receptor capacity varies widely. People respond as they are able, as opposed, perhaps, to how they should, and the original intervention thus risks losing its identity and, potentially, its potency. It is crucial for evaluators to sur-face what was actually implemented, especially if programs retain the same name but in reality have replicated very different forms of the program.

References

Analoui, F. (1993). *Training and transfer of learning.* Brookfield: Aldershot.

Baldwin, T. T., & Ford, J. K. (1988). Transfer of training: A review and directions for further research. *Personnel Psychology, 41*(1), 63–105.

Beach, K. (1999). Consequential transitions: A sociocultural expedition beyond transfer in education. In T. Tuomi-Gröhn & Y. Engeström (Eds.), *Between school and work: New perspectives on transfer and boundary crossing* (pp. 101–139). Oxford: Elsevier Science.

Bereiter, C. (1995). A dispositional view of transfer. In A. MacKeough, J. Lupart, & A. Marini (Eds.), *Teaching for transfer: Fostering generalization in learning.* Mahwah, NJ: Erlbaum.

Bozeman, B. (1988). Evaluating technology transfer and diffusion. *Evaluation and Program Planning, 11*(1), 63–104.

Bozeman, B. (2000). Technology transfer and public policy: A review of research and theory. *Research Policy, 29*(4–5), 627–655.

Cormier, S. M., & Hagman, J. D. (Eds.). (1987). *Transfer of learning: Contemporary research and applications.* Orlando, FL: Academic Press.

Dolowitz, D., & Marsh, D. (1996). Who learns what from whom: A review of the policy transfer literature. *Policy Studies, 44*(2), 343–357.

Egan, T. M., Yang, B., & Bartlett, K. R. (2004). The effects of organizational learning culture and job satisfaction on motivation to transfer learning and turnover intention. *Human Resource Development Quarterly, 15*(3), 279–301.

Gagné, R. M. (1970). *The conditions of learning.* New York: Holt.

Gick, M. L., & Holyoak, K. J. (1987). The cognitive basis of knowledge transfer. In S. M. Cormier & J. D. Hagman (Eds.), *Transfer of learning: Contemporary research and applications* (pp. 9–46). Orlando, FL: Academic Press.

Glover, S., & Butler, H. (2004). Facilitating health promotion within school communities. In R. Moodie & A. Hulme (Eds.), *Hands-on health promotion.* Melbourne: IP Communications.

Goh, S. C. (2002). Managing effective knowledge transfer: an integrative framework and some practice implications. *Journal of Knowledge Management, 6*(1), 23–30.

Greenhalgh, T., Robert, G., Macfarlane, F., Bate, P., & Kyriakidou, O. (2004). Diffusion of innovations in service organizations: Systematic review and recommendations. *Milbank Quarterly, 82*(4), 581–629.

Grol, R., & Grimshaw, J. (2003). From best evidence to best practice: Effective implementation of change in patients' care. *Lancet, 362*(9391), 1225–1230.

Haskell, R. E. (2001). *Transfer of learning: Cognition, instruction, and reasoning.* Orlando, FL: Academic Press.

Kerlin, J., Auer, J., & Reid, E. (2003). *The transfer of childcare worker education and compensation policy across states: the T.E.A.C.H. Early Childhood Model.* Washington, DC: Urban Institute.

Landry, R., Amara, N., & Ouimet, M. (2007). Determinants of knowledge transfer: Evidence from Canadian university researchers in natural sciences and engineering. *Journal of Technology Transfer, 32*(6), 561–592.

Lavis, J. N., Posada, F. B., Haines, A., & Osei, E. (2004). Use of research to inform public policymaking. *Lancet, 364*(9445), 1615–1621.

Martinez-Brawley, E. E. (1995). Knowledge diffusion and transfer of technology: Conceptual premises and concrete steps for human services innovators. *Social Work, 40*(5), 670–682.

Mestre, J. (2005). *Is transfer ubiquitous or rare? New paradigms for studying transfer.* Paper presented at the Physics Education Research Conference, Sacramento, CA.

Mossberger, K., & Wolman, H. (2003). Policy transfer as a form of prospective policy evaluation: Challenges and recommendations. *Public Administration Review, 63*(4), 428–440.

Patton, G., Bond, L., Butler, H., & Glover, S. (2003). Changing schools, changing health? Design and implementation of the Gatehouse Project. *Journal of Adolescent Health, 33*(4), 231–239.

Patton, G. C., Bond, L., Carlin, J. B., Thomas, L., Butler, H., Glover, S., et al. (2006). Promoting social inclusion in schools: A group-randomized trial of effects on student health risk behaviour and well-being. *American Journal of Public Health, 96,* 1582–1587.

Patton, G. C., Glover, S., Bond, L., Butler, H., Godfrey, C., Bowes, G., et al. (2000) The Gatehouse Project: A systematic approach to mental health promotion in secondary schools. *Australian and New Zealand Journal of Psychiatry, 34,* 586.

Roessner, J. D. (2000). Technology transfer. In C. Hill (Ed.), *Technology transfer in the U.S.: A time of change.* London: Longman.

Rose, R. (1993). *Lesson-drawing in public policy: A guide to learning across time and space.* Chatham, NJ: Chatham House.

Scriven, D. M. (1991). *Evaluation thesaurus.* Thousand Oaks, CA: Sage.

Stone, D. (2000). Non-governmental policy transfer: The strategies of independent policy institutes. *Governance, 13*(1), 45–62.

van Wijk, R., Jansen, J.J.P., & Lyles, M. A. (2008). Inter- and intra-organizational knowledge transfer: A meta-analytic review and assessment of its antecedents and consequences. *Journal of Management Studies, 45*(4), 830–853.

Williams, F., & Gibson, D. V. (1990). *Technology transfer: A communication perspective.* London: Sage.

MONICA LABELLE OLIVER is an independent evaluator in the greater Atlanta, Georgia, area.

Davison, C. M. (2009). Knowledge translation: Implications for evaluation. In J. M. Ottoson & P. Hawe (Eds.), *Knowledge utilization, diffusion, implementation, transfer, and translation: Implications for evaluation. New Directions for Evaluation, 124,* 75–87.

6

Knowledge Translation: Implications for Evaluation

Colleen M. Davison

Abstract

Translation theory originates in the field of applied linguistics and communication. The term knowledge translation *has been adopted in health and other fields to refer to the exchange, synthesis, and application of knowledge. The logic model is a circular or iterative loop among various knowledge translation actors (knowledge producers and users) with translation activities evolving and occurring at various stages. Successful knowledge translation depends on the engagement of the target audience, as well as using the knowledge to inform decisions and have a positive influence on health outcomes. Understanding this alerts the evaluator to how to maximize the likely usefulness and sustainability of their evaluation research with local stakeholders. It also invites evaluators to help appreciate why programs have the short- and long-term effects that they have, particularly any unintended or unexpected program outcomes that might have otherwise been puzzling.* © Wiley Periodicals, Inc., and the American Evaluation Association.

Globally there is a significant amount of research evidence that is being underused or not used quickly enough to inform improvements in policies, products, services, and outcomes (Landry, Amara, Pablos-Mendes, & Shademani, 2006; Pablos-Mendez, Chunharas, Lansang,

Shademani, & Tugwell, 2005; Global Forum for Health Research, 2006; Lavis, Robertson, Woodside, McLeod, Abelson, & Knowledge Transfer Study Group, 2003). Evaluators have had long-standing concerns about knowledge use (Weiss, 2000). Knowledge translation has been conceptualized as the practice, the science, and the art of bridging the know-do gap, or the gap between the accumulation of knowledge and its subsequent use or application (World Health Organization, 2006). Although not the only term used to describe the processes of research to action (Graham et al., 2006), in the past few decades, *knowledge translation* has been widely adopted in the health field (Canadian Institutes of Health Research, 2004; Pablos-Mendez et al., 2005; National Center for the Dissemination of Disability Research, 2005; World Health Organization, 2004, Lyons & Warner, 2005). This chapter examines knowledge translation from an evaluation perspective, asking such questions as: How is knowledge translation defined and conceptualized? How can it be measured? How does it differ from other knowledge-to-action processes, and what would an evaluation informed by knowledge translation look like?

Literature Search

To ground this work, a literature search was conducted for documents pertaining to knowledge translation. Of specific interest were empirical studies relating to knowledge translation as well as preexisting knowledge translation definitions, theories, and models. When a broad search was conducted using *knowledge translation* as a keyword in Medline, CINAHL, PsychINFO, ERIC, and Social Sciences Abstracts databases, several thousand documents were retrieved. Then a snowball sampling technique was used to amass the most pertinent articles from 1997 to 2006. This type of sampling begins with a number of initial, seminal citations and then evolves based on the reference lists and key citations used in the articles. Initial articles were found through a review of abstracts from the keyword search and by e-mail consultation with leading scholars in the field of knowledge translation. Jacobson, Butterill, and Goering (2003) outline a similar search strategy. Documents were organized and reviewed using a matrix method for literature reviews in the health sciences outlined by Garrard (1999).

The Origins of Knowledge Translation. Translational theory originates in the fields of linguistics and communication and is commonly associated with the translation of text or spoken words from one language to another or, less frequently, from one culture to another (Davison, 2004). It is grounded in the process of adapting source material in a particular way so as to make it more comprehensible to target audiences. The term *knowledge translation* is relatively new in knowledge change terminology; *knowledge utilization, diffusion, transfer,* and *implementation* have longer histories. According to Hiss (2004), the use of the term *translate* to describe the movement and utilization of research products (knowledge, evidence, or innovations) in the health disciplines can be traced to a 1975 U.S. National Commission on Diabetes Report, where diabetes research and training centers were called to "translate" advances in diabetes research with the least delay into improved care for patients with diabetes. The use of the term *knowledge translation* grew slowly from this time but became widely used only in the past fifteen years. Straus, Graham, and Mazmanian (2006) point out that in 1990, fewer than a hundred articles were retrieved when a search for knowledge translation was conducted within the Medline database. In February 2006, several thousand articles were found with the same search strategy. Today *knowledge translation* has become one of the most favored terms in the health field (Armstrong, Waters, Roberts, Oliver, & Popay, 2006; Davis et al., 2003; Glasgow, Lichtenstein, & Marcus, 2003; Graham et al., 2006; Canadian Institutes of Health Research, 2004; National Center for the Dissemination of Disability Research, 2005; Schryer-Roy, 2005) and is used occasionally in other fields as well: for example, in geography (Williams, 2006); social work (Stevens, Liabo, & Frost, 2005; McNeill, 2006); and education, particularly relating to medical or health education (Rikkert & Rigaud, 2004; Kyrkjebo, 2006).

Although some common characteristics appear to be emerging in the literature, Hiss (2004) notes that there has been a struggle since the introduction of the concept of KT to come to a mainstream understanding of the term. *Knowledge translation* is not used consistently, it is often not, or not well, differentiated from other knowledge exchange processes, and it is used in relation to a great number of different activities. Early conceptualizations of translation placed it at the end point of research. This was prominent in the United States in the 1980s when translating scientific discoveries into health and economic benefits began making its way into federal U.S. legislation with the Stevenson-Wyndler Technology Innovation Act and the Bayh-Dole Patent and Trademark Acts, for example (Sussman, Valente, Rohrbach, Skara, & Pentz, 2006; U.S. Congress, 1980a, 1980b). These acts existed as legislation to ensure that innovations led to "the achievement of national economic, environmental, and social goals" (U.S. Congress, 1980b).

Currently translation is more often being conceptualized as an important feature in all aspects of research, and funding is being provided accordingly. In the United States, the National Institutes of Health has launched a series of clinical and translational science awards that focus on knowledge translation through enhanced communication and information sharing between laboratory researchers and clinicians (National Institutes of Health, 2007; Dickler, Korn, & Gabbe, 2006). In Canada, the Canadian Health Services Research Foundation (CHSRF) was founded in 1997 to "facilitate evidence-based decision making in Canada's health sector" (Lomas, 2000, p. 236). This foundation aims to provide funding for activities that link health research and policymaking. The Canadian Institutes of Health Research (CIHR), formerly the Medical Research Council (MRC) of Canada, has also adopted knowledge translation as a key component of their mandate. In the case of CIHR (2008), institutional language evolved from using knowledge dissemination (prior to about the year 2000) to the use of knowledge translation and then more recently to the use of knowledge synthesis and exchange. This change has been driven by an overall reexamination of the mandate of the institution, as well as focused work by individuals within the organization responsible for providing leadership in the way institutional policy is operationalized (Canadian Institutes of Health Research, 2004, 2008). CIHR (2008) currently characterizes knowledge translation into two types: end-of-grant knowledge translation, which primarily takes place for the purpose of communicating research findings when a project is at an end point, and integrated knowledge translation, which ideally includes stakeholder engagement throughout the entire research process.

Definitions of Knowledge Translation. Three prominent definitions for knowledge translation emerged from the literature search:

> The exchange, synthesis and ethically sound application of knowledge with a complex system of interactions among researchers and users—to accelerate the capture of the benefits of research for [Canadians] through improved health, more effective services and products, and a strengthening health care system. (Canadian Institutes of Health Research, 2004, p. 2)
>
> The exchange, synthesis and effective communication of reliable and relevant research results. The focus is on promoting interaction among the producers and users of research, removing the barriers to research use, and tailoring information to different target audiences so that effective interventions are used more widely. (World Health Organization, 2004, p. 5)
>
> The collaborative and systematic review, assessment, identification, aggregation and practical application of high quality [disability and rehabilitation] research by key stakeholders (i.e. consumers, researchers, practitioners, policy makers) for the purpose of improving the lives of individuals [with disabilities]. (National Center for the Dissemination of Disability Research, 2005, p. 4)

Tugwell, Robinson, Grimshaw, and Santesso (2006) use an adapted version of the CIHR definition, adding, "KT strategies that aim to enhance equity need to target barriers to achieving optimal effectiveness across socioeconomic status" (p. 643). Their adaptation aims to address equity issues relevant to the production, movement, and application of knowledge.

Translational researchers describe knowledge translation as being concerned with two types of situations. First is KT from bench to bedside, or the movement of knowledge from the realm of the basic and laboratory sciences into a realm of social or personal relevance. Second is knowledge translation from the hospital or health clinic to the community (Hiss, 2004; Sung et al., 2003; Sussman et al., 2006). Knowledge translation is most often conceptualized as an active or planned activity related to the adaptation and application of knowledge across different settings, contexts, or populations (Green et al., 2006). In this kind of arena, transdisciplinary, multilevel thinking is key.

Key Concepts in Knowledge Translation. Knowledge translation can be understood through four important concepts:

- *Purpose.* The purpose of knowledge translation is for knowledge to be applied or used to improve the health outcomes of individuals or groups or improvements in the function of services associated with health and illness.
- *Stakeholders.* Knowledge translation is about effective communication and a complex set of interactions between various stakeholders in both the production and the use of knowledge. Although research users and research producers are often characterized as different groups, knowledge translation is a fluid, iterative process that involves varied stakeholders in evolving roles.
- *Focus.* The focus of knowledge translation efforts has largely been the products of research or the products of research synthesis. Products could also be evidence, ideas, technologies, innovations, best practices, and new knowledge, for example.
- *Process.* The basic "how" of knowledge translation has a number of conceptualizations. Choi, McQueen, and Rootman (2003) present it as being about knowledge integration and knowledge simplification, where integration might indicate systematic reviews or meta-analyses and simplification could be writing research reports in summary form or plain language (see also Choi, 2005). Knowledge translation has also been conceptualized as a set of strategies to improve awareness, communication, or interaction among various stakeholders (Jacobson et al., 2003), the development of evidence-based actionable messages (Tugwell et al., 2006), the formulation of research topics, the participatory conduct of research, or the adaptation of reports of research for different audiences and contexts (Canadian Institutes of Health Research, 2004).

Theories, Models, and Frameworks of Knowledge Translation. A number of theories, models, and frameworks have been put forward in relation to knowledge translation (these are outlined briefly in Table 6.1). Among the recurring themes are these:

- *Knowledge translation is varied and multidimensional.* Knowledge translation is not a single action or activity, and it takes many forms: it can involve knowledge producers, users, and brokers; specific messages; actions and strategies; and features of the broader context. It is often the work of teams and requires transdisciplinary, multilevel thinking.
- *Knowledge translation involves interaction.* There is an emphasis placed on the relationships between many knowledge translation actors and not only on the message source and content, but also on identifying the target audience and what that audience's own context might be.
- *The message often comes from research.* Nearly all of the theories or frameworks for knowledge translation view the work as pertaining to research

NEW DIRECTIONS FOR EVALUATION • DOI: 10.1002/ev

Table 6.1. Existing Knowledge Translation Theories, Models, and Frameworks

Theory, Model, or Framework	Details	References
Push-pull capacity theory	Knowledge moves in relation to push factors from the knowledge production or supply side and pull factors from the knowledge use or demand side.	World Health Organization, 2006; Curry, 2000; Green et al., 2006; Landry, Lamari, and Amara, 2007
Diffusion of innovations theory	Diffusion is the spread of ideas and innovations throughout systems (Rogers, 2003). Knowledge application and use differ by type of user and by the user's respective needs and incentives.	Rogers, 2003; Greenhalgh, Robert, Macfarlane, Bate, and Kyriakidou, 2004; Grimshaw et al., 2001
Two-communities or two-cultures theory	"The different worlds in which researchers and decision-makers work—employs principles of intercultural understanding" (Bowen, Martens, and the Need to Know Team, 2005, p. 209).	Bowen et al., 2005; Caplan, 1979; Lyons and Warner, 2005
Knowledge utilization theory	Variations of the six knowledge utilization models put forward by Weiss (1979, 2000): the knowledge model, the problem-solving model, an interactive model, a political model, an enlighten-ment model, and a tactical model.	Weiss, 1979, 2000
Knowledge translation within a communication system paradigm	The earliest model found in the literature. Knowledge translation is presented as one of six nested functions, activities, or processes within a larger communication system paradigm of knowledge production, management, translation, product development, product dissemination, and product adoption or utilization.	Beal and Meehan, 1978; Beal, 1980
Five-point knowledge translation framework	An often-cited framework for KT that has five points of focus: the message, the target audience, the messenger, the actual knowledge translation process and support system, and the evaluation.	Lavis et al., 2003
Five domain framework	This model consists of five domains: the user group and the context in which the population operates, the message or related issue that is to be translated, the characteristics of the research (What research evidence already exists? How	Jacobson et al., 2003

	familiar is the target audience with topic?), the researcher-user relationship, and the actual knowledge translation strategy used.	
Equity-oriented framework	The framework is grounded in the concept of health equity, and is a cascade of activities related to knowledge translation: the assessment of potential knowledge translation barriers and facilitators, the prioritization of barriers for modification, the choice of knowledge translation interventions to address barriers, the evaluation of knowledge translation, and the facilitation of knowledge management or sharing.	Tugwell et al., 2006
Canadian Institutes of Health Research knowledge translation model	The model reflects a belief that knowledge translation should be an iterative, multidimensional process that is integral to all parts of the research cycle: the interactions that take place between knowledge producers and users, the activities associated with the conduct of the research, the ability to contextualize research findings against the background of other knowledge and sociocultural norms, the act of catering reports and publishing in plain language, the ability to inform action and decision making, and the ability to influence subsequent rounds of research.	Canadian Institutes of Health Research, 2004; Armstrong et al., 2006; Tugwell et al., 2006; Schryer-Roy, 2005; Kiefer et al., 2005

knowledge and the message being associated with research products and processes. Some also refer to a messenger, a linking agent, and a support system in place to help facilitate interaction.

- *There are knowledge translation barriers and facilitators.* There are specific factors that either support or work against knowledge translation processes in different contexts. It is often implied that knowledge translation is challenging and that distinct planning and management of strategies are essential for success.

It is generally felt that a satisfactory, overarching model for knowledge translation has not emerged (World Health Organization, 2006). There is debate around whether an overarching theory or framework would be possible, or even preferable, to develop (Estabrooks, Thompson, Lovely, & Hofmeyer, 2006). This debate hinges on the facts that knowledge translation is actually a wide variety of activities, previous theory comes from a variety of disciplines, and knowledge translation can differ depending on the objectives and context of the work.

How Knowledge Translation Differs From Other Knowledge-to-Action Processes. A recent study looking at 33 applied research funding agencies in nine countries found that 29 terms were being used to describe the idea of moving knowledge into action (Graham et al., 2006). Jacobson et al. (2003) present the principles of knowledge translation as consisting of dissemination, utilization, evidence into practice, and knowledge transfer. Choi (2005) explains that knowledge translation goes beyond dissemination and diffusion. It has also been described as a component of a communication system along with knowledge production, management, dissemination, and utilization (Beal & Meehan, 1978; Beal, 1980).

Although myriad views exist around how the various knowledge-to-action processes relate to one another, and how each of them may be defined and delineated from the others, a few things are clear. First, knowledge translation is most often about movement of scientific knowledge, particularly that from health research and research syntheses, into health outcomes and health system gains. This aspect is similar to that of knowledge transfer but is not similar to other knowledge change processes such as implementation, which often refer to policies and programs that are not focused in the health field. Second, knowledge translation, more than any of the other processes, focuses on interaction between the various knowledge translation actors or stakeholders and on the involvement, or engagement, of the target audience in the process. Through engagement of the target audience, informed adaptation of the message can occur and knowledge may be more effectively understood and applied in various contexts. Although knowledge translation shares significant theoretical ground with diffusion and knowledge utilization, especially with regard to how knowledge uptake may occur, it is unique in its emphasis on user engagement. And third, knowledge translation is an iterative, multidirectional process and can occur at multiple stages in the knowledge cycle. This may be true for knowledge exchange, but it is not usually true for knowledge transfer or dissemination, for example.

Implications for Evaluation: What Is KT Success?

A list of potential evaluation indicators informed by knowledge translation was compiled from the documents reviewed for this chapter and classified according to two broad principles of knowledge translation success: interaction and knowledge use or application:

- Interactions between varied stakeholders in the production and use of knowledge, including the engagement of the target audience. Indicators might include evidence of:
  - Communication channels, processes, and context between knowledge translation actors
  - Working relationships among stakeholders
  - An ongoing forum for sharing among stakeholders
  - Opportunities for collaboration
  - Shared vocabulary among stakeholders

- Knowledge being relevant to and understood by the target audience
- A linking or brokerage role being taken among stakeholders
- Members of the target audience being engaged as coresearchers

- The use or application of knowledge, passive or active—for example:
  - Research products being used to inform policy or agenda setting
  - Knowledge being used to inform decision making, in relation to individuals or in relation to policy and practice within systems, institutions, and states
  - Changes in behavior, awareness, communication, or interaction patterns evident among varied stakeholders
  - Knowledge being used to help create and support interventions

Also important to note when thinking about evaluation and knowledge translation are:

- The context of the process: What is the issue being translated? What stage of knowledge translation is currently the focus? Who are the key actors? What are characteristics of the setting?
- The definitions of how the knowledge translation process is framed by the actors themselves
- The decision-making processes that exist
- The critical events that take place

An evaluator is looking for both positive and negative outcomes.

Translation theory originates in the fields of applied linguistics and communication. The term *knowledge translation* has been widely adopted in health disciplines. The inherent logic model is a circular or iterative loop between varied knowledge translation actors, informed by the stakeholders and by knowledge use outcomes, occurring at various stages. Successful knowledge translation depends on the engagement of knowledge users and the use or application of knowledge to inform decisions and have a positive influence on health outcomes. In this regard, knowledge translation differs from related terms because of its specific focus on end user engagement and the essential component of knowledge use or application. An evaluation informed by knowledge translation would look at indicators of interaction, engagement, and application or use.

For evaluators, a knowledge translation lens could provide a way of looking at change that would differ not only from the insights gained if no knowledge-to-action lens was used at all, but from the insights gained from the lenses of other modes of knowledge to action: knowledge transfer, utilization, dissemination, or implementation. A knowledge translation lens helps evaluators answer questions about the experience of the various actors as they interact. It also helps evaluators answer questions about how knowledge may have informed the project or intervention and how knowledge flows into, within, and out of these activities over time.

Case Study Application: Evaluating the Gatehouse Project With a Knowledge Translation Lens

The Gatehouse Project was a successful multilevel, school-based intervention aimed at promoting the emotional well-being of young people by increasing students' connectedness to school (Patton et al., 2000, 2006; Patton, Bond, Butler, & Glover, 2003).

The intervention included a curriculum component focused on increasing students' skills and knowledge for dealing with everyday life challenges and a whole-school component that sought to make changes to the schools' social and learning environment to enhance security, communication, and positive regard through valued participation. A member of the research team facilitated the project implementation process. Key elements were the establishment of a school-based health action team, the use of local data to review the school environment and drive change, targeted professional development, and opportunities for reflective practice (Glover & Butler, 2004; Patton et al., 2003; Patton et al., 2006). This process resulted in schools' identifying and implementing activities and strategies appropriate to their local context; thus, what was done varied from school to school.

Two of the key knowledge translation (KT) success indicators are the engagement of the target audience and the use or application of knowledge. What would be of specific interest to evaluators using a KT lens to examine the Gatehouse Project would be how target audiences (such as students, school staff, other community members) were involved in intervention development. Did active involvement in the intervention and research create a form of social inclusion in and of itself? Did study participants buy in because they felt valued and in control? This could be investigated qualitatively and also quantitatively by examining the health survey scores of those most involved and least involved in the project, using some predesigned metric. Also, did the intervention tap into and legitimate any special kind of knowledge and transform it into a usable resource across the project? The Gatehouse schools undertook a comprehensive needs assessment, including students' perceptions of the school environment, policies, and practices. An evaluator might ask: How did the needs of one school compare to the next, and how did this influence the way the intervention was developed at each site? What processes integrated any previous knowledge of the content area into the new intervention's design and delivery? The answers to these questions might illuminate why projects have the effects they have. But more particularly, they might help to explain any unintended, unexpected outcomes.

NEW DIRECTIONS FOR EVALUATION • DOI: 10.1002/ev

References

Armstrong, R., Waters, E., Roberts, H., Oliver, S., & Popay, J. (2006). The role and theoretical evolution of knowledge translation and exchange in public health. *Journal of Public Health, 28,* 384–389.

Beal, G. (1980, August). *Knowledge generation, organization and utilization for rural development.* World Congress for Rural Sociology, Mexico City.

Beal, G., & Meehan, P. (1978, September). *Knowledge production and utilization.* Annual Meeting of the Rural Sociological Society, San Francisco.

Bowen, S., Martens, P., & the Need to Know Team. (2005). Demystifying knowledge translation: Learning from the community. *Journal of Health Services Research and Policy, 10*(4) 203–211.

Canadian Institutes of Health Research. (2004). *The CIHR knowledge translation strategy 2004–2009: Innovation in action.* Ottawa, ON: Canadian Institutes of Health Research.

Canadian Institutes of Health Research. (2008). *The KT Portfolio at CIHR.* Retrieved August 31, 2008, from http://www.cihr.ca/e/29418.html

Caplan, N. (1979). The two-communities theory and knowledge utilization. *American Behavioral Scientist, 22*(3), 459–470.

Choi, B. (2005). Understanding the basic principles of knowledge translation. *Journal of Epidemiology and Community Health, 59,* 93.

Choi, B. C., McQueen, D. V., & Rootman, I. (2003). Bridging the gap between scientists and decision makers. *Journal of Epidemiology and Community Health,* 57, 918.

Curry, S. J. (2000). Organizational interventions to encourage guideline implementation. *Chest, 118*(2), S40–S46.

Davis, D., Evans, M., Jadad, A., Perrier, L., Rath, D., & Ryan, D. (2003). The case for knowledge translation: Shortening the journey from evidence to effect. *British Medical Journal, 327,* 33–35.

Davison, C. (2004). Translation of fixed-response questionnaires for health research with Aboriginal people: A discussion of methods. *Pimatsiwin: A Journal of Aboriginal and Indigenous Community Health, 2,* 97–114.

Dickler, H. B., Korn, B., & Gabbe, S. G. (2006). Promoting translational and clinical science: The critical role of medical schools and teaching hospitals. *PLOS Medicine, 3*(9), 1492–1495.

Estabrooks, C., Thompson, D., Lovely, J., & Hofmeyer, A. (2006). A guide to knowledge translation theory. *Journal of Continuing Education in the Health Professions, 26,* 25–36.

Garrard, J. (1999). *Health sciences literature review made easy: The matrix method.* New York: Aspen.

Glasgow, R., Lichtenstein, E., & Marcus, A. (2003). Why don't we see more translation of health promotion research to practice? Re-thinking the efficacy to effectiveness transition. *American Journal of Public Health,* 93, 1261–1267.

Global Forum for Health Research. (2006). *2005 review: Focusing research to improve global health.* Geneva: Global Forum for Health Research.

Glover, S., & Butler, H. (2004). Facilitating health promotion within school communities. In R. Moodie & A. Hulme (Eds.), *Hands-on health promotion.* Melbourne: IP Communications.

Graham, I., Logan, J., Harrison, M., Straus, S., Tetroe, J., Caswell, W., et al. (2006). Lost in knowledge translation: Time for a map? *Journal of Continuing Education in the Health Professions, 26,* 13–24.

Green, L. W., Orleans, C. T., Ottoson, J. M., Cameron, R., Pierce, J. P., & Bettinghaus, E. P. (2006). Inferring strategies for disseminating physical activity policies, programs, and practices from the successes of tobacco control. *American Journal of Preventive Medicine, 31*(4), S66–S81.

Greenhalgh, T., Robert, G., Macfarlane, F., Bate, P., & Kyriakidou, O. (2004). Diffusion of innovations in service organizations: Systematic review and recommendations. *Milbank Quarterly, 82*(4), 581–629.

Grimshaw, J. M., Shirran, L., Thomas, R., Mowat, G., Fraser, C., Bero, L., et al. (2001). Changing provider behavior: An overview of systematic reviews of interventions. *Medical Care, 39*(8), 2–45.

Hiss, R. (2004, January 12–13). *Fundamental issues in translational research.* Introductory session at the conference From Clinical Trials to Community: The Science of Translating Diabetes and Obesity Research, National Institutes of Health, Bethesda, MD. Retrieved August 16, 2006, from http://www.niddk.nih.gov/fund/other/diabetes-translation/conf-publication.pdf

Jacobson, N., Butterill, D., & Goering, P. (2003). Development of a framework for knowledge translation: Understanding user context. *Journal of Health Services Research and Policy, 8*, 94–99.

Kiefer, L., Frank, J., Di Ruggerio, E., Dobbins, M., Manuel, D., Gully, P. R., et al. (2005). Fostering evidence decision-making in Canada: Examining the need for a Canadian population and public health evidence centre and research network. *Canadian Journal of Public Health, 96*(3), 11–140.

Kyrkjebo, J. (2006). Teaching quality improvement in the classroom: Getting it wrong and getting it right. *Journal of Nursing Education, 45*, 109–116.

Landry, R., Amara, N., Pablos-Mendes, A., & Shademani, R. (2006). The knowledge-value chain: Conceptual framework for knowledge translation in health. *Bulletin of the World Health Organisation, 84*, 597–602.

Landry, R., Lamari, M., & Amara, N. (2007) Extent and determinants of utilization of university research in government agencies. *Public Administration Review, 63*, 193–206.

Lavis, J., Robertson, D., Woodside, J., McLeod, C., Abelson, J., & Knowledge Transfer Study Group. (2003). How can research organizations more effectively transfer research knowledge to decision makers? *Milbank Quarterly, 81*, 221–248.

Lomas, J. (2000). Using "linkage and exchange" to move research into policy at a Canadian foundation. *Health Affairs, 19*(3), 236–240.

Lyons, R., & Warner, G. (2005). *Demystifying knowledge translation for stroke researchers: A primer on theory and praxis.* Halifax, NS: Atlantic Health Promotion Research Centre.

McNeill, T. (2006). Evidence-based practice in an age of relativism: Toward a model for practice. *Social Work, 51*, 147–158.

National Center for the Dissemination of Disability Research. (2005). *What is knowledge translation? Focus Technical Brief Number 10.* Austin, TX: Southwest Educational Development Laboratory.

National Institutes of Health. (2007). *Clinical and translational science awards.* Retrieved November 10, 2007, from http://www.ncrr.nih.gov/clinical_research_resources/clinical_and_translational_science_awards/

Pablos-Mendez, A., Chunharas, S., Lansang, M., Shademani, R., & Tugwell, P. (2005). Knowledge translation in global health. *Bulletin of the World Health Organization, 83*(10), 723.

Patton, G., Bond, L., Butler, H., & Glover, S. (2003). Changing schools, changing health? The design and implementation of the Gatehouse Project. *Journal of Adolescent Health, 33*, 231–239.

Patton, G. C., Bond, L., Carlin, J. B., Thomas, L., Butler, H., Glover, S., et al. (2006). Promoting social inclusion in secondary schools: A group-randomized trial of effects on student health risk behaviour and well-being. *American Journal of Public Health, 96*, 1582–1587.

Patton, G. C., Glover, S., Bond, L., Butler, H., Godfrey, C., Di Pietro, G., & et al. (2000). The Gatehouse Project: A systematic approach to mental health promotion in secondary schools. *Australian and New Zealand Journal of Psychiatry, 34,* 586–593.

Rikkert, M., & Rigaud, A. (2004). Three strategies for delivering continuing medical education in geriatrics. *Educational Gerontology, 30,* 619–626.

Rogers, E. (2003). *Diffusion of innovations* (5th ed.). New York: Free Press.

Schryer-Roy, A. (2005). *Knowledge translation: Basic theories, approaches and applications.* Ottawa, ON: IDRC Research Matters in Governance, Equity and Health.

Stevens, M., Liabo, K., & Frost, S. (2005). Using research in practice: A research information service for social care practitioners. *Child Family Social Work, 10,* 65–75.

Straus, S., Graham, I., & Mazmanian, P. (2006). Knowledge translation: Resolving the confusion. *Journal of Continuing Education in the Health Professions, 26,* 3–4.

Sung, N. S., Crowley, W. F., Genel, M., Salber, P., Sandy, L., Sherwood, L. M., et al. (2003). Central challenges facing the National Clinical Research Enterprise. *Journal of the American Medical Association, 289,* 1278–1287.

Sussman, S., Valente, T., Rohrbach, L., Skara, S., & Pentz, M. (2006). Translation in the health professions: Converting science into action. *Evaluation and the Health Professions, 29,* 7–32.

Tugwell, P., Robinson, V., Grimshaw, J., & Santesso, N. (2006). Systematic reviews and knowledge translation. *Bulletin of the World Health Organization, 84,* 643–651.

U.S. Congress. (1980a). Bayh-Dole Patent and Trademark Act: A guide to the law and implementing regulations. Public Law 96–517.

U.S. Congress. (1980b). Stevenson-Wyndler Technological Innovations Act. Public Law 96–480. 94 Stat. 2311, 15 U.S.C. 3701.

Weiss, C. (1979). The many meanings of research utilization. *Public Administration Review, 39,* 426–431.

Weiss, C. (2000). *What we have learned from 25 years of knowledge utilization.* Zeist, Netherlands: Netherlands Commission for UNESCO, Management of Social Transformations.

Williams, A. (2006). Lost in translation? International migration, learning and knowledge. *Progress in Human Geography, 30,* 588–607.

World Health Organization. (2004). *World report on knowledge for better health.* Retrieved September 14, 2006, from http://www.who.int/rpc/meetings/wr2004/en/index8.html

World Health Organization. (2006). *Bridging the "know-do" gap: Meeting on knowledge translation in global health.* Geneva: World Health Organization.

COLLEEN M. DAVISON *is a Canadian Institutes for Health Research, Global Health Research Initiative postdoctoral fellow at the Institute of Population Health, University of Ottawa.*

NEW DIRECTIONS FOR EVALUATION • DOI: 10.1002/ev

Hawe, P., Bond, L., & Butler, H. (2009). Knowledge theories can inform evaluation practice: What can a complexity lens add? In J. M. Ottoson & P. Hawe (Eds.), *Knowledge utilization, diffusion, implementation, transfer, and translation: Implications for evaluation*. *New
Directions for Evaluation, 124*, 89–100.

Knowledge Theories Can Inform Evaluation Practice: What Can a Complexity Lens Add?

Penelope Hawe, Lyndal Bond, Helen Butler

Abstract

*Programs and policies invariably contain new knowledge. Theories about
knowledge utilization, diffusion, implementation, transfer, and knowledge translation theories illuminate some mechanisms of change processes. But more often
than not, when it comes to understanding patterns about change processes, "the
foreground" is privileged more than "the background." The foreground is
the knowledge or technology tied up with the product or program that prompted the
evaluation. The background is the ongoing dynamics of the context into which
the knowledge is inserted. Complex adaptive system thinking encourages greater
attention to this context and the interactions and consequences that result from
the intervention, making these the forefront of attention. For the evaluator, there
are implications of this shift in thinking. Process evaluations should be designed
to capture the fluidity of the change process. Impact and outcome evaluations
will require long time frames. Complex adaptive system thinking also encourages multilevel measures, a focus on structures, and capacity to assess the possibility of whole system transformation (whole school, whole organization) as
a result of the newly introduced program or policy. For the people involved in*

the innovation, there is a corresponding shift from a focus on their knowledge (and competence) to assessment of their learning (and system-level capability). New ways to interpret fidelity in these situations should therefore be developed. © Wiley Periodicals, Inc., and the American Evaluation Association.

I t has been proposed that theories about evaluation vary with respect to three dimensions: methods, values, and use (Alkin & Christie, 2004). In 2005 the proponents of this idea had the opportunity to put together an issue of *New Directions for Evaluation* devoted to examining evaluation theory (Alkin & Christie, 2005). The editors of that issue asked scholars of various evaluation theories to outline how they would evaluate a particular program. The result was a rich illustration of how different ways of thinking become operationalized in the data, the experience, and the contribution of a program evaluation.

In this issue, the editors have used a similar device. But there are differences. Chapter authors were asked not to consider program theory (the theory driving, or professing to drive, the program they are evaluating). Nor were they asked to consider evaluation theory (the theory they use to guide their own best practice in evaluation). Rather, they were asked to review particular theories about knowledge—specifically, the role of the theory in action and change processes. The intention was to illuminate factors that evaluators might measure or processes that they might better be able to recognize and capture in the evaluation of any program. To illustrate this, each author was asked to consider the same intervention: the Gatehouse Project, a whole-school organizational development intervention to make schools places where children feel more safe, connected, and valued. It was evaluated using a cluster randomized trial design involving 26 schools (Patton et al., 2006).

In Chapter 1 Judith M. Ottoson summarizes the five theories about the role of knowledge in change processes: knowledge utilization, diffusion, implementation, transfer, and knowledge translation (see Table 1.1 in her article). This is the first time insights across these theories have been illuminated. For example, language and how language might change as a result of a program or policy is highlighted by knowledge translation theory. Diffusion draws attention to the spread of knowledge and characteristics of those who adopt new practices. Knowledge utilization theory encourages an examination of different types of knowledge use—from instrumental use of knowledge to bring about change (where the knowledge is directly drawn on to change the ways things are done or appraised) to symbolic use of knowledge. An example of the latter might be where the power of the logo on the front of an information package saying that the content is endorsed by the College of Physicians may be more responsible for uptake of a particular new practice than the material within. The purpose of this issue is to sensitize evaluators to the subtlety of knowledge in change processes and the diversity of its manifestations. Each theory, in principle or by virtue of its origins and main application areas, shines the light somewhat differently.

New Directions for Evaluation • DOI: 10.1002/ev

This chapter is written by two of the investigators in the original Gate-house Project in Australia that formed the basis of the case study in each chapter (Lyndal Bond and Helen Butler) and another author involved in leading a replication (and extension) project in Canada (Penelope Hawe). The experience of running, or rerunning, the project and its evaluation, and its interrogation by colleagues within the broader International Collaboration on Complex Interventions, funded by the Canadian Institutes of Health Research, has yielded insights into the complexities of change processes. These complexities illustrate the inadequacy of knowledge theories alone to account for what happens within the intervention's black box, reminding the evaluator to take a wider view. These are ideas already rehearsed well in the implementation literature (O'Toole, 2000). Our own evaluation theory has evolved to embrace new methods to capture the intervention processes and effects. Knowledge still matters, and it must be understood and tracked. But we now more strongly recognize the importance of the structures within which it is embedded or dispersed.

This chapter sketches some aspects of complexity science that might usefully inform evaluation practice. True to the lessons in the previous chapters, we are mindful that new uses of words like *complexity* may simply be repositioning or lending new force to familiar concepts of the past. We endeavor therefore to confine our attention to the material consequences and added value this thinking makes to evaluation design and methods.

Growing Interest in Complexity

It does not take much more than a walk past the books displayed at an airport shop to see that words like *complexity* and *complex systems* are being used more and more to frame the problems posed by a global connected world and to describe the forms of organizations that are springing up to meet these problems.

A cursory examination of references in the scholarly literature in the past 10 years (using online research databases) shows that references to complexity have gone up by 59% in the education literature, 93% in the psychology literature, and 167% in the health literature. Complexity originated in the physics literature. Here *complexity* is not simply an adjective to describe things that are hard to understand or execute. In the field of physics, *complexity* has a particular meaning. It is a meaning that could make a substantial difference to the practice and evaluation of social programs.

It is increasingly common to talk of "complex interventions," and many authors mean these to be interventions that are multilayered and have many component parts (Riley et al., 2008). But use of the word *complexity* in this way may not truly embrace the theory of complexity as it is intended within its science of origin, physics. Disciplines use many terms differently. This matters only if important aspects of the properties we are describing become obscured. In physics, complexity is a property of a system (not an intervention), and it has far more implications beyond lots of components or multilayered parts. We think this might matter more than many of us first supposed.

For example, a *complicated* system can have many component parts, but they can be guided by specific functions and roles and simple rules (Rickles, Shiell, & Hawe, 2007). If you lose one part, a complicated system could break down or fail to work. A *complex* system also has a large number of interacting parts, but complex systems are robust to the removal of a part by adapting to change. *Chaotic* systems have few interacting parts, but they interact in ways that seem to produce random behavior from the iteration of the simple rule that governs those interactions. Complexity is the production of rich, collective dynamical behavior from simple interactions among large numbers of parts (Rickles et al., 2007). Unfortunately, many popular management and business books use the words *chaotic* and *complex* interchangeably. The key difference between chaotic systems and complex ones is in the number of interacting component parts and the resultant effect on the system as a whole. Complex systems increase in robustness over time due to the capacity to self-organize (Rickles et al., 2007), a feature called antichaos (Coffey, 1998).

There are other important properties of complex (and chaotic) systems that are worth noting and distinguishing from complicated systems. Complex and chaotic systems are nonlinear dynamical systems. A linear system can be decomposed into its component parts and "solved separately to construct the full solution" (Rickles et al., 2007, p. 934). A nonlinear system cannot. A consequence is that change in input is not proportional to change in outcome. In other words, small changes in inputs may lead to large changes in outcomes. Or conversely, large inputs can lead to seemingly very little change. Very little can seem to be happening at the system level in response to successive inputs over time, but then one might observe large change in what is known as a phase transition. Nonlinear systems are also highly sensitive to their initial conditions. This means that two complex systems (say, two health care clinics or two people) can seem quite similar at baseline and operate under the same rules yet follow very different trajectories over time. Finally the familiar saying about the types of "wholes" that are not to be decomposed to their component parts is true for complex systems because the interactions among the subunits generate properties in the unit system that cannot be reduced to the subunits. These are called emergent properties that can be arranged in an upward hierarchy so that one level of organization determines the features of the level above it (Rickles et al., 2007). Flocking is an emergent property that arises from birds interacting. Color is an emergent property of atoms. Governance and political systems arise from the congregation and interaction of people.

A noteworthy feature of complex systems is how they change and evolve in response to feedback, meaning that the output of some processes in the system becomes input elsewhere. Positive feedback increases the rate of change of a particular variable in a certain direction. Negative feedback reverses the direction of change. So key points to complex thinking are about shifting the gaze to the bigger picture—to interactions, feedback, time, nonlinearity, and properties at some levels not apparent at smaller levels. (See Table 7.1.)

Evaluators should be interested in complexity for two reasons. The first is the extent to which evaluators are involved in formative evaluation of policies and programs: reflection, interpretation, and feedback to improve program practice. Insights from complexity could help strengthen interventions. The second is the opportunity to rethink assumptions about evaluation methods as a whole. Component testing, for example, which is popular in many fields, is largely irrelevant if the whole is different from the sum of its parts—that is, if the evaluator is dealing with a complex system, not a complicated one. We now explain these assertions in more detail.

The Difference Complexity Might Make to Improving Program and Policy Practice. A useful guide to making programs and policies potentially more effective is outlined in *Harnessing Complexity,* a book by Axelrod and Cohen (2000). The title refers to changing the structure of a complex system in order to increase some aspect of its performance. The agents in a system (teachers, doctors, frontline workers) are active and constantly on the lookout for how to improve their lot. When the strategies of agents or the population in a complex system change over time toward improved performance, a complex adaptive system is in play.

Primary care is a particular growth area for complexity thought (Wilson, Holt, & Greenhalgh, 2001; Fraser & Greenhalgh, 2001; Martin & Sturmberg, 2005; Plsek & Wilson, 2001). Studies in general practice have used sophisticated mathematical techniques to diagnose the presence of complexity, using data amassed within patient records held over time to observe that the distribution of consultation activity conforms to a mathematical power law (Love & Burton, 2005). It is thought that these insights would lead to different system-level management practices than if complexity were not present. Complexity is also being used to guide individual treatment decision making (Cooper & Geyer, 2007). But how?

Table 7.1. Key Points

Complicated systems	Many interacting component parts, guided by simple rules; system may break down when a component part is removed
Complex systems	Very simple interactions among many interacting component parts; robust to the removal of a component part; increase in robustness over time due to capacity to self-organize
Chaotic systems	Few component parts, but they seem to produce random behaviors from the simple interaction of these parts

In health care, many of the principles that Axelrod and Cohen identified have been translated into guidelines, the idea being that best practice in dealing with complex systems is achieved through minimum specification rather than highly prescriptive processes. This means having devices to encourage diversification of approaches to problems, structures to encourage interaction among agents (such as networks for physicians to learn from and with each other), active feedback mechanisms to illuminate effects, and management practices that detect and select success and communicate this rapidly. Following from this, Fraser and Greenhalgh (2001) use the complexity metaphor to argue that professional education in medical practice should be less about educating people for competence and more about educating for capability. Competence, they suggest, is what individuals know or are able to do in terms of knowledge, skills, and attitude. Capability is the extent to which people can adapt to change, generate new knowledge, and continue to improve their performance (Fraser & Greenhalgh, 2001). These interacting individuals, or agents, each acting in his or her own interest and adjusting to each other over time, constitute a complex system that can be coached toward higher performance.

This shift from knowledge to learning marks an earlier shift in the education literature. Stephenson and Weil (1992), for example, cogently argued that the field of problem solving had to make the shift from a focus on dependent capability, where people worked on familiar problems in familiar contexts, to independent capability, which is the ability to deal with unfamiliar problems in unfamiliar contexts. This latter zone of action involves uncertainty, change, risk, intuition, and innovation. It requires a style of coaching in keeping with the minimum specifications idea. Indeed the successful Gatehouse Project, the focus of this issue, was implemented not with a heavily specified curriculum or required activities but with a facilitator called "a critical friend" whose focus was capacity building toward a particular goal: a school where students feel safe, connected, and valued (Bond, Glover, Godfrey, Butler, & Patton, 2001; Glover & Butler, 2004).

The Difference Complexity Might Make to an Evaluation. An acceptance of complexity and a preference to frame more toward learning and less toward knowledge per se is a phenomenon of the late 20th and early 21st centuries and a departure from the ways of thinking about science and technology of modernity (Materia & Baglio, 2005). It perhaps makes sense for some of our traditional ways of thinking about knowledge that originated in agricultural movements and the spread of post–World War II technology (such as diffusion theory) to get a bit of a shakedown or update now (Dearing, 2008). Most important, complexity ideas equip evaluators with a broader context with which to interrogate the meaning of a program or policy and challenge the face value of what a program or policy supposes.

The client of an evaluation might ask for measurement of knowledge change or knowledge use as a result of some program or policy. But while many of the knowledge theories reviewed in this volume might help identify the pattern, movement, language, diversity, users, and types of use of that knowledge, our analysis here invites further exploration. Capability or problem-solving capacity might be the true goal of the program or policy (the nonverbalized subtext), for example, helping schools look after student wellbeing. This might be surfaced in the preevaluation dialogue, the evaluability assessment, in which case there are rich and diverse opportunities for identifying how to measure, value, and use capacity building depending on the way the capacity building is theorized (Hawe, 1994).

In particular, a complexity lens invites alternate ways to think about the intervention itself. Conventional technological ways of thinking about school interventions are based on beliefs about practitioners that could almost be termed "anticapability." Dusenbury, Brannigan, Hansen, Walsh, and Falco (2005), for example, believe that as prevention programs are disseminated "the most serious threat to effectiveness is maintaining the quality of implementation intended by the developers" (p. 308). Their scheme for measuring the implementation of a drug abuse prevention program (designed and copyrighted by a researcher) has observers score teachers on six measures of adherence to the curriculum, five measures of quality of process, teacher attitudes (deduced by counting the number of negative statements made about the program and subtracting that from the number of positive statements made about the program), observer rating of teacher understanding of the program, and valence of adaptation. The last dimension is of particular interest, as it recognizes that implementers inevitably adapt programs to local contexts. Dusenbury and colleagues (2005) had their observers score whether they believed the adaptation they observed was either positive, and in keeping with program goals and objectives, or negative, that is, detracting from them. In their study, 63% of teachers adapted the program in ways that in the observers' opinion were negative. Presumably, however, the teachers thought the opposite; otherwise, they would not have made the adaptation. Whose knowledge and insights matters most? Conventional thinking and evaluation scored the teachers low and recommended more training for the teachers prior to the assessment of outcome. But perhaps if the same phenomena were occurring in the primary care field, where complexity is being embraced, one gets the sense that adaptations would be investigated, and the ultimate determinant of whether a change was adaptive in the positive sense would be determined objectively in the outcome evaluation.

Indeed, in the school education literature, the focus of reform has increasingly moved away from prepackaged program solutions toward principles, relationships, engagement, dialogue, and distributed leadership focused more on facilitating processes than directing content and action (Fullan, 1993; Hargreaves & Fink, 2006; Senge et al., 2000). Fullan (1993) conceived large-scale reform as "the transfer of capabilities rather than products" (p. 68). Drawing on ecological models, Hargreaves and Fink (2006, p. 164) argued that schools as effective organizations operate with the "fluidity and adaptability of living systems rather than with the mechanical precision of well-oiled machines." Bower (2006, p. 64) noted the importance of self-organization for sustained school improvement, which "emerges from within a school and is based upon the needs that the school has identified from internal and external feedback."

Complexity thinking, at first glance, deeply challenges conventional thinking about program fidelity. But it is not as shattering as some might think. Elsewhere we have suggested that the way an intervention is delivered does not have to be the same in every site for a randomized controlled trial of an intervention to maintain its integrity (Hawe, Shiell, & Riley, 2004, 2008). In a randomized controlled trial, for the sake of both internal validity and external validity, something has to be standardized, of course. But it can be the function the components of the intervention play rather than the form they take (Hawe et al., 2004). As long as the components of the intervention are conforming to the principles and key sequences of the change process theory being followed, the integrity of the intervention and the evaluation design is not compromised. For example, Carl Rogers's theories about listening and nondirective therapy (Rogers, 1961) could be operationalized in the case of a randomized trial of active listening. Here the intervention performs a certain function according to the theory: reinforcing the expression of ideas. But one could not standardize or prescribe a certain number of "uh-huhs" or statements like "I hear you saying . . . " in advance of the application context. Only the principle of intervention delivery could be specified. The same is true for surgical trials. Similarly, in whole-community intervention trials, one might expect to see empowerment operationalized as a set of principles and sequences (Rappaport & Hess, 1984). But it would be against the principle of the intervention to overspecify and insist on exactly which people or which organizations in each community should play which roles. To maintain validity, the intervention has to be recognizably and justifiably linked to a theory of action. It also has to be replicable across sites. Note that these are useful requirements of all interventions in evaluation research, not just those tested in randomized designs.

The guide rule of allowing local agents to adapt the form of the intervention to local context respects people's agency, that is, the view that people are essentially knowledgeable about their actions and have conscious and unconscious know-how about how to act—ideas best enshrined in the work of Giddens (1984). Gatehouse Project schools were given a long leash in how they went about implementing and operationalizing the project intervention. A process evaluation method that simply tried to measure the amount of curriculum delivered using conventional methods would have missed the point. Such ways of working require more qualitative and unstructured evaluation methods to uncover the fluidity of what happens during interventions, using such methods as interviews and narratives (see Riley & Hawe, 2005).

It should also be noted that the evaluation of the Gatehouse Project intervention showed substantial reductions in adolescent students' risk of smoking, drinking, and drug use (Patton et al., 2006); they were far greater than interventions by other investigators who have used conventional curriculum approaches, conventional means of standardizing the intervention across sites, and conventional ways of measuring implementation quality (Peterson, Kealy, Mann, Marek, & Sarason, 2000). In other words, the intervention was effective while being adapted widely to context.

The Gatehouse replication study in Canada has extended ideas about the dynamics of change processes to look at the structures in which the agents of the intervention (the teachers) are embedded using social network analysis. Social network analysis was the subject of a 2005 *New Directions for Evaluation* issue (Durland & Fredericks, 2005), and it was noted then that evaluators might wish to consider the use of this method for exploring systems perspectives and complexity ideas. We are tracking the impact of the intervention on the teacher and staff networks of interaction (Hawe & Ghali, 2008), as well as the impact on student networks over time. This is an example of where the foreground, that is, student knowledge, attitude, and skills about emotional well-being (introduced by the intervention), is being measured and interpreted against a preexisting background of the students' social networks. The main focus of the evaluation is on how the networks amplify or dissipate the intervention effects and how the lasting changes in social structure enable students to access resources across the networks. Thus, the background is brought forward (it becomes the foreground) in order to truly fathom the pattern of change.

Finally, we point to the direction complexity thinking is taking in health research. Many phenomena currently called complex interventions might be more appropriately thought of as events in complex systems (schools, communities, and primary care agencies, for example) that require evaluation reframing along the lines that we have mentioned here, as well as means to accommodate much longer observational time frames (Hawe, Shiell, & Riley, 2009). In the economic evaluation of complex interventions, Shiell and colleagues (2008) have argued that phase transitions (long periods where small inputs seems to lead to little change, followed by sudden large change) mean that conventional evaluations with 1-, 2-, or even 3- to 5-year time frames might miss the true effects of repeated stimuli to the system (the introduction of new policy or programming). Emergent properties of change processes might be lost if evaluators localize their attention to lower-level microphenomena and fail to see the bigger picture (Shiell, Hawe, & Gold, 2008). Overall the implication is that the apparent unpredictability of complexity might be offset by closer long-term observation of what already is. That is, we cannot truly evaluate the impact of any new policy or program without having a good basic knowledge of the indigenous or natural change processes without additional intervention. Reflection-in-action cycles might be more informative about change processes than the window that any single time-limited program or policy evaluation ever provides. Table 7.2 summarizes our key points.

Table 7.2. What the Complexity Lens Adds to Evaluation

A shift of focus from knowledge to capability, with consequences for measurement

Less structured "dose monitoring" as the means of evaluating implementation and more use of qualitative and narrative approaches

A focus on the structures in which knowledge is embedded (for example, through the use of social network analysis)

Long time frames that incorporate the possibility of system phase transitions

Measurement at multiple levels

More observation and analysis of the preintervention context and the natural change processes within it

No reason to abandon cluster randomized trial designs, as long as interventions adhere to a recognizable theory of action and that remains replicable across the sites (clusters)

Conclusion

Knowledge theories are robust and useful for understanding change processes. Being the product of their time, these theories initially privileged knowledge as the "magic" of an intervention, perhaps because they were born in an era when technology was prized. Hence they highlighted foreground (the new product), not the background (the preexisting context), in their interpretation of change processes. Some prominent evaluators using these models still do. Complexity thinking lends an opportunity to think more critically about the background. It invites readers to use Ottoson's Table 1.1, which lists the five knowledge theories, as the basis for theorizing the indigenous change processes in any system, context, or site prior to intervention. This way of thinking seeks to understand dynamics and hence better contextualize the meaning of any new knowledge (within a new policy or program) at the outset. This might help an evaluator act formatively to improve interventions and design evaluations that better capture the breadth and diversity of change processes and their outcomes.

That said, there is no appreciable market at present for in-house institutional ethnographers who might specialize in knowing the background or context of the places into which policies and programs might be destined. We live and work in a society where, for now and the foreseeable future, we can expect knowledge products to be produced (new programs, new policies) and for people to ask evaluators to assess their impact on an episodic basis. This means that to meet some of the challenges outlined in this chapter, evaluators will have to try to create new research spaces and new visions for research roles and methods.

In Alkin and Christie's (2004) evaluation theory terms, the complexity lens radically affects the methods of an evaluation. Complexity values the agency of the actor networks of implementation, and the evaluation is designed to capture this. Practice-based, indigenous use of knowledge for continuous system-level, adaptive change must be understood and appreciated by the evaluator within the context of interest prior to assessing the impact of any new program or policy in that context.

References

Alkin, M. C., & Christie, C. A. (2004). An evaluation theory tree. In M. C. Alkin (Ed.), *Evaluation roots*. Thousand Oaks, CA: Sage.

Alkin, M. C., & Christie, C. A. (Eds.). (2005). *Theorists models in action*. New Directions for Evaluation, no. 106, 1–128.

Axelrod, R., & Cohen, M. D. (2000). *Harnessing complexity*. New York: Basic Books.

Bond, L., Glover, S., Godfrey, C., Butler, H., & Patton, G. (2001). Building capacity in schools: Lessons from the Gatehouse Project. *Health Education and Behavior, 28*(3), 368–383.

Bower, D. (2006). Sustaining school improvement. *Complicity: An International Journal of Complexity and Education, 3*(1), 61–72.

Coffey, D. S. (1998). Self organisation, complexity and chaos: The new biology for medicine. *Nature, 4*, 882–885.

Cooper, H., & Geyer, R. (2007). *Riding the diabetes rollercoaster*. Abingdon: Radcliffe Publishing.

Dearing, J. W. (2008). Evolution of diffusion and dissemination theory. *Journal of Public Health Management and Practice, 14*, 99–108.

Durland, M. M., & Fredericks, K. A. (Eds.). (2005). *Social network analysis in program evaluation*. New Directions for Evaluation, no. 107, 1–101.

Dusenbury, L., Brannigan, R., Hansen, W. B., Walsh, J., & Falco, M. (2005). Quality of implementation: Developing measures crucial to understanding the diffusion of preventive interventions. *Health Education Research, 20*, 308–313.

Fraser, S. W., & Greenhalgh, T. (2001). Coping with complexity: Educating for capability. *British Medical Journal, 323*, 799–803.

Fullan, M. (1993). *Change forces: Probing the depths of educational reform*. London: Falmer Press.

Giddens, A. (1984). *The constitution of society*. Cambridge: Polity Press.

Glover, S., & Butler, H. (2004). Facilitating health promotion within school communities. In R. Moodie & A. Hulme (Eds.), *Hands-on health promotion*. Melbourne: IP Communications.

Hargreaves, A., & Fink, D. (2006). *Sustainable leadership*. San Francisco: Jossey-Bass.

Hawe, P. (1994). Capturing the meaning of "community" in community intervention evaluation: Some contributions from community psychology. *Health Promotion International, 9*, 199–210.

Hawe, P., & Ghali, L. (2008). Use of social network analysis to map the social relationships of staff and teachers at school. *Health Education Research, 23*, 62–69.

Hawe, P., Shiell, A., & Riley, T. (2004). How far "out of control" should a randomised trial be? *British Medical Journal, 328*, 1561–1563.

Hawe, P., Shiell, A., & Riley, T. (2008). Important considerations for standardizing complex interventions. *Journal of Advanced Nursing, 62*, 267.

Hawe, P., Shiell, A., & Riley, T. (2009). Theorizing interventions as events in systems. *American Journal of Community Psychology, 43*, 267–276.

Love, T., & Burton, C. (2005). General practice as a complex system: A novel analysis of consultation data. *Family Practice, 22*, 347–352.

Martin, C. M., & Sturmberg, J. P. (2005). General practice—chaos, complexity and innovation. *Medical Journal of Australia, 183*, 106–109.

Materia, E., & Baglio, G. (2005). Health, science and complexity. *Journal of Epidemiology and Community Health, 59*, 534–535.

O'Toole, L. J. (2000). Research on policy implementation: Assessment and prospects. *Journal of Public Administration Research and Theory, 10*(2), 263–288.

Patton, G. C., Bond, L., Carlin, J. B., Thomas, L., Butler, H., Glover, S., et al. (2006). Promoting social inclusion in schools: A group randomized trial of effects on student risk behaviors. *American Journal of Public Health, 96*(9), 1582–1588.

Peterson, A. V., Kealy, A., Mann, S. L., Marek, P. M., & Sarason, I. G. (2000). Hutchison smoking prevention project: Long term randomized trial in school-based tobacco use prevention. Results on smoking. *Journal of National Cancer Institute, 92,* 1979–1991.

Plsek, P. E., & Wilson, T. (2001). Complexity science: Complexity, leadership and management in healthcare organisations. *British Medical Journal, 323,* 746–749.

Rappaport, J., & Hess, R. (Eds.). (1984). *Studies in empowerment: Steps toward understanding and action.* New York: Haworth.

Rickles, D., Shiell, A., & Hawe, P. (2007). A simple guide to chaos and complexity. *Journal of Epidemiology and Community Health, 61,* 933–937.

Riley, B. L., MacDonald, J., Mansi, O., Kothari, A., Kurtz, D., vonTettenborn, L. I., et al. (2008). Is reporting on interventions a weak link in understanding how and why they work? A preliminary exploration using community heart health exemplars. *Implementation Science, 3,* 27.

Riley, T., & Hawe, P. (2005). Researching practice: The methodological case for narrative inquiry. *Health Education Research, 20*(2), 226–236.

Rogers, C. (1961). *On becoming a person.* Boston: Houghton Mifflin.

Senge, P., Cambron-McCabe, N., Lucas, T., Smith, B., Dutton, J., & Kleiner, A. (2000). *Schools that learn: A fifth discipline fieldbook for educators, parents, and everyone who cares about education.* New York: Doubleday.

Shiell, A., Hawe, P., & Gold, L. (2008). Complex interventions or complex systems? Implications for health economic evaluation. *British Medical Journal, 336,* 1281–1283.

Stephenson, J., & Weil, S. (1992). *Quality in learning: A capability approach in higher education.* London: Kogan Page.

Wilson, T., Holt, T., & Greenhalgh, T. (2001). Complexity and clinical care. *British Medical Journal, 323,* 685–688.

PENELOPE HAWE *is the Markin Chair in Health and Society at the University of Calgary, Canada, and director of the Population Health Intervention Research Centre. She holds a health scientist award from the Alberta Heritage Foundation for Medical Research.*

LYNDAL BOND *is the associate director of the Medical Research Council Social and Public Health Sciences Unit at the University of Glasgow.*

HELEN BUTLER *is a senior lecturer in the School of Education, Australian Catholic University, Melbourne, Australia.*

NEW DIRECTIONS FOR EVALUATION • DOI: 10.1002/ev

POSTSCRIPT

A P.S. must be brief yet important enough to be worthy of appendage to the body of writing that precedes it. The authors of this issue have taken ideas about how we understand the role of knowledge in the change process and invited us to use these in the design of any policy or program evaluation. Indeed they have shown us how to do so. What I encourage readers to do now is to consider how these same theories might help us interrogate and reframe other issues confronting evaluators, namely, the way we traditionally think about external validity as a bridge from the particular relevance for the setting in which an evaluation is conducted to its utility for other settings, populations, and times.

If we take as the primary function of research the discovery, development, and testing of new knowledge that is basic or fundamental enough to have a high degree of generalizability across settings or populations, then research will necessarily fall short of the sensitivity and specificity that local or regional policymakers, program planners, managers, and practitioners seek. The premium for research funding, as represented, for example, by the National Institutes of Health's peer review standards, is placed on the internal validity, or causal certainty, of the research findings. To achieve the comfort of such certainty, experimental controls are often imposed on the sampling and circumstances of the experiments at the expense of external validity.

Evaluation often fills these gaps in knowledge with program performance and outcomes from more or less natural experiments that are highly particular to real-time, real-context studies of programs run by typical workers who are implementing programs under more typical circumstances. What evaluation loses in causal certainty or internal validity with the relatively uncontrolled, purposive sampling and quasi-experimental circumstances of most evaluative studies, it gains in relevance of the results to that situation, that locality, that population, that sponsoring organization, and that time. But the more relevant an evaluative study is to a particular setting or population or circumstance or time, the less generalizable it may become.

When study of the diffusion, adoption, utilization, implementation, integration, and maintenance of new program knowledge is added to this mix of evidence, it offers an understanding of the range of applicability and limitations of the program, intervention, or innovation under study. This contribution to external validity could be seen as the missing link in most "evidence-based practice" guidelines. Most such guidelines are derived from systematic reviews of the published research and evaluation literature. Most of the studies that survive the screening of that literature are of the first type: more highly controlled, randomized trials that favor internal validity or causal certainty over relevance to specific circumstances or external validity for many different circumstances.

This issue of *New Directions for Evaluation* suggests in the varied richness of its consideration of this third dimension of external validation—validity of new knowledge for users besides those with whom or for whom it was tested—that the guidelines for evidence-based practice should be based on more than the rigor of the experimental designs, as most official "best practice" guidelines are prominently based. But it should not diminish the value to local policymakers, planners, managers, or recipients of evaluation results from their specific programs or interventions in specific settings with specific populations. Whether such highly relevant results for some should warrant publication and recommendations for the many must depend on how typical their setting, population, and circumstances is for the many others.

The potential new standard of publishable evaluations that could arise is not just a test of the three dimensions of external validity, for that could open the door to an infinite number of setting × population × circumstance combinations for every innovation tested, and an endless number of replications in different settings, populations, times, and circumstances. The worthiness of an evaluation can be judged in the short term and for local purposes on its relevance for a particular setting, population, and set of circumstances.

The vision offered by this issue is that the longer-range, broader merit of an evaluated innovation could rest ultimately on its diffusion, utilization, implementation, integration, and maintenance. It poses the question of whether "evidence-based practices" should await a test of their broader utilization by these criteria before they are declared best practices. It suggests, as I have argued in response to the pecuniary tendencies of federal and other program funding agencies insisting on a single-minded experimental standard of proof, that if we want more evidence-based practice, we need more practice-based evidence.

Lawrence W. Green

LAWRENCE W. GREEN is professor, Department of Epidemiology and Biostatistics, and co-leader of the Society, Diversity and Disparities Program, School of Medicine and Helen Diller Comprehensive Cancer Center, University of California at San Francisco.

INDEX

NEW DIRECTIONS FOR EVALUATION

ORDER FORM SUBSCRIPTION AND SINGLE ISSUES

DISCOUNTED BACK ISSUES:

Use this form to receive 20% off all back issues of *New Directions for Evaluation*.
All single issues priced at **$23.20** (normally $29.00)

TITLE	ISSUE NO.	ISBN

Call 888-378-2537 or see mailing instructions below. When calling, mention the promotional code JBXND to receive your discount. For a complete list of issues, please visit www.josseybass.com/go/ndev

SUBSCRIPTIONS: (1 YEAR, 4 ISSUES)

☐ New Order   ☐ Renewal

U.S.	☐ Individual: $85	☐ Institutional: $256
Canada/Mexico	☐ Individual: $85	☐ Institutional: $296
All Others	☐ Individual: $109	☐ Institutional: $330

Call 888-378-2537 or see mailing and pricing instructions below.
Online subscriptions are available at www.interscience.wiley.com

ORDER TOTALS:

Issue / Subscription Amount: $ _____

Shipping Amount: $ _____
(for single issues only – subscription prices include shipping)

Total Amount: $ _____

SHIPPING CHARGES:		
SURFACE	**DOMESTIC**	**CANADIAN**
First Item	$5.00	$6.00
Each Add'l Item	$3.00	$1.50

(No sales tax for U.S. subscriptions. Canadian residents, add GST for subscription orders. Individual rate subscriptions must be paid by personal check or credit card. Individual rate subscriptions may not be resold as library copies.)

BILLING & SHIPPING INFORMATION:

☐ **PAYMENT ENCLOSED:** *(U.S. check or money order only. All payments must be in U.S. dollars.)*

☐ **CREDIT CARD:** ☐ VISA ☐ MC ☐ AMEX

Card number _____ Exp. Date _____

Card Holder Name _____ Card Issue # *(required)* _____

Signature _____ Day Phone _____

☐ **BILL ME:** *(U.S. institutional orders only. Purchase order required.)*

Purchase order # _____
Federal Tax ID 13559302 • GST 89102-8052

Name _____

Address _____

Phone _____ E-mail _____

Copy or detach page and send to: **John Wiley & Sons, PTSC, 5th Floor**
989 Market Street, San Francisco, CA 94103-1741

Order Form can also be faxed to: **888-481-2665**

PROMO JBXND

DOING A LITERATURE REVIEW IN
NURSING, HEALTH AND SOCIAL CARE

SAGE was founded in 1965 by Sara Miller McCune to support the dissemination of usable knowledge by publishing innovative and high-quality research and teaching content. Today, we publish over 900 journals, including those of more than 400 learned societies, more than 800 new books per year, and a growing range of library products including archives, data, case studies, reports, and video. SAGE remains majority-owned by our founder, and after Sara's lifetime will become owned by a charitable trust that secures our continued independence.

Los Angeles | London | New Delhi | Singapore | Washington DC | Melbourne

MICHAEL COUGHLAN & PATRICIA CRONIN

2ND EDITION

DOING A LITERATURE REVIEW IN NURSING, HEALTH AND SOCIAL CARE

Los Angeles | London | New Delhi
Singapore | Washington DC | Melbourne

Los Angeles | London | New Delhi
Singapore | Washington DC | Melbourne

SAGE Publications Ltd
1 Oliver's Yard
55 City Road
London EC1Y 1SP

SAGE Publications Inc.
2455 Teller Road
Thousand Oaks, California 91320

SAGE Publications India Pvt Ltd
B 1/I 1 Mohan Cooperative Industrial Area
Mathura Road
New Delhi 110 044

SAGE Publications Asia-Pacific Pte Ltd
3 Church Street
#10-04 Samsung Hub
Singapore 049483

Editor: Becky Taylor
Editorial assistant: Charlène Burin
Production editor: Katie Forsythe
Copyeditor: H.A. Fairlie
Proofreader: Mary Dalton
Indexer: Judith Lavender
Marketing manager: Tamara Navaratnam
Cover design: Wendy Scott
Typeset by: C&M Digitals (P) Ltd, Chennai, India
Printed and bound by CPI Group (UK) Ltd,
Croydon, CR0 4YY

Library of Congress Control Number: 2016940072

British Library Cataloguing in Publication data

A catalogue record for this book is available from
the British Library

ISBN 978-1-4129-6203-2
ISBN 978-1-4129-6204-9 (pbk)

At SAGE we take sustainability seriously. Most of our products are printed in the UK using FSC papers and boards.
When we print overseas we ensure sustainable papers are used as measured by the PREPS grading system.
We undertake an annual audit to monitor our sustainability.

CONTENTS

LIST OF FIGURES AND TABLES

Figures

Tables

ABOUT THE AUTHORS

Michael Coughlan is an Assistant Professor in the School of Nursing, Trinity College Dublin, where he has worked since 2002. He is a Registered Nurse Tutor and has been involved in nurse education for over 25 years. He has a wide experience in guiding and supervising students undertaking literature reviews and research studies at both an undergraduate and postgraduate level. His interests include research, and haematology and oncology nursing. He has a number of publications in these areas, in addition to co-authoring two books on literature reviews and research.

Qualifications: MEd, MA, BNS, RPN, RGN, RNT.

Patricia Cronin is an Assistant Professor in the School of Nursing and Midwifery, Trinity College Dublin. She has worked there since 2004 having worked previously at City University, London. Her clinical background is in surgical and gastrointestinal nursing, which she teaches at undergraduate level. She has a special interest in enabling students to engage in research and theory and these areas form the focus of her postgraduate teaching. She has published widely, co-authoring four books and has written book chapters and journal articles related to clinical skills, gastrointestinal nursing, research and theory. Her research interest is in the area of chronic illness and what it means for the person to live with a long-term condition.

Qualifications: PhD, MSc, MA, BSc Nursing & Education, DipN (Lond), RN.

ACKNOWLEDGEMENTS

In this the second edition of *Doing a Literature Review in Nursing, Health and Social Care*, we would like to acknowledge the contribution made by our colleague Frances Ryan to the first edition of this book. We would also like to acknowledge and thank all the students who offered us their insights into undertaking a literature review.

We would like to thank the reviewers for their helpful feedback and the editorial team from SAGE for all their help in the preparation of this edition.

Publisher's Acknowledgments

The publishers would like to thank the following individuals for their invaluable feedback on the proposal and draft chapters:

Gaynor Fenton, University of Salford, UK
Claire, O'Tuathail, Ireland
Elaine Lehane, University College Cork, Ireland

Patricia Pye, Buckinghamshire New University, UK
Linda Robson, Edge Hill University, UK
Rachel Rossiter, Charles Sturt University, Australia

We would also like to thank the following students for their comments which you can find throughout the book:

Bronagh Dunning, Nursing student, Trinity College Dublin, Ireland
Colette Farrell, Nursing student, Trinity College Dublin, Ireland

Daniel Waters, Nursing student, Kingston University, UK
Suzanna Weedle, Nursing student, Trinity College Dublin, Ireland

The authors and publishers are grateful to the following for their kind permission to reproduce material:

Table 7.2: Reprinted from *Journal of Clinical Nursing*, Judith Anderson, Linda Malone, Kerry Shanahan, Jennifer Manning, 'Nursing bedside clinical handover – an integrated review of issues and tools', 2014 with permission from John Wiley and Sons.

Table 7.3: Reprinted from *International Journal of Nursing Studies*, Vol 49, Maria Grant, Alison Cavanagh, Janelle Yorke, 'The impact of caring for those with chronic obstructive pulmonary disease (COPD) on carers' psychological well-being: A narrative review', 2012 , with permission from Elsevier.

Table 7.5: Reprinted from *Patient Education and Counseling*, Vol 84, Marianne Berkhof, H. Jolanda van Rijssen, Antonius J.M. Schellart, Johannes R. Anema, Allard J. van der Beek,

'Effective training strategies for teaching communication skills to physicians: An overview of systematic reviews', 152–162, 2011, with permission from Elsevier.

Table 7.8: Reprinted from *Journal of Clinical Nursing*, Deborah Finfgeld-Connett, 'Meta-synthesis of caring in nursing', 2007 with permission from John Wiley and Sons.

Table 7.9: Reprinted from *Patient Education and Counseling*, Vol 69, Lillebeth Larun, Kirsti Malterud, 'Identity and coping experiences in Chronic Fatigue Syndrome: A synthesis of qualitative studies', 2007, with permission from Elsevier.

Figures 4.1, 4.2, 4.3, 4.4, 4.5: Reproduced with kind permission of EBSCO.

WHAT IS A LITERATURE REVIEW?

❝ Learning Outcomes ❞

Having read this chapter you should be able to:

- explain what a literature review is;
- outline the differences between writing an essay and writing a literature review;
- describe the steps involved in undertaking a literature review.

Introduction

A literature review is often simply considered as one part of a larger research study, and while this may be one reason for undertaking a review, it is only one of many reasons for doing a literature review. A literature review is an important tool that, among other things, is used for both informing and developing practice, for seeking answers from the literature on clinical problems; it can be a source of discussion on academic work. Whatever the reason for undertaking a literature review, the task is often viewed as a difficult and complicated one by students and novice reviewers. The aim of this chapter and ultimately this book is to provide you, the novice reviewer, with a comprehensive understanding of what a literature review is and, equally, what it is not. It will explore the purpose and relevance of undertaking a literature review and the differences between writing a literature review and other forms of academic assignments. An overview of the fundamental steps involved in undertaking a literature review will also be presented. Whether or not you have previously embarked on the literature review journey, this book is designed to help you understand the process and skills involved in navigating the literature and reaching your ultimate destination.

What is a Literature Review?

Whatever the reason for undertaking a review of the literature, whether it is for a clinical or academic purpose, it is essential to understand what a literature review is before you begin. A literature review is a summary of the outcomes, and critical appraisal of a number of research studies on a defined topic (Baker, 2016). Rather than having to read a multiplicity of studies on a topic, a comprehensive review should provide the reader with a succinct, objective and logical summary of the current knowledge on that particular subject. The literature should have been gathered in a systematic manner, to ensure all the relevant information has been included, and the critical appraisal allows the reader to make a judgement on how robust the original studies were. A literature review is not an essay where studies can be selected to support a particular view or opinion. Nor is it a series of critiques or lengthy descriptions of a number of studies. Quite simply, the literature review provides a critical discussion on the topic of interest while pointing out similarities and inconsistencies in existing relevant literature. It is important to note that while a literature search is the means of helping you to unearth literature that is appropriate to your review topic, a literature review is the larger process which includes identifying the topic of interest, gathering, critically appraising and summarising the literature.

The term literature review today encompasses a number of different approaches to searching, gathering and presenting literature (Cronin et al., 2015). These range from the traditional or narrative review which is similar to the literature review in research study to the more complex systematic review. Systematic reviews can involve meta-analysis or meta-synthesis to analyse the data discovered, and are regarded as research in their own right. The different types of literature reviews will be discussed in more detail in Chapter 2, while Chapter 3 discusses the process of undertaking a systematic review.

The Steps Involved in Undertaking a Literature Review

When undertaking a literature review, there are a series of sequential steps that need to be considered. The first step is to identify the aim or purpose of the review. If your literature review is part of a larger research study, then the aim or review problem will correspond with that of the study. The aim or review problem will help the reader identify what you are interested in investigating and why. This step is also important as it gives you, the reviewer, a concrete topic of interest. Without a clear aim or problem there may be no focus to the review, and the result may be a hodge-podge of diverse studies with no identifiable objective. The focus of your review also needs to be reasonably well defined. If it is too broad you may have difficulty managing the amount of literature and if the focus is too restricted then you may not be able to find enough literature for your review. Both of these are common problems encountered by novice reviewers and both can be managed through initially identifying a suitable review problem or aim. Chapter 4 offers advice on identifying a topic of interest and refining it. If you are undertaking a systematic review, you will need to identify a research question at this stage which is more specific and focused than the aim or review problem in a traditional narrative review (see Chapter 3).

The next step involves searching the literature. The search of the literature should be undertaken in a planned and organised way. To demonstrate this you should clearly delineate how the search will be undertaken. You should identify the key-words for your search and any combinations of these, the databases you intend searching and any other strategies you intend to employ such as limiting your search or using the reference list from some of the studies you selected. It is important to be as comprehensive as possible in describing your search strategy so that if another reviewer wished to replicate your search they would have the necessary information to do so.

When you have searched the literature the next task is to identify which studies are applicable to the topic you are investigating. Depending on the type of review you are undertaking some of the studies identified in the search may not meet the aims of the review and may need to be excluded. If the number of studies identified is small, it may be possible to evaluate each study individually; however, for larger numbers, studies are usually assessed on their title and then the abstract. Studies that meet the criteria are then usually downloaded for in-depth study. The steps of searching and selecting the literature are discussed in more detail in Chapter 4.

The next stage is becoming familiar with the literature you will be including in your review. This includes reading, note-taking and summarising the study. It is important at this stage to make a complete bibliographical reference of the studies in your review to keep with your notes and to make distinctions between what is paraphrased and what are direct quotes. Price (2014) states that poor note-taking at this point can potentially lead to allegations of plagiarism where paraphrased or quoted citations are not properly acknowledged. Reference management tools such as EndNote can be useful at this stage as the reference details can be stored for application when writing the review; notes can also be made and a pdf copy of the article attached to the reference for further review.

It is during this stage of the process that themes from the literature start to emerge. It is important to consider these carefully as these will determine how your review is presented. Remember you are attempting to summarise the findings of the studies in your review, so the themes you select should allow you to do this. Reading and organising the literature in your review are discussed in Chapter 5.

Analysis and synthesis are the next stages in undertaking a literature review. Having decided what literature is to be included in your review, you need to critically appraise that literature to identify its strengths and any limitations. The reader is depending on you to discern which studies are robust and which findings should be interpreted with caution. You also need to demonstrate that you are critically reading and not simply taking studies at face value. Bear in mind that a literature review should be objective so you need to support your analysis with references to the literature. Synthesis involves combining the information from the different studies in your review. This will involve comparing and contrasting the different studies and their findings, and per-haps identifying potential reasons for differing results and developing new perspectives in relation to the topic being reviewed. Issues related to appraising and combining the literature will be discussed in Chapters 6 and 7 respectively.

The final part of writing your review is to complete the summary, conclusion and recommendations. While these appear to be and are in a sense different components, they are often combined under one heading. The summary is a concise overview of the outcomes from each theme, which leads into the conclusion. The latter should reflect the problem or topic that was being reviewed. Recommendations can be in relation to further studies that need to be undertaken, or a justification for a proposed study if the review is part of a larger piece of research. Chapter 8 discusses writing your review and referencing is discussed in Chapter 9.

The Importance of Reviewing the Literature

As stated earlier, literature reviews are undertaken for a number of different reasons. One of the most common reasons is as part of a larger study. The rationale here is that the researcher needs to establish what studies have already been done, and what is already known in relation to this topic. This information can then be used to identify the knowledge gaps that exist, develop the research question or hypothesis, and help the researcher decide the most appropriate methodological approach to the study. Robust literature reviews can also be useful in developing practice guidelines and procedures. They can also be valuable as sources of support for evidence based practice and improving quality of care (Baker, 2016).

Student Comment

'A literature review allows you the opportunity to improve your knowledge on a chosen topic of interest in a structured academic format.'

(4th year undergraduate general nursing student)

Summary

A literature review is a systematic search and identification of literature on a specific topic. The literature therein is objectively appraised and summarised in order to offer new insights on the topic to the reader. Literature reviews can be undertaken for a number of different reasons, for example as part of a larger research study, or as a means of answering a clinical problem. Literature reviews can also be helpful sources of knowledge to both practitioners and students who are faced with a vast volume of literature on a topic and minimal time to search the databases. A comprehensive literature review can give the practitioner a succinct overview of the literature, offering insights as to how the studies were conducted, comparing and contrasting outcomes and answering clinical questions.

There are a number of different types of literature review ranging from the classical narrative review to systematic reviews. However, despite their differences, the principles which underpin searching for and selecting literature, and appraising and combining the research outcomes, are similar for them all.

❝ Key Points ❞

- A literature review is a process that involves systematically gathering, appraising and summarising studies relevant to a problem or topic.
- A review of the literature may be undertaken as part of research study, to inform practice or policy development, or for academic purposes.
- The steps in the literature review process involve selecting a topic, searching and selecting the literature, appraising and combining the findings of the studies, and finally presenting the review.

TYPES OF LITERATURE REVIEW

❛ Learning Outcomes ❜

Having read this chapter you should be able to:

- explain the purpose of different types of literature review;
- describe the major differences between the various types of literature review;
- outline how the stated purpose of a literature review directs the type of review to be undertaken.

Introduction

Student Comment

'I can see that there are different types of review, such as traditional/narrative review, systematic review, meta-analysis and meta-synthesis. Each type has different challenges but I would think the major challenge is in actually choosing which type of review to use...'

(2nd year undergraduate mental health nursing student)

This chapter focuses on the various types of literature review that you may encounter when reading the literature, and it is important that you can distinguish between them for a number of reasons. First, in recent years there has been a noticeable increase in the terms that have been used to describe the 'literature review' and, to those of you who may be accessing academic literature for the first time, the discussion can be daunting and confusing in terms of differentiating between them. Second, throughout your undergraduate programme and beyond, being able to analyse and critique published literature is fundamental. Much has been written about how to do this in respect of research reports but there has been limited guidance on how to make a judgement about the quality of a literature review. It is suggested here that the ability to determine if a reviewer has conducted a 'good' review starts with determining if there is congruence between the type of review they said they were going to do and what they actually did. Third, in the event that you have to conduct a review, it is important that you have clear indicators of the requirements of your particular review.

This chapter begins with a brief outline of how the conceptualisation and categorisation of the literature review has developed. This is followed by an overview of the various types of literature review as well as offering some clarity around the use of terms. Examples are offered throughout to enhance understanding.

The Changing Literature Review

Traditionally, literature reviews have been seen as being embedded in the various stages of the development, conduct and reporting of a research study or as a vital part of an academic assignment. However, in recent decades several factors have combined to transform and expand their role and functions, including:

- the knowledge explosion;
- evidence-based practice;
- hierarchies of evidence.

The Knowledge Explosion

The increasing sophistication of online technology and the advent of online databases has led to an explosion of available literature which is enormously beneficial when compared with the pre-electronic days, when many hours were spent in libraries searching catalogues, hand-searching journals and photocopying material. However, for practitioners who are interested in a topic for whatever purpose, the sheer volume of available literature means that the business of discerning and subsequently assessing and judging it is complex. Moreover, busy practitioners may be time constrained or may not have the wherewithal to undertake the level of analysis required to determine the quality of a series of individual or discrete studies. Consider, for example, the individual skills you need just to be able to access material electronically. At the very least, you have to have some computer literacy and you have to be able to discern 'credible' sources of material. Despite the assumption that computer literacy is a universal skill, we have over our years in education met many students who are daunted by the prospect. We have also noted that many in the early stages of their education do not have the skills to discriminate between that which is considered an acceptable source of information or evidence and that which is not. If these issues are put in the context of limited time and resources, locating and retrieving the evidence can be an intimidating process, and that is before you even consider what you are going to do when you have collected the material.

Go to any well-known search engine and type in any of the following terms:

- postoperative pain;
- mobility assessment;
- assessment of swallowing.

Note how many 'hits' you get but also look at the sources of the material and see if you can judge whether or not they are 'credible'.

Evidence-based Practice

In the context of the information explosion and possible overload, Hamer and Collinson (2005) argue that it is almost impossible for healthcare practitioners to stay up to date. Yet we have a professional obligation to provide the best care possible based on the best available knowledge and evidence. The rise in the popularity of evidence-based healthcare (EBH) that corresponded with the ever-increasing availability of information is a reflection of this obligation. Early work in EBH was largely in the field of medicine, and the evidence-based medicine movement (EBM) promoted summarising the evidence from clinical research in order to reduce the emphasis on 'unsystematic clinical experience and pathophysiological rationale' (Guyatt et al., 2004: 990).

Therefore, evidence-based practice (EBP) is about 'the conscientious, explicit, and judicious use of current best evidence in making decisions about the care of individual patients' (Sackett et al., 1996: 71). Muir Gray (2001) characterises this as doing the right things for the right people at the right time where clinical expertise and consideration of the individual patient's needs, situation, rights and preferences are factors that influence whether the 'evidence' is applied. Therefore, good evidence is not the only determinant of the right thing to do, and issues such as patient empowerment, cost pressures, changing public expectations and political consensus impact on the translation of strong evidence into practice. Later in the chapter the significance of this will be demonstrated when considering various types of literature review.

Nonetheless, despite those who claim EBM/EBP suppresses clinical freedom, there is now almost universal recognition from practitioners, managers and policy-makers that in order to deliver effective healthcare scientific evidence is an essential element. However, given the limitations identified above with the sheer volume of information and the skills and time needed to source and summarise the evidence the question is, how can practitioners determine what is best evidence?

Hierarchies of Evidence

A long-held view in healthcare research is that some 'types' of studies produce 'better' or more reliable results than others. Thus, there are hierarchies of evidence where some evidence is valued more highly, based primarily on the type of research used to generate it (Hamer and Collinson, 2005). For example, in healthcare research that examines the effectiveness of clinical interventions, the randomised controlled trial (RCT) is ranked as the 'gold standard' study design (see Box 2.1 for a definition). This is because researchers undertaking these types of study attempt to minimise the effect of factors (variables) that might affect the results. Therefore, they can claim that the findings are more likely to represent the 'true effect' of the intervention (Evans, 2003). Although much has been written about the limitations of RCTs in evaluating healthcare interventions (see Parahoo, 2014: 395), they are still considered to be at the highest level of evidence.

Nonetheless, in the last 20 years or so, there has been a general recognition that the findings of individual or single studies, even if they are gold-standard RCTs, are not always an adequate basis for changing healthcare practice. Moreover, despite their best intentions, studies may not have been conducted as rigorously as they should and may be unintentionally biased. Thus, there has been a drive to synthesise or 'pool' the findings from several studies in order to determine the overall strength of the evidence that exists about a particular issue.

Box 2.1   Definition of Randomised Controlled Trial

A simple definition of a randomised controlled trial is that it is an experiment for the purpose of testing the effectiveness of an intervention, for example a new medication. Those who are taking part are randomly assigned to either the intervention group (to receive the new medication) or the control group (not to receive the new medication). The results are compared between the two groups.

As a result of this drive to pool results from more than one study, a form of literature review known as the 'systematic review' has become prominent in the health sector and is now a fundamental factor in clinical, healthcare, managerial, educational, social and public policy decision-making. A number of organisations have emerged that have supported the conduct and dissemination of systematic reviews. In 1992, the Cochrane Centre in Oxford (now the UK Cochrane Centre (http://uk.cochrane.org/)) was founded in order to facilitate summarising evidence about the effectiveness of healthcare interventions. In the following year The Cochrane Collaboration (www.cochrane.org) was launched and since then it has become an internationally recognised organisation with over 37,000 contributors from more than 130 countries (see examples from their reviews in Box 2.2).

Box 2.2   Reviews from The Cochrane Collaboration

'Advocacy interventions to reduce or eliminate violence and promote the physical and psychosocial well-being of women who experience intimate partner abuse' (Rivas et al., 2015).

'Crisis intervention for people with severe mental illnesses' (Murphy et al., 2015).

'Restricting oral fluid and food intake during labour' (Singata et al., 2013).

In recent years, the National Institute for Health Research (www.nihr.ac.uk) has funded the Centre for Reviews and Dissemination (CRD) (www.york.ac.uk/inst/crd/), whose focus is the synthesis (pooling) of evidence that has relevance for policy development across a range of health topics. In addition, the NIHR's dissemination centre (www.disseminationcentre.nihr.ac.uk/) makes available new summaries of research that has been identified as important to clinicians, patients and managers. Recent summaries from the NIHR dissemination centre are presented in Box 2.3.

Box 2.3   Systematic Review Summaries from NIHR Dissemination Centre

'Music as an aid for postoperative recovery in adults: a systematic review and meta-analysis' (Hole et al., 2015).

'Interventions to improve the experience of caring for people with severe mental illness: systematic review and meta-analysis' (Yesufu-Udechuku et al., 2015).

Another organisation that has relevance for healthcare is the Evidence for Policy and Practice Information and Co-ordinating Centre (EPPI-Centre) (http://eppi.ioe. ac.uk/cms). The EPPI-Centre is based in the Social Science Research Unit in University College London and its primary focus is to inform policy and professional practice through sound evidence in the areas of social policy including education, health, social care, developing economies, sport, environment and crime. Some recent examples are cited in Box 2.4.

Box 2.4   Reviews from EPPI Centre

'The views of young people in the UK about obesity, body size, shape and weight: a systematic review' (Rees et al., 2013).

'Depression, anxiety, pain and quality of life in people living with chronic hepatitis C: a systematic review and meta-analysis' (Brunton et al., 2015).

As a result of these developments, the traditional literature review has changed irrevocably. Primarily, this is because when organisations concerned with systematic reviews set themselves the task of summarising the evidence from research they deemed it necessary to develop criteria for ensuring the quality, consistency and transparency of the review process. As a result, 'protocols' were introduced into the world of literature reviewing and became the hallmark of the systematic review.

An outcome of this is that literature reviews themselves are now 'ranked', with systematic or protocol-driven reviews being most highly valued. It is argued that this is because the process of undertaking such a review is highly structured, logical and transparent, with all decisions being clearly explained throughout. Therefore, regardless of their underlying purpose, all literature reviews are now judged against the standard or benchmark of the systematic review. Even the literature review that you undertake on a topic for an assignment will likely incorporate elements of the systematic review process. To some extent, this has had implications for reviews that do not meet the criteria for a systematic review. For example, the 'traditional' (also variously described as 'narrative', 'descriptive', 'standard') review has seen its position eroded to a point where it is regarded by some as being the least structured and thereby the least significant. Moreover, the rapid rise of the systematic review has resulted in an associated growth of published literature reviews and with it a plethora of terms that are used to describe various 'types' of review (see Box 2.5).

While this proliferation of all types of reviews has contributed to the development of more systematic and rigorous methods, Arksey and O'Malley (2005) argue that the labels appear to be applied loosely and there is a lack of consistency in terms of definition. In addition, there are a number of publications where the focus is on authors promoting the merits of their own approach. In some instances, rather than adding clarity, this merely serves to confuse the issue further. Therefore, when reading about each type of review presented in this chapter, you should consider the examples offered and reflect on whether the differences are apparent or whether you think the labels are merely a matter of semantics.

Student Comment

'There are many different words and terminologies used for the same type of review. It takes some time to become familiar with the words they use...'

(4th year undergraduate general nursing student)

Box 2.5 Some Terms that Are Used to Describe Types of Literature Review*

- Narrative.
- Traditional.
- Descriptive.
- Standard.
- Integrative.
- Scoping.
- Qualitative.
- Concept analysis.

- Realist.
- Rapid evidence.
- Systematic.
- Meta-analysis.
- Meta-synthesis.
- Meta-summary.
- Meta-ethnography.

(*This list is not exhaustive or complete.)

Therefore, in this text we present the argument that all literature reviews share the fundamental characteristics of collecting, evaluating and presenting available evidence on a given topic. We also share Arksey and O'Malley's (2005) contention that there is no single type of 'ideal' literature review but a range of methods that need to be adopted appropriately depending on the focus of the review. Therefore, while some authors present reviews on a continuum from least to most systematic or structured in terms of their approach, we have chosen to present each as a discrete 'type'. Differences between each will be highlighted but comparisons in terms of their value are avoided.

Types of Literature Review

Traditional/Narrative Review

As indicated above, interchangeable terms that are used to describe this type of review include standard, traditional, narrative and descriptive. In this text, the term narrative is used for ease of description and because it is the term that appears most commonly in the literature.

Prior to the emergence of systematic reviews of interventions, the narrative review was the primary means by which literature on a given topic was presented. However, as outlined above, it is regarded by some as lacking any defined method for searching and retrieving the literature and is therefore described as being the least rigorous. It is unlikely that you will see such reviews published today as they will not meet the more systematic and rigorous methods that have evolved (Whittemore and Knafl, 2005).

The increasing emphasis on reviews that are methodical means that the narrative review must, at least, meet the basic standard of having a clearly outlined method by which it was conducted. The result of these developments means that sometimes what are essentially narrative reviews are described in a publication title as 'systematic'. This term may be used by the authors to indicate that the review was undertaken methodically rather than actually following a systematic review process.

Properly conducted narrative reviews remain a vital part of the science of any discipline. Overall, their aim is to identify, analyse, assess and interpret a body of knowledge on a topic. The particular focus and the breadth and depth of literature to be included in the review varies according to the context in which it is being conducted. For example, a literature review is a normal part of undertaking a research dissertation or thesis, and its function is to situate and justify the selection of the topic in the context of the existing literature. In funding proposals, reviews tend to present the current literature while also identifying gaps in existing knowledge. A narrative review may be presented also as a chapter in a book with the purpose of presenting the state of existing knowledge on a topic. It can be undertaken as a stand-alone, substantive review that is valuable in offering a connection between different aspects of a particular topic or even proposing a different or new interpretation of it. The narrative review is also the basis of many academic assignments and results in student learning through exploration of a specified topic.

Consequently, the topic areas for narrative reviews can vary from relatively broad to specific. In general, however, they are less precise than the type of question or problem that would be posed in any protocol-driven type of review such as a systematic review. For example, Williams and Manias (2008) conducted a literature review on pain assessment and management in patients with chronic kidney disease. Although there was some specificity in respect of the focus on chronic kidney disease, pain assessment and management are very broad topics which resulted in literature being retrieved from a wide range of sources.

Because the focus is broader the type of literature sourced in a narrative review tends to be broad also. In Williams and Manias' review, the authors did not confine themselves to empirical research studies but included every type of publication that addressed pain and kidney disease or renal failure. These incorporated review and discussion papers as well as textbooks, and resulted in four renal textbooks and 93 articles being retrieved for full review. Of these, 12 were research papers using diverse methodologies and approaches relating to pain control in patients with chronic kidney disease. The key point here is that in a narrative literature review, you are not constrained by the type of literature you can use. However, it is fundamental that at the very least there is clarity about how you came to identify such literature and why you chose to include it.

For instance, even when you are undertaking a literature review as part of an academic assignment you will be expected to outline the parameters you put in place when you searched the literature. These include delineating the databases you used, the key search terms you employed and how you combined them, the time limits you applied and any language restrictions you put in place. In addition, it is likely you will be expected to outline what you found, such as the volume and type of literature and how you arrived at the final selection.

In a well-conducted narrative literature review critiques or evaluations of the included literature have always been an important element. Nonetheless, these tended to be integrated within the discussion and the transparency of the process was not always evident. However, in contemporary narrative reviews, a further influence of the systematic review is the likelihood that you will see statements or evidence of the evaluation of the methodological quality of any research studies that have been included. Although it is not an absolute requirement it is seen as enhancing the rigour of the review and may well be something you will be required to do when undertaking such a review.

It is also important in contemporary narrative reviews that the process by which the analysis of the included literature was undertaken is described (e.g. thematic analysis – see Chapter 7). It is worth noting that it is often these aspects that are poorly developed. For those who wish to publish their reviews, it is unlikely that they will be accepted for publication unless they meet these parameters. Further details on these processes are addressed in Chapter 7.

Outlining the methods you adopted is also important because there is a risk of what is known as 'selection bias', where the reviewer only chooses literature that supports their standpoint. Nonetheless, the narrative review does not have to be a review of all the available literature and, in fact, it would be unrealistic to attempt to do so. What is fundamental is that the literature selected is relevant, that no key report is excluded and that the body of literature is adequately represented in the final review (Sandelowski, 2008). Therefore, many contemporary reviews tend to have a particular stance or focus that makes the review of the available literature more manageable (see Box 2.6).

Box 2.6   A Narrative Literature Review

'Adult family member experiences during an older loved one's delirium: a narrative literature review' (Day and Higgins, 2015).

Day and Higgins (2015) identified that there was little understanding of delirium and support for families in acute and maintenance care settings. Therefore, they reviewed the literature on the experiences of family members when an older loved one had delirium in acute, community and residential care settings with the purpose of identifying issues for practice and research. The review was undertaken as follows:

Database Searches

- *Electronic databases*: Medline, EMBASE, PsychINFO, CINAHL, Proquest and Informit (Health Collection).
- *Search engine:* Google Scholar.
- *Handsearches*: Reference lists from retrieved literature.
- *Grey literature:* One thesis (by the first author), Project Report, Book Chapter.

Search Terms

Multiple search combinations of: 'delirium', 'acute confusion', 'experience', 'older person', 'elderly', 'aged', 'geriatric', 'family', 'relative', 'spouse', 'carer'.

Parameters

Publications in English available to June 2014.

Findings

Four studies (qualitative and/or quantitative methods), a project report and book chapter.

Themes Identified

- 'Unexpected, rapid and unpredictable changes in demeanour'.
- 'Losing connection to the older person now and maybe forever'.
- 'Distressing times'.
- 'Not knowing about delirium nor how to help'.
- 'Supportive and unsupportive relationships with healthcare staff'.

Integrative Review

Another form of review that you may see in the literature is the integrative review. A brief overview is included here because it is likely you will encounter these in your reading and it is important to have some understanding. Integrative reviews are, to some extent, a response to a perceived need for more systematic and rigorous approaches to reviewing the literature.

According to Broome (2000), an integrative review is one which summarises past research and draws conclusions on a given topic. In this definition the term research is interpreted in its broadest sense and literature that is sourced is not limited to empirical (primary) research studies. Theoretical or conceptual literature is also considered important (Whittemore and Knafl, 2005). The purpose of an integrative review may be to provide a more comprehensive understanding of a concept or healthcare issue particularly where uncertainty or a lack of clarity exists. It can also be used to create a new perspective or conceptualisation of a topic (Torraco, 2005). Thus, an integrative review has the potential to re-frame thinking or views of a phenomenon and contribute to the development of the knowledge base of a discipline by informing practice, policy and research (Whittemore and Knafl, 2005).

Therefore, integrative reviews are often framed by a theoretical concept or model. For example, in the review presented in Box 2.7, the theoretical model of dignity was used as a frame by categorising data under the main themes and sub-themes of the model. This is an essential distinction between an integrative review and a narrative review. However, it can be difficult for the reader to distinguish between them, particularly where the latter has clearly stated and similar purposes.

The steps of an integrative review begin with the identification of a concept of interest. In a recent integrative review Johnston et al. (2015) identified dignity-conserving care in palliative care settings as the concept or phenomenon of interest (see Box 2.7). Clearly identifying the problem and purpose of the review is considered essential in an integrative review as it provides the focus and boundaries for all subsequent stages. The purpose of Johnston et al.'s review was to synthesise available evidence around dignity-conserving care actions in palliative care settings. It was an update of an earlier narrative review and driven by a stated lack of clarity amongst nurses about how to effectively use dignity-conserving care actions.

As with any good review, the literature searching strategy should be rigorous as it helps prevent problems associated with incomplete searching and selection bias. Search strategies, inclusion and exclusion criteria, and results of searches must be clearly outlined. Following extraction of the appropriate data (literature), decisions regarding evaluation of its quality are undertaken. This is particularly complex in any review, including an integrative review that draws on material from diverse sources such as empirical and theoretical literature. Moreover, it is likely that any integrative review will include research studies that are difficult to compare because they may have used a wide range of different methodologies or research designs. Both Broome (2000) and Whittemore and Knafl (2005) acknowledge this and recognise that this part of the process of undertaking an integrative review must be developed further. Nonetheless, some system for evaluating quality is essential for transparency regarding the outcomes of the review. Similarly, the process by which data analysis is undertaken can be complex and will depend on the type of literature that is being reviewed. Regardless, when reading the final report, you, as the reader, should be able to discern the approach taken. Read the précis of the integrative literature review in Box 2.7 and complete the associated activity.

Box 2.7   An Integrative Review

'Dignity-conserving care in palliative care settings: an integrative review' (Johnston et al., 2015).

Aim and Objectives

To identify appraise and synthesise relevant, available evidence related to care actions that conserve dignity in palliative care settings. People with palliative care needs are individuals who require care to manage their physical, psychological, social, and spiritual health needs.

Inclusion/Exclusion Criteria

- Included adults who are receiving care in Western Palliative Care settings.
- Included peer-reviewed literature that describes the results of empirical and theoretical research studies, published in English since 2009 (current review is an update).
- Specifically focusing on: dignity-conserving care; individuals with palliative care needs; individuals with life-limiting conditions; frail older population; dignity and dignity-conserving care as a nursing intervention.
- Excluded research about mental illness and/or dementia.
- Excluded physician assistance suicide and euthanasia.
- Excluded anecdotal, reflective, impressionistic and opinion piece literature.

Search Strategy

Electronic databases: Medline, CINAHL, EMBASE, ASIA and PsychINFO.

Search Terms

Using MeSH headings such as 'human dignity', 'humanism', 'personhood', 'self-concept', 'palliative care', 'terminally ill', 'advanced cancer'. Free terms were also used.

Findings

Electronic database search found 646 articles.

Search Outcomes

- Application of inclusion and exclusion criteria resulted in 116 articles being selected for full-text review, following which a further 85 were excluded.
- Thirty-one articles were included in the final analysis and synthesis.

Data Analysis and Appraisal

- Included articles appraised for the strength of providing guidance for care actions that nurses could use for dignity-conserving care in practice.
- Identified care actions were linked to appropriate themes in the Dignity Care Model. Nine main themes were identified (level of independence; symptom distress; dignity conserving perspective; dignity-conserving practices; privacy boundaries; social support; care tenor; burden to others; aftermath concerns) under the Dignity Model Themes of 'illness-related concerns', 'dignity-conserving repertoire' and 'social dignity inventory'.

Examine the information provided in each aspect of Johnston et al.'s (2015) integrative review and answer the following questions:

- Are the aims and objectives of the review clear?
- Are the inclusion and exclusion criteria appropriate?
- Is the search strategy clearly outlined?
- Do the search terms used help achieve the aims and objectives of the review?
- Have the authors outlined how they evaluated the literature?
- Do the authors outline how they arrived at the themes for the subsequent presentation of findings?
- How do you think this example differs from Day and Higgins (2015), as cited in Box 2.6?

Scoping Review

Although they have been used for a number of years across a range of academic disciplines, the scoping review is a relatively new phenomenon in healthcare. In the literature you will also find them described variously as 'scoping studies', 'scoping method', 'mapping of research', 'rapid scoping reviews' and/or 'scoping projects' (Davis et al., 2009; Colquhoun et al., 2014). These authors also suggest that scoping reviews/studies are poorly defined and they vary considerably in terms of their aims, the process by which the review is conducted and their methodological rigour. Usually, however, they consist of one or more discrete components, the most common of which is that they are not driven by a predetermined protocol (Armstrong et al., 2011). They can also involve consultations with stakeholders and literature mapping, conceptual mapping and/or policy mapping (Anderson et al., 2008). Again, it is a good idea to have some idea of what these reviews entail as it is likely you will come across them in your reading.

According to Arksey and O'Malley (2005: 21), there are at least four common reasons why a scoping study might be undertaken and these have been incorporated into key criteria for the commissioning of a scoping study by the NIHR Service Delivery and Organisation Research and Development programme (SDO Programme) (see Box 2.8).

Box 2.8   Reasons for Undertaking a Scoping Review/Study

- To 'map' the extent, range and nature of research activity in an area of study. In this type of scoping, the research may not be described in detail but might include mapping of concepts, policies, evidence and/or user views (separately or in combination).
- To determine the feasibility of undertaking a full systematic review or further empirical research. Feasibility is about determining if there is sufficient literature to undertake a systematic review or even if they have already been conducted.

(Continued)

(Continued)

- To summarise and disseminate research findings to policy-makers, practitioners and consumers.
- To identify gaps in the current research literature. In this type of scoping study, conclusions are drawn regarding the overall state of research activity in a particular area of study.
- To develop methodological ideas and/or theoretical approaches best suited to future research studies of a particular topic.
- To clarify conceptual understanding of a topic where definitions are unclear or where there is lack of agreement.
- To advise on and justify further research studies.

(Arksey and O'Malley, 2005; Anderson et al., 2008)

As is evident from Box 2.8, the reasons for undertaking a scoping review are diverse and there is considerable variety in terms of both the breadth and depth of literature extracted. It is also worth noting that scoping can be part of a preliminary investigation into an area or may be a stand-alone project. In healthcare, their ultimate aim is to facilitate asking the right questions in the context of health service organisation and management, healthcare practice and policy, and determining the research agenda in particular areas. They have been found to be particularly useful in identifying services that are available for discrete groups in the population (Anderson et al., 2008). However, it is important to emphasise that scoping reviews are not appropriate for answering clinical questions (CRD, 2009).

Given the wide range of functions that come under the umbrella term of scoping review/study it is difficult to outline in any definitive way the steps that should be followed. However, Arksey and O'Malley (2005) proposed a methodological framework for conducting a scoping study with the intention of assuring a rigorous and transparent process. More recently Levac et al. (2010) suggested enhancements to this process while retaining Arksey and O'Malley's essential framework (see Box 2.9).

Box 2.9   Methodological Framework for Conducting a Scoping Review

- Identify the research question.
- Identify the relevant studies.
- Select the studies.
- Chart the data.
- Collate, summarise and report the results.
- Optional stage: consultation exercise.

(Arksey and O'Malley, 2005: 22)

Identifying the research question or focus of the review is the first step that enables the reviewers to define which aspects of the research are deemed most important. These subsequently guide the choice of search strategies. The CRD (2009) assert that the search strategy in a scoping review should be as extensive as possible with the purpose of identifying all relevant literature. Because of the complexity of the processes, it is recommended that a scoping review is undertaken by a multidisciplinary team rather than an individual. Searches should include a range of relevant databases, handsearching and efforts to seek unpublished literature by, for example, contacting established organisations and via networks and conference materials. Initial search terms and strategies may be revisited as the reviewers become familiar with the literature.

As with all types of review, parameters for searching are decided at the outset, particularly in terms of time limits and language. Other aspects, such as budget and time constraints, may also limit the comprehensiveness of the review. In selecting studies, inclusion and exclusion criteria are developed but this may be after the initial search of the literature has taken place.

Data are usually charted according to an analytical framework that facilitates sorting the material into relevant themes. Collecting standard information such as authors, year of publication, aim, methods, study populations, intervention type, outcome measures and results is an example of one such framework. Following charting of the data, collating, summarising and reporting of the results are undertaken. These are often configured around the themes that have emerged from the review. This stage of the process is complex, time consuming and laborious given the breadth of literature sourced and the likelihood that the reviewer will still have a large amount of material to present.

An important factor is that scoping studies provide a descriptive account of the available research. They do not attempt to formally appraise the quality of the evidence in primary research reports. Neither do they make recommendations from the evidence about what is the most effective type of intervention. However, Arksey and O'Malley (2005) caution against assuming a scoping study is an easy alternative. There is the potential to generate a large number of studies that include a disparate number of designs and methodologies, and reviewers have to have the ability to analyse and present them in a coherent way.

A final optional step in a scoping review is consultation. Many contemporary scoping studies that are concerned with the identification of research priorities include consultation with stakeholders. Stakeholder consultation is an important element in contributing to service development and promoting user involvement in research (Anderson et al., 2008). See Box 2.10 for an example of a scoping review.

Box 2.10 A Scoping Review

'Social media use among patients and caregivers: a scoping review' (Hamm et al., 2013a) (conducted in parallel with a review of the use of social media among health care professionals and trainees, Hamm et al., 2013b).

(Continued)

(Continued)

Research Question

- What social media tools are being used to improve health outcomes in patient populations?
- For what purposes are social media tools being used in patient populations?
- For what patient populations and disease conditions are social media tools being used?
- What types of evidence and research designs have been used to examine social media tools?

Objectives

- To map the existing literature examining the use of social media in patient and caregiver populations.
- To determine the extent and type of evidence available to inform more focused knowledge synthesis.
- To identify gaps for future research.

Inclusion/Exclusion Criteria

- Included primary research on healthcare issues related to patients or caregivers and examining the use of a social media tool (social media defined as collaborative projects, blogs or microblogs, content communities, social networking sites and virtual worlds) since 2000 (corresponding to the development of Web 2.0).
- Included studies that focused on electronic discussion forums and bulletin boards.
- Excluded studies that examined mobile health (e.g. tracking or medical reference applications), one-way transmission of content (e.g. podcasts) and real-time exchanges mediated by technology (e.g. Skype, chat rooms).

Search Strategy

Electronic databases: MEDLINE, CENTRAL, ERIC, PubMed, CINAHL Plus Full Text, Academic Search Complete, Alt Health Watch, Health Source, Communication and Mass Media Complete, Web of Knowledge and Proquest.

Search Terms

A plethora of MeSH terms and keywords associated with 'social media' in combination with health care education/promotion terms and various 'research designs'.

Literature Located

Included 284 studies in the final review.

Analysis

Descriptive synthesis to map aspects of the literature identified in the key review questions. Studies were grouped according to tool used, audience and study design Descriptive statistics were calculated using StataIC.

Findings

- Most common intended use of social media was for self-care.
- A wide range of (disease) conditions were covered in the included studies.
- Most studies were descriptive but included a range of designs.
- 65.5 per cent of included studies demonstrated there was evidence of utility of social media while 5.3 per cent said there was not.

Concept Analysis

There has been a considerable amount of concept analysis work undertaken in healthcare in the last decade, particularly in the disciplines of nursing and midwifery. Concepts are mental images of phenomena (things), and it is through language that we give labels to these mental images in order that we can communicate with each other. For example, when we say the word 'horse', each of us has an image of what a horse looks like. It is through our experiences, perceptions and learning that we come to equate the mental image with the label 'horse'. However, language is complex and contextual and the meaning of a word can change over time, from one group to another or from one geographic area to another. Whilst the image of a horse may be reasonably universal there are many other concepts that are not as concrete, and meaning is only understood by the context in which the word is used. Many of the concepts in use in healthcare are what are known as behavioural concepts which are concerned with understanding health and illness experiences (Cronin et al., 2010). Examples include phenomena such as coping, self-care, suffering, hope, reassurance, anxiety, adherence, compliance and concordance. Imagine that a patient is about to have surgery and you determine from their behaviour and responses that they are anxious. As a result, you perceive that they need reassurance. Your mental image of both anxiety and reassurance will ultimately determine how you respond to the patient in question. It may well be an appropriate response on your part, but difficulties may arise when another person responds in another way because their understanding of the meaning of anxiety and reassurance is different, which can result in a lack of consistency in the standard and quality of care being delivered.

Make a list of concepts that are used in practice where you think there may be a lack of clarity.

Outline your reasons why you think such a lack of clarity may pose problems.

ACTIVITY 2.3

This lack of consistent understanding of a concept and its use in practice or research are the main reasons for undertaking a concept analysis. Simply stated, concept analysis is a method by which concepts that are of interest to any discipline are examined in order to clarify their characteristics, thereby achieving a better understanding of its meaning (Cronin et al., 2010).

Clear methodologies for undertaking concept analysis have evolved, and the most popular and most cited methods are outlined in Table 2.1. Although there are additional methods that include a 'fieldwork' stage, the focus here is on stand-alone concept analysis methods that are literature review based. While a detailed discussion of the methods outlined in Table 2.1 is beyond the scope of this book, some points regarding concept analysis are worth noting.

The concept selected for analysis should be relevant for practice and/or the research of the discipline. There should also be some ambiguity or lack of consensus as to its meaning or use within the context in which it is to be used. For example, in general usage most people will have an understanding of the concept of 'fatigue'. However, it has emerged in recent years that 'fatigue in chronic illness' is ill-defined and has different characteristics from the fatigue we experience as a normal aspect of living. See Box 2.11 for McCabe's (2009) example of a concept analysis of fatigue in children with long-term conditions.

As with other types of literature review, a clear search strategy must be devised and explained, and all uses of the concept (physical, psychological, social) identified. This is important as the literature in a concept analysis will include sources such as dictionaries, thesauruses, the media, history and popular literature as well as discipline and non-discipline specific publications. This stage is likely to produce large amounts of data, particularly if the concept is in use in a variety of settings or disciplines. For example, the concept of fatigue is not confined to healthcare and is also a key consideration in areas such as sport and engineering.

Regardless of the method being used, the next stages involve review, analysis and synthesis of the literature to identify characteristics of the concept that appear repeatedly. This is a difficult and time-consuming process that generally follows a thematic analysis approach (see Chapter 7) where recurring themes are identified. At the same time, analysts are expected to derive antecedents and consequences of the concept. Antecedents are those things that cause the concept to happen, and consequences are what occur as a result of the concept (see Box 2.11).

Where concept analysis differs notably from other types of review is that, following analysis and synthesis of the literature, a model case or exemplar is presented to illustrate a pure example of the concept. It can be drawn from real life, found in the literature or in some instances constructed by the analyst.

Table 2.1 Two Approaches to Concept Analysis

Walker and Avant's method (2011)	Rodgers' Evolutionary method (2000)
1. Select a **concept**.	1. Identify the concept of interest and associated expressions (including surrogate terms).
2. Determine the aims or purpose of analysis.	
3. Identify **all uses** of the concept that you can discover.	
	2. Identify and select an **appropriate realm** for data collection.
4. Determine the **defining attributes**.	
5. Identify a **model** case.	3. Collect relevant data.
6. Identify **borderline, related, contrary, invented** and **illegitimate** cases.	4. Analyse the data.
	5. Identify an **exemplar** of the concept.
7. Identify **antecedents** and **consequences**.	6. Identify **implications,** for further
8. Define **empirical referents**.	development of the concept.

Subsequent steps vary according to the method being used. For example, Walker and Avant (2011) argue that identifying 'other' cases that are not pure examples of the concept helps to illustrate the differences between it and other concepts that may be related or similar, whereas Rodgers (2000) does not advocate this. Walker and Avant (2011) also promote identifying empirical referents, which are explicit criteria that show the concept exists. This can be in the form of an instrument that measures the concept. For example, in McCabe's (2009) concept analysis this would be an instrument to quantify the existence of fatigue in children with long-term conditions. Empirical referents are most often used as a basis for undertaking research.

Concept analysis is not for the faint-hearted as it is a lengthy process and can be frustrating due to the task of dealing with potentially vast amounts of literature. Recent analyses have tended to be more context specific, such as in McCabe's example, not only because the appearance of a concept may differ depending on the situation in which it is being considered but also because it reduces the amount of literature that has to be sourced. Nonetheless, another analyst might arrive at different outcomes because of the potential variation in the literature sourced and the level of critical thinking and analytical skills of the reviewer (Cronin and Rawlings-Anderson, 2004). Outcomes of concept analysis are always tentative as concepts change and develop with use or as practice situations change. A good example of this is Bissonnette's (2008) analysis of the concept of 'adherence', in which she attempted to identify how and if the concept differed from the previously used concept of 'compliance'.

Box 2.11   A Concept Analysis

'Fatigue in children with long-term conditions: an evolutionary concept analysis' (McCabe, 2009).

Concept of interest

Fatigue in children with long-term conditions.

Aims

- To identify gaps in knowledge.
- To provide a clear definition of the concept.
- To clarify the current status of the concept and its use.

Surrogate terms

- Energy/Vitality.
- Tiredness.

(Continued)

(Continued)

Data sources

- *Electronic databases*: CINAHL, Medline, PsychINFO.
- Confined to English language from 1985 to 2007.
- Five additional sources identified during review.
- *Key words*: 'fatigue', 'child', 'childhood', 'adolescent', 'tiredness', 'fatigue syndrome'.

Literature retrieved

- CINAHL and Medline references (346).
- PsychINFO references (145).

Final sample

Sixty-two papers and two book chapters:

- Nursing references (34).
- Medical references (11).
- Psychology references (19).
- Research reports (43).
- Review papers (18).
- Expert opinions (3).

Data analysis

Thematic analysis with coding for attributes, antecedents, consequences, definitions, related concepts and surrogate terms.

Antecedents

- Imbalance in 'healthy routine' (nutrition, sleep, physical activity).
- Physiological disequilibrium.
- Stress, worry and fear.

Attributes

- Feeling of physical and emotional exhaustion.
- Decreased energy.
- Co-morbid pain or painful syndromes.
- Persists over time.
- Impacted by developmental stage.

Consequences

- Inability to engage in usual activities.
- Necessary to devise strategies to replenish or restore energy.
- Altered mood.
- Sleep disturbances.
- Social relationships impacted.

- School attendance/academic achievement.
- Negative quality of life.

Exemplar

No exemplar identified in this analysis.

Definition

A subjective experience of tiredness or exhaustion that is multidimensional and includes physical, mental and emotional aspects (McCabe, 2009).

Recommendations

- Ongoing international study to explore the experience of fatigue in children and advance understanding of the concept.
- Further exploration of the mechanism of fatigue in children so that appropriate interventions can be devised.
- Accurate measures of fatigue (behavioural and physiological).

Realist Review

Realist reviews (sometimes referred to as realist synthesis) have emerged in recognition of the complexity of healthcare interventions and the realisation that what may be determined to be the most effective intervention might work differently or not at all depending on the situation or circumstance in which it is being implemented. Social, environmental, economic and individual factors can all influence the effectiveness of an intervention and the focus of realist review is to examine these factors.

Realist review was developed originally for complex social interventions to examine how context influences the relationship between an intervention and its outcome. This is represented sometimes as context–mechanism–outcome (C–M–O) and asks how given contexts (C) have influenced or interfered with mechanisms (M) to generate the observed outcome(s) (O) (Greenhalgh et al., 2011). It focuses essentially on discovering what works, how it works, for whom it works, to what extent it works and under what conditions (Pawson et al., 2005). To date, much of the focus of realist reviews is in the areas of health policy and practice.

A realist review to examine how district nurses provide nursing care to patients in the palliative phase of their illness is presented in Box 2.12 to provide an illustration of how such a review may be undertaken. As with all types of literature review, the realist review should begin with a clear question. However, this is not necessarily fixed and can be amended or additional questions can emerge as the data (literature) is retrieved and analysed. Sometimes, it may be appropriate to undertake a preliminary search of the literature to identify its nature and scope before finally deciding on the review questions.

In their realist review Walshe and Luker (2010) were interested in the nature of district nursing practice (generalist registered nurses providing home care) with patients who are in the palliative phase of their illness. What made this a realist review was that they were not only interested in the care provided but why district nurses provided this care, whether the home context influenced the care given and whether it influenced patient outcomes.

An important difference between realist and other types of review is the role of theory or mechanisms that underpin the types of interventions. The realist reviewer approaches the literature with the intention of searching for theories of why an intervention may work and why it may have gone wrong (Pawson et al., 2005). Simply stated, this is about identifying the basis for believing a particular intervention or programme will be successful. At this stage of the process the review team undertakes a comprehensive examination of theories underpinning the intervention/programme being studied, following which a list or subset of theories to be tested should be drawn up. In Walshe and Luker's (2010) review they found that 'explicit theories' of district nursing practice in palliative care were not evident but that 'implicit theories' or assumptions about what is important could be found in research papers, administrative, legislative and planning documentation. Therefore, they constructed a list of statements about what appears to be important to district nursing practice with palliative care patients drawn from textbooks, policy and research. Once this process is complete, the search for empirical evidence commences.

Realist reviews will normally draw from a wide variety of research designs about the process of implementing the intervention or programme. As with all reviews, the search strategies and retrieval mechanisms, including inclusion and exclusion criteria, must be rigorous and transparent.

The synthesis (analysis) stage is highly complex because of the variety of literature that is generally included and the need to evaluate the evidence with the purpose of judging the integrity with which each theory was tested. The focus is not on the topic *per se* but on whether or not the included study addressed the theory being tested (Pawson et al., 2005). Thus, the relative contribution of each source is assessed, explained and a judgement is made. In Walshe and Luker's (2010) review, each of the statements they had constructed about district nursing practice with palliative care patients was evaluated against the studies included in the review.

The outcome of a realist review is not a final judgement on what works but is a revision about how it was thought the intervention would work (Pawson et al., 2005). This may result ultimately in changes to programmes in given settings. Walshe and Luker's (2010) review concluded that the implicit assumptions underpinning the studies about district nursing practice with palliative care patients are not realised enough to be useful in taking forward district nursing theory and models. Therefore, their recommendations largely centred on expanding the direction and focus of research in this area in order to inform improvements (see Box 2.12).

In keeping with many of the types of review outlined in this chapter, a realist review is a difficult undertaking. The reviewers must have a sound knowledge of the subject matter as well as an understanding of the issues that are of concern to policymakers. In addition, reviewers need to have a deep-seated knowledge of research appraisal and skills of synthesis to ensure the rigour of the process. Given these factors and the possibility that review will involve a vast array of literature, it is unlikely that it would be attempted by an individual.

Box 2.12   A Realist Review

'District nurses' role in palliative care provision: a realist review' (Walshe and Luker, 2010).

Aim

To construct a detailed account of the role of the district nurse (generalist registered nurse providing nursing care primarily in home settings) in providing palliative care, to determine if and how district nursing care provides effective care to such patients at home.

Inclusion/Exclusion Criteria

- Included research studies of the district nursing role in the provision of palliative care.
- Included papers studying community nursing work in any country.
- Included papers in English.
- Excluded papers studying specialist palliative care or advanced cancer care.

Search Strategy

- *Electronic databases*: Ovid, Medline, CINAHL, British Nursing Index, Embase, PsychINFO, EBM reviews from 1990.
- *Citation Tracking*: To identify earlier work and those appearing in the reference lists of retrieved papers
- *Grey literature*/Snowball sampling: To explore new propositions about district nursing care of those in the palliative phase of illness.

Search Terms

District nurse and combined with 'home health nursing', 'community nursing staff', 'home care services', 'home visiting', 'home visiting programs', 'public health nursing', 'community health services'.

Palliative care and combined with 'palliative', 'terminal', 'terminal care', 'terminally ill', 'terminal care services', 'end of life', 'end of life care', 'hospice', 'hospice care', 'hospice and palliative nursing'.

Literature Retrieved

- Forty-six studies that examine district nurse palliative care provision from the perspective of the district nurse and others (including family carers and patients).
- Studies included 33 from UK, 8 from Scandinavia, 3 from Australia and 2 from Canada.
- Thirty-three studies using qualitative interviews, 6 using observation of some kind and 8 using questionnaires.

Data abstraction and synthesis

- Each study reviewed to identify information, which ultimately contributed towards the identification of implicit concepts and theories of district nursing and palliative care (p. 1171).

(Continued)

(Continued)

- Studies reviewed to gather data that supported or refuted the theoretical statement that had been developed.
- Identified issues that had not yet been considered.

Results of Synthesis

Studies were examined against the following theoretical statements:

- District nurses value and respect patients in the palliative phase of illness.
- Palliative care is important to district nurses.
- The quality of district nurse–patient relationships is important and has a direct effect on the quality of patient care.
- Palliative care is holistic care.
- Palliative care can be stressful and emotionally difficult.
- Home is important as a care context.
- District nursing care is invisible.
- District nursing service is demand led.
- Relationships with colleagues are important.

Outcomes

- On the basis of the review it was not possible to reformulate the theoretical statements about district nursing into a model to guide district nursing practice roles.
- There are clear gaps in understanding about how district nurses provide palliative care because of the nature of the research designs, i.e. primarily small-scale, interview-based, qualitative studies.
- More research is needed that includes patients and families as these are noticeably absent.
- More inter-professional research.
- More research using a broader range of designs, e.g. observational methods to study what district nurses 'do'.
- Undertaking research that is clearly underpinned by theory.

Systematic Review

Discussion of the systematic review in this chapter is limited to an outline as further detail on the process of undertaking such a review is presented in Chapter 3. Summarised evidence about a particular intervention and its effectiveness has become an invaluable source of information for practitioners and decision-makers. Traditionally, as stated earlier in the chapter, systematic reviews have been concerned with reviews of effectiveness of interventions – that is, answering questions about 'what works' (CRD, 2009). They are generally classed as 'research on research' or secondary research because they do not collect new data but use the findings from previous research (Maxwell, 2006; Parahoo, 2014). Thus, most systematic reviews have the prefix 'meta', meaning 'after' or 'beyond', to indicate that they are second-order – that is, they come after and are based on previous or first-order studies (Zhao, 1991: 378). Systematic reviews are most likely to be undertaken when uncertainty exists regarding an intervention and the primary studies on the topic may have conflicting or disparate findings. The findings from the studies are pooled and analysed, and conclusions are drawn about the overall strength of the evidence.

The systematic review differs essentially from other types of literature review in that its methodology is explicit and precise. It follows a clearly outlined protocol that is standardised and replicable, thereby ensuring the quality, consistency and transparency of the review process. A further important feature is that the protocol, including decision-making in terms of what studies are eligible for inclusion, is normally constructed before the review is begun. Recently, however, it has been acknowledged that in some instances a more emergent or iterative process, but which is still clear and rigorous, may be appropriate in some situations. Explicit criteria are used to judge the quality of the studies being reviewed and only those that are deemed to be of high quality are included. This process assists with reducing bias, thereby enhancing the reliability of the conclusions drawn.

Originally, the systematic review in healthcare was limited to undertaking a review of the findings of research from RCTs as they are considered to be at the highest level of evidence. However, within the systematic review community, there has been a notable shift and the boundaries of what is accepted as meeting the criteria for a systematic review have changed. This is because there is increased recognition that not all healthcare questions can be addressed by RCTs. In many instances, either RCTs do not exist or they would be an inappropriate approach to address the review question.

The outcome of this increased recognition is that the logic of the systematic review process has been extended to include a greater variety of research questions, types of evidence, range of research designs and methods for synthesising the evidence (EPPI, 2010). For example, recent developments have examined the impact of data from qualitative research and the expansion of the systematic review to include such data.

A further development has been the emergence of the systematic review of reviews. With the rapidly expanding number of systematic reviews, there may be situations where decision-makers are faced with more than one review on a topic or where there are questions regarding the quality and scope of the original review. As a result, systematic reviews of systematic reviews are now being conducted. Whilst the protocol and process are similar to that of an original systematic review, the literature sourced is confined to systematic reviews.

Summary

This chapter has outlined the various types of literature review you may encounter when examining published literature as part of your academic work, when exploring an issue related to your clinical practice or as part of the process of preparing a research proposal of your own. The types of review presented in this chapter are commonly published in academic journals but, as indicated earlier, this is not an exhaustive list as the range is ever expanding. The world of literature reviewing has become far more complex because of the recognised need to synthesise the increasingly vast amounts of available information and knowledge on a wide variety of topics. The advent of protocol-driven reviews as a means to manage this has resulted in a drive for more rigorous and systematic approaches to undertaking literature reviews. However, this has resulted in much debate and discussion about the merits or otherwise of these and non-protocol driven reviews such as the traditional, narrative review. It has been demonstrated also that undertaking a 'good' review is a difficult and time-consuming endeavour and many of the types presented here are likely to be beyond the scope of individual students and practitioners. Nonetheless, having read this chapter you should have a better understanding of the key, distinguishing features of the various types of literature review.

Key Points

- There is no single type of 'ideal' literature review but a range of methods that need to be adopted appropriately depending on the focus of the review.
- All literature reviews share the fundamental characteristics of collecting, evaluating and presenting available evidence on a given topic.
- In recent decades, factors such as the knowledge explosion, evidence-based practice and hierarchies of evidence have combined to transform and expand the role and function of the literature review.
- Systematic or protocol-driven reviews are valued most because the process of undertaking such a review is highly structured, logical and transparent.
- The advent of systematic or protocol-driven reviews has seen the position of the traditional or narrative review eroded, which is regarded by some as being the least structured and thereby the least significant.
- All literature reviews are now judged against the standard or benchmark of the systematic review with the result that all are likely to incorporate elements of the systematic review process.
- The rapid rise of the systematic review has resulted in an associated growth of published literature reviews and a plethora of terms that are used to describe various 'types' of review.
- The range of types of literature review is ever expanding in keeping with the various purposes for which they are being developed.
- Undertaking a 'good' literature review can be a difficult and time-consuming process and is one that requires the reviewer to develop skills in selecting, retrieving, organising and analysing a body of literature.

SYSTEMATIC REVIEW

❝ Learning Outcomes ❞

Having read this chapter you should be able to:

- describe what is meant by a systematic review;
- outline the steps involved in conducting a systematic review;
- explain variations in the steps of the systematic review process.

Introduction

In the previous chapter an outline of the tenets of systematic review was presented in order to enable you to begin to discern how it differs from other types of literature review. This chapter develops these principles further and presents the process of conducting such a review. It is worth mentioning, however, that it is unlikely that you will be undertaking a systematic review as part of your undergraduate study as the process is complex and demanding. For the most part such reviews are conducted in teams and can take a year or more to complete. Nonetheless, when you are searching the literature you will almost certainly source articles or publications that are entitled 'systematic review'. It is important, therefore, that you have an understanding of what they are in order to be able to appraise them and determine if they meet the explicit criteria to be termed as such.

The focus of this chapter is an exploration of the systematic review methodology. As discussed in the previous chapter, a systematic review is a process whereby data (findings) from previously conducted, primary studies related to a particular topic are appraised, re-analysed and synthesised (Parahoo, 2014). An important point is that systematic reviews are research studies and like all research enquiries they require an explicit and transparent methodology, which in turn facilitates the aim of reaching an unbiased conclusion (Engberg, 2008).

It is important to reiterate the point made in Chapter 2 that the systematic review is evolving and the types of questions being addressed and the methods for synthesising the evidence from a wide range of study designs have expanded (Gough et al., 2012). Traditionally, systematic reviews were focused on synthesising (pooling) the findings of studies, primarily randomised controlled trials (RCTs) that examined the effectiveness of a range of interventions. In recent years, however, a number of methods for synthesising studies that are not RCTs have emerged. This has generated some debate about whether these different types of syntheses can be described as systematic reviews, particularly, where the findings are those from qualitative studies. What has emerged from these discussions is a sort of consensus that what makes a systematic review systematic is the use of a 'protocol' that uses an explicit and transparent method. This means that not all reviews that are classed as systematic review follow the same method for synthesising (pooling) the data. For example, those that are undertaking systematic reviews of the effectiveness of interventions will generally progress in a linear way through the recognised stages of study identification, quality assessment and synthesis. Others, such as those that use mixed or qualitative data, may adopt a more emergent approach that does not follow these stages exactly. Nevertheless, what is fundamental to all systematic reviews is that the authors explicate the process in order that readers can determine whether the review has been undertaken rigorously in accordance with their declared approach. It is important when reading this chapter to keep these points and variations in mind.

The Review Protocol

Preparing the review protocol is perhaps the most important part of conducting a systematic review because the thoroughness of the planning and preparation will ensure the process remains rigorous. The review protocol is similar to a research proposal produced prior to commencing a primary study in that it details the purpose of the review, presents the formulated question and objectives, and outlines the processes for searching the literature, assessing and interpreting the data and presenting and disseminating the results. Although a protocol is developed in detail in advance of conducting the review, modifications are possible and may even be essential to ensure the findings are of value. Should changes be deemed necessary, these must be detailed in the final report.

Background

Prior to developing the protocol, it is important to address some background issues. The primary consideration is to determine if the review is necessary. This includes situating the review and offering justification for why it needs to be undertaken. This will often be in relation to the potential significance and implications for clinical practice. Determining if the review is necessary also involves undertaking a search of the literature to see if the same or a very similar systematic review has been completed already. This is referred to sometimes as a scoping review or scoping search (see Chapter 2). Reviews may exist on the topic but may not be of good quality or may require updating if they were conducted some time ago. If a good-quality systematic review was conducted recently then there is little merit in doing another. In this instance, the reviewer could change the focus of the review question to include a different population, intervention or outcome. It is also worth noting that a scoping search may identify that there is no research available on the topic. This means that a systematic review is not feasible because in order to do so primary studies must exist.

A further background consideration is deciding about the team or panel to be involved in the systematic review. As indicated in the introduction, systematic reviews are often undertaken in teams. These teams can comprise an expert panel or critical colleagues and/or service-users, depending on the research question (Bettany-Saltikov, 2012). Prior to commencing the review decisions regarding the composition of the team should be made. It is possible, however, to undertake a systematic review individually, say as part of a dissertation, but the role of your supervisor is crucial in terms of providing advice and guidance to ensure the process is as valid and unbiased as possible.

Review Question, Aim, Objective

The first step in undertaking a systematic review is to identify a researchable question on a selected topic. As with any research study, the topic or research question can be generated from a number of sources. It may arise from a problem identified in clinical practice; it may be generated from an identified knowledge gap or may emerge from the existence of inconsistent or contradictory findings from individual studies. Systematic reviews are also commissioned by funding bodies where there are defined research priorities.

Review questions can be broad or narrow. Questions that focus on general management of a disease may be broad, whilst those that focus on the effectiveness of a particular intervention on a particular population or subset thereof may be narrow. However, if a question is very broad, it is often necessary to break it down further into more specific questions. For example, in the review presented in Box 3.1, the objective would be considered broad but the three objectives subsequently posed add more specificity and focus. A further point to consider is that the question or objectives should be sufficiently narrow to make the review feasible. A feasible review is one where it is possible for all related studies to be identified. If the topic is too broad it may render it impossible to manage in terms of the numbers of studies that would have to be included.

It is fundamental that the research question and/or objectives are clearly focused. Some reviews frame the questions in terms of population, interventions, comparators, outcomes and study design (PICOS). What this means is that the review question includes reference to each of these elements. It is worth noting, however, that not all elements will always be relevant. For example, some review questions will not indicate the type of study design to be included (CRD, 2009). In addition, PICOS is normally used for reviews related to therapeutic interventions. Where qualitative studies are reviewed the acronym PEO (population, exposure, outcomes) can be used (Bettany-Saltikov, 2012). Box 3.1 outlines how these were included in an update of a Cochrane review to determine the effectiveness of planning the discharge of patients from hospital.

Population

In formulating a good question, the review team specifies the characteristics of the population or participants to be included. This incorporates outlining any inclusion or exclusion criteria in terms of age, gender, educational status or the presence of a particular disease or condition. The inclusion or exclusion of any of these factors is determined primarily by the topic of interest but should be broad enough to ensure that relevant studies are captured. For example, if a reviewer is interested in the chronic pain experiences of older adults who live in a residential setting, it is important that caution is exercised if an age range is to be specified. This is because some studies will have included all participants living in the residential setting without specifying their ages. If the reviewer includes a parameter whereby only those over the age of 70 are to be included he or she may be excluding some studies that are relevant to the phenomenon of chronic pain in this population. In the example cited in Box 3.1 the reviewers included all 'patients in hospital'.

Intervention/Comparators

Detail regarding the interventions to be included in the review should be specified also. These may include factors such as the type of intervention, where the intervention is delivered and the person administering the intervention. For example, in the review outlined in Box 3.1, while the intervention was broadly classed as an 'individualised discharge plan' the reviewers subsequently detailed specific criteria that delineated what they meant in the PICOS elements.

In reviews that use qualitative data you will not see the term 'intervention' but may instead see use of 'exposure' (the E in PEO – see above). Exposure refers to what it is the participants are experiencing, e.g. chronic pain, cancer, compromised mobility etc. For example, in a review that is focused on older adults' experiences of chronic pain, the exposure is 'chronic pain'. What is important is that the reviewer has offered a clear definition of the phenomenon, i.e. chronic pain, so that there is clarity when assessing whether a study meets the criteria for inclusion or not.

If comparisons are to be included in a review these should be described. In reviews that are examining experiences and where the data largely derive from qualitative studies, you will not see the inclusion of comparators. However, in studies that are focused on intervention such as in the example cited in Box 3.1 it is an expectation that comparators are indicated. In this example the reviewers indicated that 'standard care with no individualised discharge plan' constituted the comparator. Although it could be argued that the term 'standard care' was not specific enough, the essential delimiter for this review was the absence of an individualised discharge plan. However, in other instances, defining terms is important in order to be able to compare the findings of various studies. For instance, in a review undertaken by Spilsbury et al. (2011), the review question included reference to 'quality of care'. Given the complex nature of this concept it was fundamental that the reviewers specified clearly what they understood by this term.

Whiting (2009) highlighted that there are different types of comparisons and it is critical to specify which type will be examined so that the appropriate studies are sourced. For example, she outlines that the reviewer could focus on studies that compare one type of intervention with none at all (as in the cited example). Another possibility is to include studies where the focus is on identifying whether one form of intervention is preferable to another.

Outcomes

Higgins and Green (2011) state that outcomes can be related to a number of factors including mortality, clinical events, patient-reported outcomes, adverse effects, burden on patients and carers, and economic factors. In a systematic review that focuses on the effectiveness of an intervention the outcome section may include statements such as 'assess the effects', 'determine the clinical effectiveness' or 'assess the clinical effectiveness'. In systematic reviews that are examining the subjective experiences of a group of people and using the findings of qualitative research studies words such as 'experiences', 'perceptions', 'views', might be presented as outcomes. What is important is that it is the review team that determine the types of outcome measures to be included.

The outcomes in the discharge planning example in Box 3.1 were linked directly to the objective and questions for the review. For example, length of stay, readmission rate, complication rate and place of discharge were seen as factors that could determine whether discharge planning improved the appropriate use of acute care in hospital while mortality rate, patient health status, patient and carer satisfaction, and psychological health of the patient and caregivers could establish whether discharge planning improved or (at least) had no adverse effect on patient outcome.

Study Design

Essentially, the type of review question directs the type of studies to be included but, as indicated previously, these are not always specified in the review questions and objectives. However, they are often stated in the PICOS elements and developed in more detail in the remainder of the protocol. This is a key part of the process because individual systematic reviews usually include only one type of study design as it is difficult to make comparisons or pool the findings from different types of study design. For example, if the intention is to synthesise the findings from a number of studies that have examined the effectiveness of an intervention then the preferred study design is the randomised controlled trial or controlled trial. This is because these study designs tend to use the same methodology and methods for undertaking studies, thus making it possible to compare and pool the findings. However, studies such as RCTs and observational studies use different methodologies and methods and it is important that reviewers do not attempt to 'pool' the data from these dissimilar study designs because they are inherently different. Not only is comparison difficult but it would also have implications for the validity of the findings.

To date most systematic reviews have been concerned with determining the effectiveness of interventions and RCTs are the preferred type of study design for these reviews as this approach is seen to produce the most reliable and valid results. This is because the RCT study design has the most robust procedures for reducing susceptibility to bias. However, it may be that RCTs related to the topic area do not exist or are limited in number and, in these instances, quasi-experimental or observational studies that are not at the level of RCTs may be included (CRD, 2009).

There has been some discussion among the systematic review community about the contribution that data from qualitative research can make to reviews of effectiveness (CRD, 2009; EPPI, 2010). This follows the recognition that although RCTs and quasi-experimental approaches may determine the most effective intervention, there are other factors that impact on its implementation, such as the experiences of people receiving it (CRD, 2009). Three options are suggested by CRD (2009: 222) for how qualitative evidence can be included in or alongside quantitative effectiveness reviews. Briefly these are: using the evidence from qualitative studies in the discussion of the quantitative synthesis; using the qualitative evidence to interpret the quantitative synthesis; or using a formal system combining the evidence from qualitative and quantitative studies. If qualitative evidence is to be included in or alongside an effectiveness review, it is important to outline in the protocol how this will be done.

To date, most systematic reviews incorporating qualitative evidence have been undertaken separately and many address questions that are not related directly to effectiveness. For instance, review topics or questions that are concerned with people's experiences incorporate designs such as descriptive survey or qualitative research studies. For example, Brunton et al. (2011), in their research synthesis of women's experiences of having their first child, selected studies that focused on open-ended qualitative approaches because they were more in keeping with the aims of the review.

A final point about study designs is that in the initial stages reviewers may not be in a position to determine which study designs are to be included and, therefore, they may not appear in the PICOS elements.

Box 3.1   PICOS Elements of a Systematic Review

'Discharge planning from hospital' (Gonçalves-Bradley et al., 2016).

Main Objective of the Review

To assess the effectiveness of planning the discharge of individual patients moving from hospital.

Specific Objectives

- Does discharge planning improve the appropriate use of acute care?
- Does discharge planning improve or (at least) have no adverse effect on patient outcome?
- Does discharge planning reduce overall costs of healthcare?

Type of Participants

All patients in hospital (acute, rehabilitation or community) irrespective of age, gender or condition.

Intervention – Individualised Discharge Plan

Discharge planning was defined as the development of an individual discharge plan prior to patients leaving hospital for home or residential care:

- pre-admission assessment (where possible).
- case finding on admission.
- inpatient assessment and preparation of a discharge plan based on an individual patient's need.
- implementation of the discharge plan, which should be consistent with the assessment and required documentation of the discharge process.
- monitoring in the form of audit to assess whether the discharge plan was implemented.

Comparators

The control group had to receive standard care with no individualised discharge plan.

Outcomes

Main Outcomes:

- Length of stay in hospital.
- Readmission rate to hospital.

Other Outcomes:

- Complications related to the initial admission.
- Place of discharge.
- Mortality rate.
- Patient health status including psychological health.
- Patient satisfaction.
- Caregiver and healthcare professional satisfaction.
- Psychological health of patient.
- Psychological health of caregivers.
- Healthcare cost of discharge planning:

  o   hospital care costs and use;
  o   primary and community care cost.

- The use of medication for trials evaluating a pharmacy discharge plan.

Study Design

Randomised controlled trials.

Identifying Studies for Inclusion

The first step in identifying studies for inclusion in the review is detailing the criteria by which they will be included or excluded. In essence, these criteria constitute the search strategy and define the parameters of the review. They include defining search terms, describing how the literature is searched and outlining delimiters such as publication types, timelines and language. They are in addition to any criteria that have been identified already in the PICOS or PEO elements. The inclusion and exclusion criteria are normally determined in the planning stage of the review so as to reduce the potential for bias. This is based on the view that if decisions are made in advance (a priori) then the reviewers are not influenced or swayed by the findings of individual studies. However, there are times when a more emergent process may be adopted and, whilst this may be seen as contrary to the systematic review process, the key factor is that the reviewers adhere to the principles of being transparent and explicit (Marshall et al., 2011).

Decisions regarding inclusion or exclusion criteria must be justified as they are likely to have implications for the overall validity of the findings. For example, if a reviewer chooses to source publications in English only, important evidence may be missed, which will have implications for the overall outcome of the review. However, factors such as time and resources may limit the reviewers' ability to source all studies related to the topic. For instance, retrieving published or even unpublished research in another language may be time consuming and there may be the added cost of translating that work. The important point is that these are recognised as possible limitations and will impact on how, for example, the findings can be generalised. Areas that are commonly addressed in systematic reviews in respect of inclusion or exclusion criteria are outlined in Box 3.2. Further detail on each of these can be found in Chapter 4.

Box 3.2   Inclusion/Exclusion Criteria

Search Terms

Specification of the key terms.

Identifying Sources of Literature

- Electronic databases.
- Manual/handsearching.
- Bibliography and references lists.
- Grey literature.

Publication Type

- Journals.
- Books or book chapters.

- Reports.
- Theses (published/unpublished).
- Conference abstracts.
- Conference papers.
- Interim reports.
- Unpublished work.
- Consulting with experts in the field.

Language Delimiters

Inclusions/exclusions by virtue of the language of publication.

Timelines

Deciding on time limits for the review.

When reviewers are making decisions about their search strategy there are a number of factors that should be kept in mind. In respect of search terms, for example, Marshall et al. (2011) report how terminology, such as 'language', 'communication' and 'speech', commonly used in speech and language therapy, has wider application in lay contexts and other disciplines. In instances such as these there is potential for large amounts of irrelevant literature to be generated and considerable skill is needed to manage this. In reality, very few searches are straightforward and reviewers will often include or seek the services of a librarian because of their professional expertise in searching and retrieval.

Even though electronic databases have eased the process of searching the literature, no single database records all healthcare publications. Moreover, not all published research is indexed in the main databases, thus making it more difficult to retrieve. In addition, it should be remembered that not all research is published in journals. Therefore, there is a need to search widely and include a range of sources such as those outlined in Box 3.2.

There are also issues with publication and language bias that should be kept in mind. For example, research that has positive results is published more frequently than those with negative results (Whiting, 2009). Also, language bias refers to the tendency for authors to seek publication in English language journals if the results are positive or statistically significant (Bettany-Saltikov, 2012).

Catling-Paul et al. (2011: 1647–8) used the search strategy outlined below in their systematic review of 'clinical interventions that increase the uptake and success of vaginal birth after caesarean section'. Examine the search strategy and assess it for completeness or any possible biases.

(Continued)

ACTIVITY 3.1

(Continued)

Keywords used

'Intervention' and 'Pregnancy Outcome' with 'Vaginal Birth After C(a)esarean/Caesarian', 'VBAC', 'Trial of Labo(u)r', C(a)esarean/Caesarian Section' and 'C(a)esarean/Caesarian Section, repeat'.

Unrestricted search

- CDSR (Cochrane Database of Systematic Reviews).
- CINAHL (Cumulative Index to Nursing & Allied Health).
- Ovid MEDLINE(R).
- MIDIRS (Maternity and Infant Care).
- PsycINFO was undertaken to determine any studies that evaluated an intervention for vaginal birth after caesarean section (VBAC).
- Government health websites and obstetric and midwifery professional organisation websites.
- Reference lists of relevant articles, including any guidelines and reviews.

Included

- Studies written in English that evaluated an intervention for increasing either the uptake of and/or the success of VBAC.
- Studies that involved a comparison group (randomised controlled trials, cohort studies, case control studies and before-and-after studies); and published up to December 2008.

Excluded

- Studies that did not report VBAC uptake or success rates were excluded.
- Only primary sources were considered appropriate for this review. Systematic reviews were used to source further publications but were excluded as they were not primary sources.

Study Selection

Following retrieval of the literature, the reviewers detail how studies were selected for inclusion. Study selection is normally done in two stages, which involves an initial screening followed by screening of the full papers. The initial screening includes judging the titles and/or abstracts of the studies against the inclusion criteria. Those that do not match the criteria are rejected immediately. Where there is some doubt, it is better to access the full paper rather than exclude too early. The second stage involves detailed screening of the full papers against the inclusion

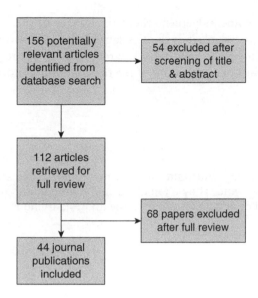

Figure 3.1 Example of Flowchart from Database Search

criteria. It is important that more than one person considers the eligibility of a study for inclusion. This will reduce the risk of relevant papers being discarded inadvertently. It may be helpful to construct a flow chart of how studies were selected (see Figure 3.1).

Throughout the searching and retrieval of literature, it is fundamental that all decisions are carefully recorded and, in particular, when studies are excluded. It is also important to 'manage' the retrieved literature, and there are many bibliographic software packages available for that purpose.

In some systematic reviews, a descriptive mapping exercise may be undertaken whereby an overview of the research literature available on a given topic is presented (Gough et al., 2012). This may be done as part of a two-stage review where the original topic is very broad. Through descriptive mapping, the reviewers develop a clearer picture of the subject following which they narrow the focus or refine the original review question. In other instances, where what are deemed to be an unmanageable number of references are retrieved and if the review team does not have the capacity or resources to conduct an in-depth review of all the retrieved material, the scope of the review is narrowed. It may also be that narrowing or refining the topic will ultimately have more useful outcomes for end-users (Gough et al., 2012).

Quality Assessment

The next step in the process of undertaking a systematic review is to assess the quality of the studies that are included. In all literature reviews, there is an expectation that reviewers make some judgement about the quality of the work. However, how well and the extent to which it is done is largely dependent on the reviewers and their skills. In a systematic review, it is a key requirement of the process because the strength of the findings or conclusions of the review are dependent on the quality of the included studies.

Student Comment

'I found the quality and data analysis methods (in systematic reviews) difficult to understand. They often discussed methods and models I would not have heard of and it slowed down my analysis trying to figure out what it meant.'

(4th year undergraduate general nursing student)

In systematic reviews where the included studies are quantitative, the criteria for judging quality are largely concerned with determining whether sufficiently robust steps were taken to reduce methodological bias in the design, conduct and analysis of the study. What this means, in essence, is that various aspects of the primary studies must be examined to determine the 'truthfulness' or 'believability' of the original findings. It also enables the reviewers to judge whether variations between the results of one study and another can be explained by differences in quality.

While the emphasis will vary depending on the focus and type of review being undertaken, the criteria for judging studies that fall under the umbrella of quantitative designs generally include:

- deciding if the chosen research design was appropriate for answering the research question or aim;
- identifying the risk or presence of bias (internal validity);
- other issues related to study quality such as:

    o considering the reliability and validity of the measuring tool or instrument used;
    o statistical issues around sampling and analysis;
    o the quality of reporting of aspects of the study;
    o assessing if the intervention has been used appropriately;
    o generalisability (external validity).

(CRD, 2009: 33)

Although there is a wide range of instruments available to critically appraise studies, a number of specific tools have been developed or adapted for use in systematic reviews. For example, in those that use quantitative or numerical data the Cochrane Collaboration 'Risk of Bias' tool or the Evidence for Public Health Practice Project

(EPHPP) tool are recommended. Therefore, rather than having a broad-based tool that appraises 'quantitative' studies in general, a design-specific instrument poses methodological questions that are relevant and explicit to the design of the study being assessed. This is crucial because, as stated previously, systematic reviews involving 'quantitative' studies tend to focus on one or very similar research designs such as a review that only includes RCTs. A further important difference between these and many generic tools is that they have been validated and they provide a score.

However, in systematic reviews that incorporate qualitative studies it is likely that more than one type of research design is included. This is because there is such an array of qualitative research designs that it would be difficult to find studies that use the same one to address a particular topic. For example, if researchers were interested in older adults' experiences of chronic pain the design of the study could be grounded theory, phenomenological, qualitative descriptive or ethnographic, among others. The result then could be several studies that are broadly based on the same topic but which have not adopted the same methodological approach. This can create difficulties when undertaking quality assessment in systematic reviews that are attempting to pool the findings from these various types of qualitative studies. Some consider that it is not possible or appropriate to develop standardised criteria or a single tool that addresses all qualitative research given their diverse philosophical, theoretical and methodological positions (Tong et al., 2012). However, Gough et al. (2012) propose that in these types of reviews what is important is that the assessment tool should not only consider the methodological rigour of the included studies but should also focus on findings when appraising their quality.

What this means is that reviewers should evaluate the methodological quality of the included studies and make a judgement as to whether or not the study meets the acknowledged standards for the chosen research design. In this way, the rigour or trustworthiness of the study is established. Secondly, the reviewers should make a judgement about whether the interpretation of the study findings is grounded in the data and whether the conclusions are warranted given the methods adopted (Gough et al., 2012).

In systematic reviews of qualitative studies, the quality appraisal tool may be one that was originally developed for a different purpose. An example of this is the Consolidated Criteria for Reporting Qualitative Research (COREQ) (Tong et al., 2007) tool, which is a 32-item checklist that is used for assessing the quality of the *reporting* of qualitative research but which has been used successfully to undertake quality assessment in systematic reviews. Other reviewers have developed their own quality assessment tools, an example of which is Brunton et al.'s (2011) 10-item checklist which incorporates questions about methods adopted in the study and the relevance of the findings for the review question.

Important aspects of undertaking the quality assessment will be deciding what checklist will be used, what quality criteria will be adopted and how a scoring system will be applied. As part of the appraisal of studies, reviewers may choose to develop a scoring system for each criterion in the quality assessment. The scores are aggregated and the studies are classed, usually, as being of a high, medium or low quality. For example, Brunton et al. (2011) had a scoring system whereby points were awarded depending on whether the study met the criteria fully (1.0), partially (0.5), or not at all (0.00) with a maximum score of 10 available. Studies that scored above 8 were considered to be of high quality, those that were between 5 and 7.5 were of medium quality and those below 4.5 of low quality.

Decisions about the impact of the scoring of studies should be clear. For example, it may be that studies that are considered of a medium or low quality may not be excluded but that a system is developed to 'weight' the evidence. What this means is that studies that are of good quality and are larger in terms of their size might be given more 'weight'. Therefore, when reading a systematic review you should be able to discern how the reviewers have done this.

In addition, the assessment is usually undertaken independently by more than one person. Therefore, it is important to decide how many people will be involved, how decisions regarding the final inclusion and/or exclusion of studies will be made and how disagreements will be resolved. The advisory group or panel can also advise in terms of ensuring that the quality assessment has been undertaken appropriately. If a systematic review is being undertaken as part of postgraduate award, then the role of the supervisor in assisting with and reviewing the quality assessment process is central.

Data Extraction

Data extraction is the means by which information is taken from the studies included in the review. It is known at this point that all selected studies are relevant to the research question and have met the inclusion criteria. Now the reviewers return to each study and extract the information that will answer the review question. Information about the characteristics of the studies, the methodology and methods employed and the findings are extracted. Data synthesis (pooling) is undertaken on extracted data so it is essential that the process is rigorous, accurate and transparent. When the data extraction process commences evidence may emerge that there are missing data or that some detail has not been reported due to publishing restrictions. In this event, reviewers will often attempt to retrieve these data by contacting the original authors.

Normally, a data extraction form is utilised to record the information. There are pre-existing tools that can be modified to suit the purpose of the individual review, or alternatively, reviewers may have developed their own tool. What is important is that the reviewers have tailored the criteria to the individual review. Publications such as the CRD's (2009) guidance for systematic reviews, the Cochrane Handbook (Higgins and Green, 2011) and the supplemental handbook guidance by Noyes and Lewin (2011) all provide guidance for what should be included in data extraction forms for various types of systematic review.

According to Noyes and Lewin (2011), data extraction in reviews that include quantitative studies is a relatively linear process in that items are determined in advance and include aspects such as the PICO (participants, interventions, comparators, outcomes) elements. These are included in the data extraction tool/template and applied to each included study.

In reviews that include qualitative studies the reviewers may have used the PEO (participants, exposure, outcomes) criteria. However, a decision must be made as to what counts as qualitative evidence for the purpose of data extraction. In the majority of qualitative studies, researchers present their findings using key themes identified during the analysis process and it is how these are handled in a review that determines what is extracted. Noyes and Lewin (2011) outline two main approaches. The first is where the reviewers only extract 'direct quotes' pertaining to each of the themes identified in the study. Therefore, if a particular theme does not have any included quotes, which may be the case given the word limits in journal publications, those data are not included. The limits of such an approach are evident as it may result in important themes being excluded from the review.

The second approach involves including all pertinent qualitative data located in the findings of a report. This incorporates the researcher's (original author's) description of the findings as well as the direct quotes used to illuminate it. Depending on the number of included studies this approach may result in a significant amount of data. Nonetheless, this approach is likely to provide a more comprehensive picture of the evidence.

As with quality assessment, more than one person may perform the data extraction in order to reduce bias and enhance the reliability of the process and strategies. However, there is an inherent risk that those extracting the data may not do so consistently. Therefore, it is important to pilot the data extraction form on a sample of the included studies to make certain that the reviewers are consistent in their interpretation but also to ensure the tool itself is capturing the pertinent data (CRD, 2009).

Data Synthesis

Discussion of data synthesis here is limited to an outline as further detail on the process is presented in Chapter 7. When all the data have been extracted, the information is synthesised, which at its simplest means that all the evidence is pooled. Data synthesis has been likened to data analysis (Hamer and Collinson, 2005) and how it is conducted depends on the purpose of the review and the type of studies that have been included in it. For example, if a review included RCTs only then a statistical analysis known as meta-analysis is usually undertaken, for which there are software packages available to manage the process. The data (findings) from each of the studies are pooled and then re-analysed together as one large data set. For example, six randomised controlled trials may have been undertaken that examined the effects of a particular antibiotic on people with a chest infection following hospitalisation. Each of these studies will have undertaken statistical analysis of their data to determine if the antibiotic was effective and if so, how effective. However, results from one study may not be sufficiently 'strong' to say for certain if the antibiotic is effective enough to warrant its use. In a meta-analysis, the data from each of these studies are combined (pooled) in order to calculate one overall result known as a 'single summary statistic' or 'effect measure' (Booth et al., 2010: 294). This enhances the ability to draw meaningful conclusions because combining the results increases the chance of detecting that a 'real' effect is statistically significant (CRD, 2009).

However, a meta-analysis is not undertaken in studies where non-experimental (observational) quantitative approaches have been undertaken. This is often because these studies are heterogeneous (diverse/different) and might have used a range of different research designs. In these situations, reviewers may undertake what is known as a narrative synthesis where a narrative rather than a statistical approach is used to pool the data from the findings. It is important to note here that narrative synthesis is an approach that is used more frequently when referring to synthesis of quantitative research (Barnett-Page and Thomas, 2009) (see Chapter 7 for further detail).

Within the qualitative research community a large number of methods and terms have emerged in recent years to describe the various means for synthesising qualitative research. This proliferation of terms and methods and the surrounding debates can be confusing for the reader (Tong et al., 2012) and perhaps for those who are considering undertaking a systematic review of qualitative research and want to choose the best method. However, whilst an absolute consensus does not exist, the term meta-synthesis has emerged as one that encompasses various approaches to synthesising qualitative research studies (Barnett-Page and Thomas, 2009; Paterson et al., 2009). Some of these methods include but are not limited to meta-ethnography, meta-study, meta-narrative, meta-summary, thematic analysis, thematic synthesis, textual narrative synthesis, critical interpretive synthesis, ecological triangulation, framework synthesis and grounded theory. To date, meta-ethnography is the most commonly used method. A useful summary of the some of these methods is provided by Barnett-Page and Thomas (2009) and Ring et al. (2010).

Whilst there are variations in how synthesis of qualitative research is conducted, most methods are concerned with interpretation, that is, deconstructing the research findings from each study, discovering key features and combining them again in a transformed whole. The outcome then is a new interpretation that is greater than the sum of the individual studies (Flemming, 2007; Finlayson and Dixon, 2008). These new insights are often represented as concepts or theories. Lindahl and Lindblad's (2011) meta-synthesis of 'family members' experiences of everyday life when a child is dependent on a ventilator' is a useful example of the process. Meta-summary differs as a method of synthesising qualitative data since it has been described as 'aggregative' where the results are assembled, pooled and summarised for the purpose of determining the frequency of each finding rather than being interpreted (Finfgeld-Connett, 2010).

Undertaking a meta-synthesis using whichever method is a complex and challenging endeavour, not least in respect of the analysis phase. Not only is the process time consuming but debate continues about combining studies that are philosophically, theoretically and methodologically diverse. Some consider that this should not be done, while others believe that it is synthesising the findings that is the main focus (Bondas and Hall, 2007). In addition, the reviewer may be faced with the difficulty of combining studies that have different populations and/or contradictory or conflicting findings. Nonetheless, a key factor is that like the synthesis of quantitative data, it is important that whatever method is chosen it is conducted rigorously and is transparent to the reader.

Presentation and Discussion of Results

As with all research, once the analysis (synthesis) stage has been completed the reviewers turn their attention to presenting and discussing the results of the review. The results should provide the answer to the review question. The manner in which the results are presented can vary but usually includes detail about the outcome of the search strategy, the quality assessment and the data extraction.

Most reviews begin with a textual, descriptive summary of the findings, which is supported by a collation of information about each study and presented in a grid or table. (See Boxes 3.3 and 3.4 for how this might be done.)

Box 3.3   Example of a Summary Table

Title	Author/ Year	Full reference	Methods	Participants	Interventions	Outcomes	Risk of bias

Box 3.4   Example of a Summary Table

Title	Author/Year	Full reference	Aims	Method	Population	Quality rating

The purpose of the discussion is to facilitate interpretation of the findings of the review. Essentially, it should include the analysis of the findings, the meaning of the findings and the strengths and weaknesses of the review.

Some reviewers prefer to integrate the presentation of findings with a discussion of them while others present them separately. Either way, it is important that the discussion reviews the findings in light of the original aim and objectives and the relevant theoretical and background literature (Bettany-Saltikov, 2012). This should involve comparing and contrasting the results with the work of others in the field and making interpretations or judgements as to their implications, say for practice or policy. The discussion may also address theoretical considerations, such as making a claim for a new conceptualisation of a phenomenon. For example, in Harrison et al.'s (2014) meta-synthesis of how patients respond to, appraise and understand the experience of acute exacerbation of chronic obstructive pulmonary disease (COPD) a number of themes were identified from data extracted from eight qualitative studies. The identified themes were grouped under two conceptual themes, namely *Acute Effect* and *Sustained Regulation*, both of which were determined to be reflective of two domains of disease management. This synthesis of the findings of these studies offered a conceptualisation for understanding patients' experiences of acute exacerbation of COPD that contributed to the discussion of the implications of these findings for the support and management of people who live with COPD (Harrison et al., 2014).

The discussion should include, where applicable, a commentary on aspects of the studies included in the review, such as their ethical integrity or their quality and whether they had an influence on the findings. Clear recommendations for professional practice, theoretical development and further research/enquiry should be presented also. Particular attention should be given to these recommendations, as they are often the key area of interest to practitioners, policy-makers and consumers of services. Just as in any research, it is important that remarks on the methodological limitations of the review are included but also that the discussion should present the strengths, difficulties and/or challenges that were encountered throughout.

How the report is written will vary depending on whether the review was conducted for a commissioning body, as an academic piece of work such as a dissertation, or for a journal article. Some commissioning bodies, libraries and journals have their own recommendations for how results of systematic reviews are presented. In addition, guidelines such as those found on the EQUATOR network (Enhancing the Quality and Transparency of Health Research) (www.equator-network.org) provide guidance for authors on reporting and publishing so that the quality of their work is enhanced. Currently, for systematic reviews this includes the Preferred Reporting Items for Systematic Reviews and Meta-Analyses (PRISMA) (Moher et al., 2009), the Meta-analysis Of Observational Studies in Epidemiology (MOOSE) (Stroup et al., 2000) and the Enhancing Transparency in Reporting the Synthesis of Qualitative research (ENTREQ) statement (Tong et al., 2012). Other organisations such as the Cochrane Collaboration, CRD and EPPI all provide guidelines on reporting.

Dissemination of Review Findings

The final and vital part of a systematic review is dissemination of the findings, which is essential to ensuring the message reaches its intended audience, be they practitioners, end-users, policy-makers, organisations or commissioners of research. Inherent in this is the need to recognise that dissemination is an active process that should have been planned at the protocol stage. It is also important that the manner in which the message is conveyed is understood by the recipients. This may mean that the results of the review are disseminated more widely and through different media than the traditional academic journals or conferences (CRD, 2009).

Summary

This chapter has provided an overview of the process of undertaking a systematic review. Systematic reviews were identified as research studies that follow an explicit and transparent methodology whereby evidence from previously conducted primary studies is re-analysed and synthesised. The steps involved in undertaking a systematic review were presented. Although systematic reviews were traditionally associated with reviews of effectiveness of interventions, this chapter has outlined how the method has been evolving, and the types of questions being addressed and the methods for synthesising the evidence from a wide range of study designs have expanded. Whilst this chapter largely follows the standard protocol, variations, particularly in the synthesis methods, have been presented to demonstrate how the process has advanced in recent years. Undertaking a systematic review is a complex endeavour but you should now have some insight into the method and be able to distinguish the range of purposes for which such a review might be undertaken.

❝ Key Points ❞

- A systematic review is a research study that follows an explicit and transparent methodology to re-analyse and synthesise evidence from previously conducted primary studies.
- Systematic reviews were developed originally to review effectiveness of interventions using RCTs and quasi-experimental approaches. However, their use is continually expanding and now includes studies, such as qualitative research, that are not related directly to effectiveness.
- Regardless of the type of studies that are being reviewed, a review protocol (plan) must be prepared prior to undertaking any systematic review. The protocol details the purpose of the review; the research question and objectives; the search strategy; the plan for analysis, interpretation and presentation of the data; and how the results will be disseminated.

(Continued)

(Continued)

- A systematic review begins with the development of a research question that may be framed using PICOS or PEO elements.
- Study design, identification of studies for inclusion in the review, selection of studies, quality assessment, data extraction, data synthesis, presentation and discussion of results, and dissemination constitute the main features of a systematic review although there are variations, particularly in respect of how data is synthesised.

SELECTING A REVIEW TOPIC AND SEARCHING THE LITERATURE

❝ Learning Outcomes ❞

Having read this chapter you should be able to:

- identify and refine your review topic/problem;
- categorise the different types of literature;
- develop a search strategy;
- undertake a literature search.

Introduction

As previously stated, a literature review can be undertaken for a number of reasons. Nonetheless, whatever the reason for undertaking the review the first step is always identifying the topic to be reviewed. Undertaking a review of the literature, whether as part of a larger study or as a piece of work in its own right, needs careful consideration. It is a process that demands commitment, time and effort if it is to be completed in in a robust manner and to an acceptable standard. So it is advisable to select a topic that is meaningful and will keep your interest throughout. There are factors that may influence your choice of review topic. For example, if your review is an academic assignment, the topic of the review may have been predetermined, there may be a time frame in which the review must be completed or there may be a word limit on the review. If you are undertaking an assignment and have a limited time frame to gather literature and write a review, a topic that has accessible material may be a more prudent choice than a topic with a dearth of literature.

Undertaking a literature review is time consuming, and writing the actual review can take as long as if not longer than actually searching for and selecting the literature to include. Novice reviewers often fail to recognise this and focus too much of their time on gathering literature which can leave them with insufficient time to write and present their work in a way that does it justice. The purpose of a word limit is to encourage a writer to be focused and concise so it is important to have a clear aim or purpose when you are selecting your topic of interest.

Identifying a Review Topic/Research Problem

The first step in undertaking a literature review is to identify the topic that is going to be studied. Selecting an appropriate topic is probably the most important step you will make. A problem or topic that is poorly conceived may leave you over-whelmed with a vast quantity of literature to manage and perhaps considering abandoning the review. On the other hand a topic or problem that has been appro-priately refined is manageable and can stimulate interest, inspire you to ask questions and seek answers, and generally keep you motivated. However, identifying a suitable topic is not as easy as it first appears so it can be worthwhile spending some time considering the topic and seeking advice before undertaking your review. There are numerous sources from where ideas for a review topic can be drawn. Some of the more common ones are presented in Box 4.1.

Student Comment

'Researching a topic that interests you makes doing a literature review a much more enjoyable experience. For me, it should be about something that fills a gap in practice, a way of improving the quality of life or health outcomes for those you aim to support. You're going to be reading copious amounts of literature on the topic, so make it a topic worth reading about.'

(4th year undergraduate intellectual disability nursing student)

Professional/clinical practice is often a source for review topics or problems, both for novice and experienced reviewers, because it relates to issues that are often per-sonally encountered. However, an initial idea may be very broad and it may be necessary to refine a broad topic or problem using the literature or through discuss-ing the issue with clinical or subject specialists. Brainstorming with colleagues is also an alternative way of clarifying what exactly is to be investigated.

Box 4.1   Review Topic/Problem – Sources

Professional/Clinical Practice

Practice is always a good source for a review topic or problem. It may be an issue you encountered in your own practice or it may be one you heard being discussed. In either case the professional nature of the topic is more likely to stimulate your interest, and be rel-evant to and inform your practice. Zhang et al. (2014) is an example of a review in this area.

Academic/Professional Literature

Another useful source of ideas can be gleaned from reading the literature. Discussions in research studies, literature reviews or opinion articles, for example, can often stim-ulate questions that need answers, and topics are frequently identified for further research or review.

Quality Assurance Issues

Healthcare professionals have a duty to maintain and improve the quality of the care they offer their clients. Quality assurance topics can include identifying ways of improving care, patients' perceptions of care, or reviewing methods of measuring quality to identify the most appropriate method for a particular clinical environment. Holly and Poletick's (2014) review is an example of one undertaken to improve quality of care.

Contemporary Concerns

Current social and cultural problems such as bullying, hospital overcrowding or equality of access to health or social care are the types of topics that may be identified here. Sources can include the media and government publications or publications from other organisations. Quinlan et al.'s (2014) scoping review is an example of this.

(Adapted from Polit and Beck, 2012)

Refining and Clarifying the Topic of Interest

Initially a topic of interest can be quite broad and may need to be refined so that the purpose of the review becomes both clearer to the reader and more manageable for the reviewer. If the topic you have chosen is too broad you may find that the quantity of literature you have to deal with is vast (Brusco, 2010) and may have a multitude of sub-categories that further complicate your literature search. For example, a search on CINAHL for the term 'substance abuse' yielded 28,230 hits and multiple sub-categories, some of which can be seen in Box 4.2. A review of the sub-categories can be helpful in refining your search and offer an insight into how much literature is available on the topic. Knowing how to refine your search yet have sufficient literature for your review is particularly important where the review is an academic assignment with both a specific word count and time frame.

Box 4.2   Sub-categories for Substance Abuse

- Substance abuse detection.
- Substance abuse rehabilitation programs.
- Substance abuse, perinatal.
- Substance abuse, intravenous.
- Substance abuse.
- Substance abuse control.
- Inhalant abuse.
- Substance withdrawal, controlled.
- Substance abuse and Mental Health Service Administration.
- Substance withdrawal syndrome.
- National Institute on Drug Abuse.

Select a classical literature review from a professional journal. Is the topic of interest/ research problem explicitly identified? Does the reviewer indicate why he/she is interested in this topic?

Searching the Literature

Sourcing literature is the next step once a clear topic of interest or the research problem has been decided. Literature can be sourced from a number of different media including both published and unpublished documents, such as journal and newspaper articles, theses, and television and radio documentaries. A competent review is one in which the search for literature has been undertaken in a systematic or methodical manner, and the literature gathered is appropriate to the research problem or topic of interest identified. While this is not to infer that it must be a 'systematic review' it does imply that elements of this type of review should be clearly identified. These include:

- a well-defined aim or purpose for your review, so it is clear to the reader what is being studied;
- details of how the literature was categorised and selected for the review – including the databases and search engines used, other searches undertaken, the keywords or search terms used and how the search was limited. This is necessary if the search is to be replicable.

For you as a reviewer, an explicitly defined aim is important at this stage because the more specific you can be in identifying your area of interest, the more likely it is that the material identified in the literature search will be relevant to the purpose of your review. The more relevant the literature the more likely the expectation of depth of reading and discussion about the topic will be achieved. An aim that is clearly defined can also help in the identification of relevant themes or concepts that underpin this idea or hypothesis, and this can be useful in determining the most appropriate databases or literature sources as well as the most suitable keywords.

Types of Literature

All literature is not the same. Literature can originate in a number of different ways and present different forms of knowledge. This knowledge can be categorised under a number of different headings including research, theoretical, philosophical, experiential/ practice, and policy knowledge (Price, B., 2009). The focus of the review or the review question will determine which type of literature will best suit the review, so it is important to be aware of the purpose and function of the different categories of literature. However, there is usually more than one type of literature used within a review, for example theory or practice may be used to support or justify research.

Research literature, as the term suggests, comprises literature that is influenced by the different research paradigms including positivist, naturalistic and critical theory, as well as results from systematic literature reviews, and meta-analysis and meta-synthesis studies. When using research literature it is important to understand the context in which the research was undertaken, such as positivist research focusing on empirical data, when discussing the findings. If the purpose of your review is to discover facts or identify principles then research data will be an essential part of your literature search (Price, B., 2009).

Theory-based literature is different from research in that theories attempt to explain phenomena or predict responses to a particular situation, such as how an individual may respond to grief or loss (Kübler-Ross, 1969). However, in a sense a symbiotic relationship exists between these two forms of knowledge in that theory needs evidence to support it, and the focus of research studies is often to test a theory. Thus this type of literature can be an important literature source from the perspective of being the focus of the review or simply setting the background for the review.

Underpinning nursing are the beliefs and attitudes that nurses hold in relation to concepts such as health and illness, how the person is perceived, and caring. Books and articles dealing with these types of concepts fall under the heading of philosophical literature. Also included here are issues of an ethical or moral nature such as withholding treatment and euthanasia. Once more, depending on the focus of the review, this philosophical knowledge may be the main literature source or may form the background for research studies in a related area.

Experiential/practice literature is usually written by individuals with an expertise within an area and who wish to share their experiences with others in the field. This literature can be presented in the form of case studies (Price, B., 2009), as discussion papers or other forms of expert opinion (Aveyard, 2014). This type of literature can be useful for adding context or background to a review but should where possible be supported by research literature.

Policy and procedure literature includes local, national and international guidelines and policies that advocate best practice. Policies and guidelines are usually evidence based when developed, but need to be updated on a regular basis. Most policies will have a review date to ensure that the evidence is current, so it is worthwhile checking the review date has not expired. Evidence to support the policy or procedure may be the focus of the review or this type of literature again may be used to set the context for a review or highlight a standard that should be achieved.

Sourcing the Literature

There are a numerous sources from which to access literature, and where possible multiple sources should be used. For small academic literature reviews it may be acceptable for students to confine their searches to a limited number of professional databases; but for larger, in-depth studies a broader use of literature sources is expected. The potential for missing important publications can be decreased by using multiple sources (McGinn et al., 2014). This is particularly the case where work is poorly indexed, for example where the author uses an amusing or entertaining title for a publication. It is therefore important, if a search is to be systematic, that as many search methods and sources as possible are used to gather literature. A number of literature sources are included in Box 4.3.

Box 4.3   Sources of Literature

- Electronic databases and internet search engines.
- Catalogues /printed indices.
- Grey literature.
- Textbooks and dictionaries.
- Manual searches.

Bibliographic Database and Internet Searches

Bibliographic databases and search engines are the major sources of information and literature for reviewers and researchers, and literature searches are now predominantly undertaken online. Most libraries have now opted for online access to journals which enables multiple copies of a journal or article to be accessed simultaneously and also reduces problems with storage and replacing missing issues. Bibliographic databases are organised collections of literature stored in an electronic format and indexed using search terms, such as keywords or author, which a reviewer can use to access related literature. The collections can be derived from journals, books, dissertations, reviews and conference proceedings. Depending on level of access to a database the reviewer can access full text, the abstracts and references of works selected, or just a reference list of works that match that search term. Some databases offer a level of access for free; however, the level of access is usually limited. To access a database a membership subscription is normally required. Universities, colleges and organisations such as hospitals usually have institutional subscriptions to one or more databases and provide varying levels of access to staff and students associated with that institution. Some databases that may be of interest are shown in Table 4.1.

Search engines are computer programs that have been designed to search the Internet for information specified by the searcher. The information is then presented in the form of a 'web page' that can then offer specific information or redirect the searcher to other sites. Because different search engines, such as Bing, Dogpile, Google, Google Scholar and Yahoo, use their own unique software programs to trawl the Internet, using the same search terms on different search engines can sometimes yield different results. It is therefore worthwhile using a variety of search engines.

In recent years there has been a large increase in the numbers of peer reviewed open access journals on the Internet. These journals can be accessed without a subscription and are not always available on institution library sites. Search engines such as the Open Access Search Engine (www.oajse.com/) can be helpful for identifying open access journals related to a particular speciality. Searches for specific open access journals or articles can also be made using traditional search engines.

Table 4.1 Databases Related to Nursing, Health and Social Care

Database	Main Content	Access
Allied and Complementary Medicine Database (AMED)	Journals related to allied health literature, complementary medicine and palliative care.	Subscription required
Applied Social Sciences and Index and Abstracts (ASSIA)	Journals related to health, social policy, race relations, education, psychology and sociology.	Subscription required
British Nursing Index (BNI)	Nursing journals, mainly of UK origin.	Subscription required
Centre for Reviews and Dissemination (CRD)	Systematic reviews and meta-analysis for evidence-based medicine.	Free access
Cochrane Library	Database of systematic reviews.	Free access (UK and Ireland)
Cumulative Index to Nursing and Allied Health Literature (CINAHL)	Journals related to nursing and allied health issues.	Subscription required
EMBASE	Journals related to biomedical and pharmacological issues.	Subscription required
Joanna Briggs Institute	Evidence-based research relating to nursing and allied health care.	Subscription required
Maternity and Infant Care	Journals related to midwifery and infant care up to one year.	Subscription required
MEDLINE/PubMed	Journals related to life sciences, particularly biomedicine. Free access to this database is available through PubMed.	Free access
Proquest Nursing and Allied Health Source	Covers journals related to nursing and allied health, including physical and occupational therapy, and rehabilitation.	Subscription required
PsycINFO	This database contains peer-reviewed journals related to mental health and the behavioural sciences.	Subscription required
Social Care Online	This site offers access to UK government documents and reports, and journal articles related to social care and social work.	Free access
Web of Science	A multidisciplinary database containing journals related to medical and social issues among others.	Subscription required

Search engines can also be useful tools when searching for documents and reports from government agencies, professional bodies, voluntary and professional agencies and self-help groups. They can also be used to access databases and other useful sites. However, it is important to be aware that web pages may not always contain accurate information and may also include personal views and unsupported comments (Ely and Scott, 2007). It is therefore important to ensure the accuracy of the information and use only trustworthy websites. A number of library websites offer advice on how to check the accuracy of sites on the web such as Virginia Tech (www.lib.vt.edu/instruct/evaluate/).

Catalogues/Printed Indices

Before the 1990s and the advent of the Internet and electronic databases, information regarding professional literature was stored in large tomes known as catalogues or printed indices, which were available for searching in most university and college libraries. Before becoming an online database CINAHL was one such index. While electronic cataloguing of earlier journals has happened to a degree and some databases like MEDLINE contain journals back to the 1940s, for most databases data is only available back to 1982 (Rebar et al., 2011). For any searches that pre-date the electronic databases, catalogue searches will need to be undertaken. Data was stored in catalogues by author and keywords and each catalogue had a linked thesaurus of terms. They were printed annually so searches using this medium have to be undertaken one year at a time.

Grey Literature

Grey literature is the term given to literature that is of a standard to be protected by intellectual property rights, but which is not controlled by commercial publishers (Schöpfel, 2010). It includes data from conference proceedings, unpublished works such as Masters and PhD studies and unpublished studies or excluded data from published studies. While this information can be important and show an alternative perspective on a topic, at undergraduate and even at Masters level, the benefits have to be weighed against the cost in time to undertake the search. Other considerations include the cost financially if this literature has to be accessed through inter-library loan, and whether it is a requirement of the course to include such data in the review. Universities and third-level institutions usually have databases or archives that can be accessed to identify the grey literature that is generated in their own establishments. Information can also be accessed through the Internet, and the GreyNet (www.greynet.org) and the Index to Theses (www.these.com) databases. However, searching for grey literature can be time consuming, especially if the searcher is unclear about what exactly is being sought.

Textbooks and Dictionaries

Textbooks can be a valuable source of information to help you select a topic for your review and can offer a good resource for background reading and preparation. University or college libraries usually have a large cache of textbooks, some of which may be online, so the library collection catalogue is a good place to start your search. When using textbooks, however, it is important to remember that these can quickly become dated. Twelve months or more may have elapsed between the first draft of a chapter of a textbook and its appearance in a library or online. Libraries also hold older editions of books, so do ensure you have the textbook that is most appropriate to your needs. Dictionaries and thesauruses can be helpful for defining terms and concepts, and can prove useful when you are attempting to identify keywords.

Manual Searches

Another way in which literature can be identified is through manual searches. Manual searches are done to supplement the primary database search and to identify any studies that may have been missed (Chapman et al., 2010). Chapman et al. (2010) state that manual searches help to reduce the risk of retrieval bias that can occur from poor indexing or selective publication. There are a number of ways to undertake a manual search and those included here are by no means exclusive. The most common method of undertaking a manual search is through reviewing the reference lists of articles and literature reviews you have identified from your database searches. Articles that have been recently published can be particularly useful as their reference lists are more likely to contain other recently published literature. This method of searching is often referred to as a snowball search (Ridley, 2008) or as 'pursuing references of references' (Chapman et al., 2010: 23). Another useful manual search method is to identify studies that have cited the seminal works within the topic area you are reviewing. Some databases and search engines, for example Web of Science and Google Scholar, will allow readers to track seminal articles. Studies that are citing these seminal works are more likely to be of interest.

While reference lists from other studies and reviews can be useful when undertaking a manual search, it is important to remember that these are secondary sources. It is important to retrieve the original primary source rather than depending on observations or analysis made by secondary authors. Unless you review the primary work yourself you have no means of authenticating the accuracy of the comments made by reviewing authors. Using a secondary source should only occur if the primary work is unavailable, and its use should be presented in a way that the reader can recognise the author is citing from a secondary source.

As you become familiar with the literature in your topic area you will possibly be able to identify authors who have an expertise in, and write extensively on, this subject. Databases have the capability of doing what are known as author searches which can help you identify other works by those authors. This type of search is usually difficult to undertake until you have become familiar with the literature in your area of interest. Another means of manual searching is a trawl through the research journals (Chapman et al., 2010). This can be particularly useful if the topic of interest is related to a specialist area supported by one or more dedicated journals. This search may involve reviewing the content index for each issue of that journal to identify relevant articles.

Manual searches are time consuming and in most incidences only produce a small number of articles that were not identified in, original searches of the databases (Chapman et al., 2010). Nevertheless they do have a role to play in reducing retrieval bias and this is of particular importance if undertaking a systematic review.

ACTIVITY 4.2

Appraise the literature review you selected in Activity 4.1. Is the search strategy clearly identified? Can you determine how the search was undertaken? Did the reviewer give sufficient information for the literature search to be replicated?

Now read the description of the literature search undertaken by Camak (2015) in Box 4.4.

Box 4.4   Documenting a Literature Search

A literature review was conducted using the following terms: 'caregivers', 'stroke', 'burden', 'depression', 'family nursing', 'mental health nursing', 'stress', 'older adults', 'family caregiving', 'discharge planning', 'emotional distress', 'caregiving burden', 'decision making', 'patient education and practice' and 'nursing'. The databases used were: CINAHL, PubMed, MEDLINE, Expanded Academic, NIH.GOV, FCA. org and CDC.gov. A total of 42 articles published within the past five years were retrieved with 22 published during the years of 2009 and 2014 selected for reference in this article. Of the 42 articles retrieved, 34 were research articles. Of the articles selected, each article was evaluated for its contribution to the body of literature related to caregiver burden and the role of the nurse in addressing caregiver needs. Finally, 15 research articles, two literature reviews and two reports from the Centers for Disease Control and Prevention [CDC], one report from the National Institute of Health [NIH] and two reports from FCA organisation were selected.

(Camak, 2015: 2377)

Recording Your Literature Search

The next thing to consider before undertaking your search is how you will record it. Keeping accurate notes on how the search was conducted – for example, the databases searched, the keywords used, and the number of articles identified – will make writing up the methodology of the search much easier. The methodology should describe the search to the extent that another reviewer could undertake the same search and identify much the same works. It will probably never elicit the same result, as databases are continuously being updated. However, the person replicating the review should be able, at least, to locate the same literature you did. An example of how a literature search might be documented can be seen in a review by Camak (2015) who describes her search in relation to the burden borne by elderly family members caring for stroke sufferers (see Box 4.4).

Searching and Selecting the Literature

The advent of electronic databases and search engines has made locating literature a lot easier. However, literature searching can be more difficult than it first appears and novice researchers often find the process frustrating. Difficulties that are regularly encountered relate to an apparent scarcity of, or no literature on an area of interest, and the contrasting scenario where the individual is overwhelmed with the quantity of literature. Searching is a skill that has to be learned and developed; however, Avdic and Eklund (2010) state that there is evidence to suggest that students believe they are more skilled in searching than they actually are. It is therefore important to seek help and advice in relation to your search, particularly if difficulties arise. The process of searching the literature can also be made easier and more fruitful if you can identify the main ideas or concepts that underpin the purpose or research question and further categorise these into keywords (Lahlafi, 2007). Lahlafi (2007) also suggests being strategic, and identifying which databases or other literature sources are likely to be relevant to the search and focusing your search in these areas initially.

Student Comment

'Sourcing material for the literature review was a daunting experience especially as the literature on my topic was limited. I soon learned that there are so many ways to source literature. You can look through all the relevant databases, e-journals and grey literature and even explore your library's archive of printed journals. If you look hard enough you would be amazed how much you can find. It's just about learning where and how to look.'

(4th year undergraduate intellectual disability nursing student)

The principles supporting a search on the different databases are similar, although there are some minor variations. EBSCOhost offers access to a number of databases including AMED, CINAHL and PsycINFO. When a database such as CINAHL is accessed the searcher is presented with a screen and a number of choices which can be selected from beneath the 'search box' (see Figure 4.1), including a basic or advanced search option.

The simplest search method is the basic search. A search term is entered into the search box and the search mode and expanders are selected. The screen default is Boolean/Phrase which supports both Boolean and exact phrase searching. A help box to explain the terms is available by clicking the '?' button. The search can also be limited by selecting explicit categories of literature – for example articles where full text or an abstract is available through the database, or literature in the English language only. If the 'Suggest Subject Terms' box, which is above the search box, is ticked the key word or phrase will be further defined. This can be helpful if the search term is broad and needs further refining. Both of these options can be switched off by clicking on search options and un-ticking the suggested subject terms box.

The basic search mode is ideal when the search consists of single words. However, in some instances a phrase can be regarded as a series of single keywords which can lead to a large number of hits, many of which may not be relevant. One method of overcoming this is the use of parentheses ( ) or double inverted commas " ". When a search term is enclosed within the parentheses or inverted commas the database recognises that these words should be regarded as a single term rather than individual words (see Figure 4.3). Alternatively, the advanced search option can be

Figure 4.1   Basic Search Screen CINAHL

selected (see Figure 4.2). Up to 12 search terms can be combined to limit, expand or clarify a search. The combining of keywords is achieved through the use of Boolean operators. Boolean operators will be discussed in more detail later in this chapter. When using the advanced search there are a variety of different search fields that can be selected. So searches can be performed for a combination of single or multiple authors, particular journals, as well as keywords in the text or other parts of an article such as the title or abstract. These search fields can be selected by using the dropdown tab which is beside each search box.

Figure 4.2   Advanced Search Screen CINAHL

When undertaking a topic search it is important to use the most accurate keywords to ensure the data gathered is the most relevant. There can be variations in the keywords used by database providers when indexing literature; however, data is stored under multiple headings so therefore the more keywords you use, the more likely you are to identify the literature you require. Most databases have thesauruses of indexing terms to help users identify the most appropriate keywords. One of the most well-known indexes is MeSH (Medical Subject Headings) which is used by Medline/PubMed and can be helpful for identifying keywords. The MeSH browser can be accessed at: https://www.nlm.nih.gov/mesh/MBrowser.html. Another useful way of identifying keywords or phrases is to look at any articles that are available on the topic. Authors are often asked to identify the keywords that define their work, and also through reading works related to the topic other terms can materialise. Clinical experts again can be useful sources of alternative terms.

Another point that should be considered when identifying keywords is spelling related to language. CINAHL and MEDLINE are both American (US) databases, so the spelling of certain words will differ from the English (UK) spelling. While most databases use word recognition software to compensate for difference in common spelling, when using words with alternative spelling such as haemophilia (hemophilia), tumour (tumor) and oesophagus (esophagus), especially where multiple databases are being accessed, it is best to use both spellings in case the alternate spelling is coded separately.

Boolean, Truncation and Wildcard Operators

Boolean operators are commands which are used to combine keyword searches so as to select or exclude articles that have particular keywords. The most frequently used Boolean operators are AND, OR and NOT and are written using block capitals. An example of how the number of hits can be expanded or limited using Boolean operators can be seen in Figure 4.3.

Figure 4.3   Using Boolean Operators

In the initial searches the key words Diabetes Type 1 and Diabetes Type 2 had 999 and 1,885 hits respectively and Gestational Diabetes had 209 hits (Figure 4.5). After the initial literature searches were complete, 'search history', which is an option on the basic/advanced search line, was selected. The searcher then had to decide how best to combine these searches using Boolean operators. In this instance, the Boolean OR was initially used to combine the two searches. This ensured that either of the keywords were present and any repetition of literature was eliminated (Figure 4.3):

> (Diabetes Type1) OR (Diabetes Type 2)

The result was 2,603 articles were identified. The Boolean AND was then used to limit the search. Both keywords had to be present and if only one keyword was present the article was excluded. This reduced the number of hits to 281. It was then decided that gestational diabetes would not be included in the search and so NOT was used to reject the articles related to this keyword. This final search identified 270 articles:

> (Diabetes Type1) AND (Diabetes Type 2) NOT (Gestational Diabetes)

On occasions it may be useful to use related keywords when searching the literature. Truncation involves using the root of a keyword to identify other possible forms of that word and include them in your search. In the CINAHL database this can be done by including an asterisk with, for example, the word 'diet*'. The database will now also search 'dietary' and 'dietetic'; however, it will also include other terms such as 'dietician', which may not be wanted. Another set of operators which are associated with truncation are called 'wildcards'. In CINAHL a question mark can be used to replace a letter. The database will then seek this word with every alternative letter replacing the question mark – for example, 'wom?n' will result in the search using 'woman' and 'women'. Another wildcard is # which can be used for alternative spellings where a letter may or may not exist – for example, 'tumo#r' will search using both 'tumour' and 'tumor'. While the Boolean operators identified are available in most databases, truncation and wildcards do vary between databases. It is always a good idea to seek advice from a librarian who will be best placed to offer advice. Alternatively, most databases have help features that, when accessed, will guide the user through the use of these strategies.

Limiting the Search

Sometimes, even when the search parameters have been clearly refined, a search can result in a large number of hits within the literature. While this may be useful in some cases, in other instances – particularly where an assignment has a strict word limit or there is a short time frame in which the work must be completed – it may be problematic. Limiting the search is about making the number of hits more manageable and there are a number of ways of doing this. It is important at this stage that you keep good records of all the searches undertaken. The simplest method of doing this is to save them within each database you have used.

Boolean operators have already been mentioned as one method of limiting the number of articles identified. A number of study limiters are also available on the EBSCOhost as part of Search Options and appear under the heading 'Limit your results' (see Figure 4.2). The effect of using the limiters 'Language': English, 'Publication Type': Research and 'Journal Subset': Nursing, can be seen when comparing the 'Diabetes' searches in Figure 4.4 and Figure 4.5.

Depending on the quantity of literature available it is recommended that the majority of studies included in your review should be as contemporary as possible. Limiters can be set on age of the study by identifying parameters in relation to the date of publication. Exceptions are made for works that are regarded as being seminal or having a major influence in the field. Alternatively, if the topic under review has been the subject of only a small number of recent studies, older works may need to be included. In this instance, however, the rationale for including the older studies should be acknowledged.

Publications can also be limited to peer reviewed, research studies. Peer reviewed and research studies are two independent limiters so either or both can be applied. When undertaking a literature review, the vast majority of the works included should be research studies. While literature reviews, opinion articles and editorials may be helpful in identifying literature and setting the scene, the works being reviewed should be mainly research based. Another common method of limiting a search is by language. Depending on the database used, studies published in any number of languages may be accessed, but may not be of use if there is no means of translating them. It is not unusual to see searches limited to the English language for this reason.

Figure 4.4 Diabetes Search without Limiters

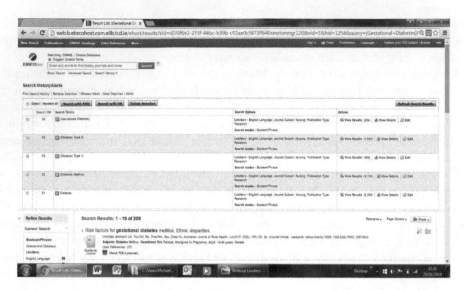

Figure 4.5   Diabetes Search with Limiters

The above are only a few of the methods of limiting or narrowing a search. However, when using these tools it is important to consider the outcome. Limiting a search to 'Linked Full Text', for instance, may be sensible if you only have access to those journals that are available on a particular database; however, universities and colleges usually subscribe to numerous online journals, some of which may not be available as full text on the databases you are searching. By limiting your search to Linked Full Text you could lose the opportunity to identify those articles. Limiting your search to studies with abstracts, however, can be very useful as you can then check how relevant these articles are before you download or search the university or college online journals for them.

Evaluating the Search Strategy

When doing a literature search, it is important to regularly evaluate how well the strategy being employed is working. It is unusual to be completely successful on a first search, so it is useful to review the phrases and keywords used to see how effective they were in identifying the appropriate articles. It may be that some keywords or phrases need to be further refined as they may be too broad and getting too many results, or are identifying results that appear unrelated to the topic being reviewed. If too few useful results are being received it may be the keywords or phrases being used are too narrowly focused, or it may be that that particular database is not the most suitable one for what is being sought. Throughout this process it is a very good idea to save your searches.

Summary

The aim of this chapter was to lead the novice reviewer through the first stages of undertaking a literature review, from identifying a problem/topic of interest through the process of doing a literature search. A number of sources from where the topic could arise were identified, one of the most popular sources being professional/ clinical practice. Once the topic was identified the importance of refining the topic to make the search more manageable was discussed. The next step was to identify appropriate keywords or phrases that could be used to search for literature. The most commonly used sources of literature today are the professional databases and the Internet. Nonetheless, there are other sources and ways of searching, and these are both useful and essential in some instances. When undertaking the search it may be necessary to expand or narrow the search parameters, depending on the success of the search, and some methods of limiting the search were identified and the use of Boolean operators was discussed. Evaluating progress in the search is important as modifications to the search invariably have to be made and it is better to do this early to improve results. Remember that searching the literature is a skill and it may not always be possible to identify articles on a topic; that is not to say they do not exist, it may be simply that the wrong search term was used. It is important, there-fore, to recognise that 'not being able to identify any studies' related to a particular topic is not the same as saying 'there are no studies' on that topic. The latter state-ment is probably wrong.

Once the literature has been found the next stage is sorting the literature to see how relevant it is and organising it so that the articles are categorised in some ordered way for easy access. This will be discussed in Chapter 5.

❝ Key Points ❞

- The first and arguably the most important step in undertaking a literature review is to identify the review topic or problem.
- Review topics that are too broad can lack a focal point and become unwieldy, therefore it is important to refine the topic to make it more focused and manageable.
- Literature should be searched for, identified and selected in a systematic manner. The databases and other sources of literature used, as well as the key words and search strategies, should be identified in the review.
- It is important to continuously evaluate your strategy to ensure the data that you are gathering matches the purpose of your review.

READING AND ORGANISING THE LITERATURE

5

❝ **Learning Outcomes** ❞

Having read this chapter you should be able to:

- screen the results of your literature search;
- identify strategies for effectively reading and summarising your included literature;
- explain how you might organise your literature for easy retrieval for when you come to write the review.

Introduction

Once you have completed your literature search you will have identified literature that will be relevant, on the face of it, to the focus of your review. This chapter considers the process by which you will identify the final publications for inclusion in your review. It also outlines strategies for reading and summarising the literature effectively with a view to producing a finished piece of work that is concise and comprehensive. An introduction to the use of bibliographical software packages as a means of organising your literature is presented to aid easy retrieval.

Screening the Results of the Literature: Selecting Appropriate Papers

The first part of this chapter examines the process by which you screen the results of your literature search and decide which ones will ultimately be included in your review. This is because no matter how good your search of the literature it is more than likely the results will include publications that are not relevant to the particular focus of your review. Rather than limiting your search further to reduce the number of publications and run the risk of excluding important material you should screen your results.

For example, in the previous chapter Camak's (2015) search (see Box 4.4), related to the burden borne by elderly family members caring for stroke sufferers, initially identified 42 publications that were considered relevant. Following screening 22 were included in the final review. The process described here outlines how you might get from your initial retrieval to your final selection.

Throughout this book, we have made reference to the processes adopted in undertaking systematic reviews and how they have influenced how contemporary narrative reviews are conducted. These influences are evident also in how we screen and select appropriate literature for final inclusion in the review. It is an expectation now that the screening and selection of papers for inclusion in any review is both rigorous and transparent. This means that you must be able to say why you excluded publications during the screening process.

In order for you to be able to screen your results you must have saved your searches and it is possible to do this within any of the databases you have used. When you are ready to undertake the screening these searches can be retrieved easily. According to Ridley (2008) it is not unusual to feel overwhelmed initially by the sheer volume of literature you have retrieved. Therefore, it is important to be clear about the key elements of your question and aim and have them to hand throughout the screening process. This will this ensure that your selection process is rigorous and that you do not include irrelevant publications because you consider the findings 'interesting' or because they support your own personal views, which is a form of bias that is referred to sometimes referred to as 'cherry-picking'. In addition, having the review question or aim close to hand will enable you to discard irrelevant citations quickly.

If possible, you should have the question or aim separated into its constituent parts and listed as such. Acronyms such as PICO or PEO, outlined in Chapter 3, can be helpful here but at the very least you should be very clear about your population, that is the people who are the focus of your review (e.g. children, adults, people living in residential care), the setting or context in which you are interested (e.g. acute care, community, residential care) and the phenomenon of interest (e.g. stroke, diabetes, palliative care). For example, in Camak's review, the population were elderly family members who are caring for people who have had strokes. The setting was not specified although there was a suggestion that it was home or place of residence, and phenomena or outcomes of interest were lived experience of caregiving, caregiving burden, educational needs of caregivers, relationship of caregivers with nurses and interventions to address the needs of caregivers.

You may also want to specify at this stage the 'types' of literature in which you are interested. If you do this it makes the process of reducing the number of citations clearer. Many contemporary narrative reviews tend to only include research studies, systematic reviews and literature reviews of various types. However, care should be exercised about excluding literature that provides the background or context of the focus of your review. For example, you may be undertaking a review related to self-management of type 2 diabetes, in which case it will be important for you to include background literature about the condition, the concept of self-management and the recommended best practice before you discuss the current state of knowledge and research on the topic.

Initial screening involves simply reading the title of each of the citations on your saved searches and making a decision to discard on the basis that the title does not meet your inclusion criteria. This often reduces the amount of literature considerably but you should, where possible, keep a record of those you have excluded. It can also happen that the same title will appear in more than one database search so you should exclude duplicates and just keep one copy of any citation. If you are unsure about retaining or discarding a title, it is better to do the former and screen the abstract. In fact, many reviewers review title and abstract simultaneously as the additional information in the abstract is likely to help the decision-making process. If having reviewed the title and abstract and you are still unsure or have some doubt, it is better to access the full paper rather than exclude too early.

Student Comment

'Often the abstract did not provide enough information – it would lead me to believe a study was related to my topic but on reading the study in full it did not.'

(4th year undergraduate general nursing student)

The next stage, therefore involves detailed screening of the full text papers against the inclusion criteria. However, before you do this you should download the citations you wish to retrieve for full text review. This can be done manually but it is not recommended as it is laborious and time-consuming. All databases have a system whereby the references can be sent to a number of places such as a file, email, or citation manager software packages (see Figure 5.1). You simply tick each citation in which you are interested and when finished they can be exported to the place of your choice. Examples of citation managers or reference management packages type include EndNote (www.endnote.com), Procite (www.procite.com) and Reference Manager (www.refman.com) which are discussed in more detail later in the chapter.

Once you have done this it will be necessary to access the full text of the publication. As stated in Chapter 4, many of these are available through university or college libraries. Where they are not available online you may be able to source them in hard copy format in the library holdings. Alternatively, the library may be able to source it for you but this may incur a cost. They can also be purchased from the publisher but the cost can be prohibitive particularly if you have to source more than one.

Once you have retrieved the full texts you will need to store them. You can download full-text articles to your computer or laptop or if you are using a reference management package such as EndNote you will be able to attach them to the citation in the system. Each publication must now be read for the purpose of determining if it is to be included in your final selection of articles. If you are diligent in undertaking this process and only include those publications that meet the specific focus of your review, that is, meet your inclusion criteria, it will reduce the amount of reading unnecessary material. When you are discarding any articles at this stage, you

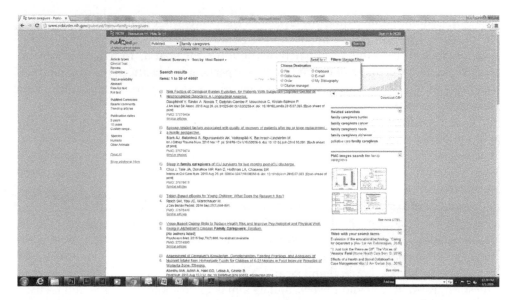

Figure 5.1 Choosing a Destination for your Citations

should record the reasons for exclusion. Constructing a flow diagram such as that presented in Chapter 3 is a useful way of displaying the process (see Figure 3.1).

Reading and Summarising the Literature

Once you have decided on the publications that will be included in your review the next step is to read each citation with the ultimate aim of extracting pertinent information. It is this extracted information that will provide the substance for the main discussion of your topic. Often students do not allocate sufficient time for this process but if you are to produce the best review it is important to be systematic and thorough in this phase. It is prudent also to keep your question in a prominent place at all times to avoid deviating from the precise topic. This prevents you from getting side-tracked by extraneous material that serves no purpose. For example, the publication you are reviewing may include material related to your review question but it may also have content that is not directly related. Tempting as it might be to digress, particularly when you think the material is interesting, you should make every effort to remain focused throughout.

Student Comment

'I found it difficult not to mention other key findings from a piece of research and only mention aspects that related to my topic. For example, mentioning other populations or samples they had studied when I was not examining it in my review.'

(4th year undergraduate general nursing student)

Reading is about familiarising yourself with the content but is also the beginning of the process of assessing the content of the literature you have included. Often, however, we tend to read indiscriminately without a clear goal as to what we want to achieve. In addition, most of us tend to read aspects of publications that are interesting, such as the findings, and we tend to ignore what we consider difficult or less interesting aspects, such as the methodology and methods.

Yet a good literature review will not only present the findings of a study but will include comment and judgement on the methodological elements. Therefore, it is important to be clear about why you are reading and to be systematic in how you read and how you extract pertinent data from each of the included publications.

A number of techniques have been developed to assist students with reading academic literature and most of these can be located easily through your study skills online support in your own university or on the Internet. However, the most commonly recommended strategy is the SQ3R system as it is flexible and can be adapted for use with books, book chapters and articles. The acronym stands for Survey, Question, Read, Recall and Review, and its aim is to promote organised and focused reading. While it may appear labour intensive at first, it is a useful strategy for learning to read effectively and purposefully. It encourages questioning and analysis and allows connections to be made between new knowledge and existing knowledge. This is a worthwhile step to undertake and can provide valuable information for the analysis and synthesis stage of your literature review.

Student Comment

'I actually found the reading to be quite enjoyable. If you are interested in your research then it is less of a chore. Finding key terms that can be found in documents was an easy start. Limiting your reading to both the introduction and then conclusion/discussion is a quick way to get through large amounts of articles.'

(2nd year undergraduate mental health nursing student)

Survey is the first step and involves acquiring an overview of the text by scanning it for content. Reading the abstract, introduction, discussion and conclusion gives a general idea of the main thrust of the article and an initial understanding of the key concepts that underlie each piece of work. This first impression is important as it will give you an indication of the value of the literature, while saving time that might be wasted reading irrelevant articles. Skimming the main headings and sub-headings provides information on the main points of the text. This is likely to be the strategy you will use when screening the articles for inclusion as it provides a general overview of what is contained in the article and will give you an indication of its appropriateness for your own review.

Following a preview of the articles you have acquired, the second step is to ask questions of each paper. For a literature review the questions you ask should be those that will enable you to answer your review question. These can be about the aims, the methodology and methods used, the findings that are relevant to your review and the recommendations and limitations. The source and reference should also be included as this will enable easy retrieval of references when you come to write the review. Developing or adapting what are known as data extraction tools (see Chapter 3) can be very useful at this stage as they are a means of recording the required information from each of the included articles. Moreover, they enable you to ask consistent questions of each paper and can be retrieved easily when preparing a Summary Table (see Chapter 7) of the findings of your review (see Chapter 7). See Table 5.1 for an example of a Data Extraction Tool.

Table 5.1 Data Extraction Tool

Reviewer:
Reference:
Aim/Research question:
Study design: **Setting/context:**
Sample:
Data collection
Data analysis

Page/Column   **Data extracted from the findings of the study**
number

Devise a framework for summarising your literature. This should include your research topic and question as a starting point. Decide on the other relevant points to include, such as the source and reference of the paper and its purpose, the type of study and its relevance to your literature review, the methodology used, major findings and limitations, and your own key points and comments.

ACTIVITY 5.1

The third step of the process is to read the publications in more depth and is about finding the answers to the questions you have posed. As you read and reread, you will become more critical in your approach and will be able to differentiate between what is relevant and what is not. Reading at a deeper level allows connections to be made within the literature. You will be able to identify which studies are largely saying the same thing, e.g. similar findings, or those that contradict or offer a new perspective on the topic. You may also begin to establish reasons why the findings might be different. For example, if your topic was related to barriers to help-seeking for people with a chronic illness you may find that social barriers vary depending on where a study was conducted. Ultimately, you may conclude that social barriers are always a feature of help-seeking but the interesting or pertinent point may be that they differ across different populations because they are culturally determined.

However, reading is a task that requires concentration and application if it is to be effective and it is likely that you will have to read each article several times to develop a good understanding of its content.

Student Comment

'I always needed to read a study more than once to understand it.'

(4th year undergraduate general nursing student)

Student Comment

'Reading through the literature initially is a daunting task. I found the more I read the less daunting it became because I was able to do a thematic analysis.'

(4th year undergraduate general nursing student)

It is important then that you allocate time when you can read without interruptions. This is especially important when you are reading difficult content such as the methodology and methods sections of research studies.

Reading and note-taking are interconnected. While you are reading, notes should be taken, summarising the main points. Using key words to identify important points will help you make connections between papers and references. These can then be organised into distinct themes, which will give structure to the review. If you are reviewing how a topic has developed over time, then reviewing the literature in chronological order is a good way to organise it.

Whether you read your publications on a computer or print a hard copy is a matter of preference. However, it is important that you have the facility for making notes on the text. This is why you may wish to have a hard copy. How you take notes is a matter of personal choice. Ridley (2008) suggests three methods: annotating a hard copy of a text, pattern notes and linear notes (Ridley, 2008: 51). Annotating a hard copy of a text involves using a highlighter pen to highlight important points. Key words may be written in the margins to denote significant issues. Different colours can be used for different themes and your own comments.

Student Comment

'Organising the literature when trying to write on themes was difficult. I found myself constantly shuffling through the printed articles trying to find what I was looking for. I quickly realised that colour coding the themes and findings made it much easier.'

(4th year undergraduate general nursing student)

Pattern notes typically involve using diagrams or mind maps, where the main idea is drawn in the centre of a page, with themes and sub-themes branching out from it. Using diagrams or mind maps can also allow you to see relationships between ideas or themes emerging from the literature.

Linear notes use headings and subheadings to illustrate the important points (Ridley, 2008). Headings may also be useful when it is proving difficult to organise and make sense of what you have read. A heading could be a subsection of your research question or topic, whereby you can group all the articles relevant to that section in one place such as using different pages for each section. Headings used in an ordered manner will ultimately help the literature review flow in a logical sequence.

In the stage of recall, it is a good idea to try and outline what you have read in your own words while referring to the questions you have posed. In other words, what does the material say about your topic? While this may be a strategy that is used more frequently when reading and preparing for examinations, it can also be very useful for helping you to summarise what you have read. You can do this by writing down what it is you understand from the content of the article. This is important in a literature review because the main body of your discussion requires that you present the findings of the literature. If you have created summaries in your own words, you will have the basis for writing the main body of the review. Moreover, writing in your own words gives you immediate feedback about how well you have understood the content and is also a mechanism for avoiding plagiarism.

The first two Rs (reading and recall) are primarily concerned with understanding the content. The third R permits you to review what has been read in a more in-depth fashion. This stage facilitates an interaction with the text, allowing you to make connections with your own questions and what you have read. Making additional, more detailed notes at this stage enables you to make comparisons with other literature and can also alert you to possible areas that warrant further investigation. You may choose to combine the recall and review stages when you are engaging with the papers in your review.

Organising the Literature

It is possible that you will retrieve and have to manage a large amount of information and this can be a daunting task. Therefore, throughout the processes of screening, retrieving, reading and note-making it is important to be organised. It is a good idea at the outset to devise strategies for ensuring that all of your material for your review can be sourced and retrieved easily.

As mentioned earlier in the chapter, it is important that you keep records of the literature you have retrieved for your review. Organising and collecting citations can be a frustrating task and organisation at the outset will prevent extra work when you begin to write.

While this is sometimes done manually or by recording the references on a personal computer or laptop, databases and citation manager systems have made saving your searches and downloading your references and the full text of the article relatively easy. Specific training is usually available and is recommended for the use of these packages. It is worth spending the time becoming familiar with them as in the long term it saves time searching for references and helps you avoid the common problem of referencing errors associated with manual inputting. Moreover, creating a digital library means your work is centralised, which removes the effort of trying to locate reference lists often scattered randomly in your personal computer. Keeping track of your retrieved literature is important because referencing errors prevent the reader from gathering information from your work; they also reflect poorly on the perceived rigour of the work (Smith and Baker, 2007).

There are many citation manager packages available for use, examples of which include EndNote (www.endnote.com), Procite (www.procite.com) and Reference Manager (www.refman.com). As stated above they allow you to store, organise and cross-link references, insert citations and create references lists or bibliographies in different formats (Smith and Baker, 2007). Using the 'cite as you write' feature allows you to insert citations directly into your text and in doing so the reference list or bibliography is automatically created. This prevents omissions but also ensures that the citation is referenced appropriately and in full.

In addition to organising your references you also need to keep track of your retrieved literature. As indicated earlier it is possible to attach the full text of a publication to its citation in a reference management system. Your personal notes regarding your references may also be inputted into these packages. It is likely also that you will download full-text articles to a file on your computer or print them so that making notations is easier. It is important to mention that whatever system you use, be it recording references on a file on a computer or using a software package, keeping a backup is essential and is a good habit to develop.

When you are organising your literature in preparation for analysis, having a hard copy of the included literature can make it less difficult. The analysis stage is primarily where you integrate the findings from all the publications (see Chapter 7). You will have made notes on each publication and extracted the findings or information that are relevant to your review question. Now you need to pull them together to form themes. Most of us find this an easier task if we have the original publication in view as the process involves thinking, reviewing and grouping and sometimes re-grouping the findings so that those that are reporting on the same aspects of the topic are categorised together (see the section on thematic analysis in Chapter 7).

Summary

Reading and organising the literature is a skill, and at times your own personal style will be challenged. However, it is important to get into the habit of doing this in a structured way from the beginning. This chapter has examined how to identify literature that is relevant for your review, through the process of screening titles, abstracts and the full-text articles. The importance of careful reading, note-taking and summarising were emphasised and strategies for doing so efficiently and effectively were outlined. The importance of organising, managing and storing your literature and references in a systematic way was also highlighted and the benefits of doing so with the assistance of bibliographic software packages were delineated. If you have done this well you should now have an organised and manageable body of literature that is ready for appraisal and analysis.

❝ Key Points ❞

- Your research question is an integral part of keeping your work focused and the literature you include in your review should relate to your specific question.
- Screening is a process of examining the literature by title, abstract and full-text to identify those publications that are most relevant to your review topic/question.
- There are a number of techniques for reading academic literature but the most commonly recommended strategy is the SQ3R which stands for: Survey, Question, Read, Recall and Review.
- Taking notes is an important part of summarising the literature and three strategies for doing so include annotating a hard copy of a text, pattern notes and linear notes.
- It is necessary to develop a system for organising and managing your literature and references from an early stage. Bibliographic software packages are an effective means of doing this.
- Always keep an up-to-date backup of your work.

CRITICALLY APPRAISING THE LITERATURE

❝ Learning Outcomes ❞

Having read this chapter you should be able to:

- compare and contrast findings in the literature;
- differentiate between articles using a post-positive and a naturalistic research methodology;
- critically appraise quantitative and qualitative research, and systematic reviews;
- critically appraise non-research articles.

Introduction

Now that the studies that meet the parameters of your review have been selected, the next step is to consider how to clearly yet succinctly present these studies. The studies need to be examined so that those with related findings can be identified and their results compared and contrasted. These related findings can become the foundation that forms a theme or subheading within your review. Themes or subheadings are important as they pull those studies with commonalities together and help to prevent your review becoming a rambling collection of isolated research studies.

The studies in your review also need to be critically appraised. The reader does not have the benefit of reading the original articles so is depending on you, the reviewer, to distinguish between those studies that are robust and those studies whose limitations may have influenced their outcomes. It is important to realise that there is no such thing as the perfect research study. Every research study has some limitations. It is expected that the strengths of a study will exceed its limitations, and that the limitations are minor, in which case the study is usually regarded as being good.

Comparing and Contrasting the Literature

Having searched the literature and selected the studies relevant to your review, you will probably realise that you now have a large number of studies to include in your review with a limited word count in which to present them. The most practical way of managing this situation is to develop a framework in which to present these studies. When you perused the literature that you were going to select, you will probably have noticed that certain related issues and concerns were discussed in many of these studies. These related issues and concerns, if suitable, may form the basis for one of the themes or subheadings under which some of your literature may be presented and discussed (Wakefield, 2014). An example of the themes presented and used by Hayes et al. (2015) in their review of disruption during medication administration can be seen in Box 6.1. Some studies address issues that may be represented by more than one theme, and in such cases the same article will appear under more than one subheading.

Box 6.1   Use of Themes/Subheadings

'Relevant literature included a combination of qualitative, quantitative and mixed methods studies. Broad and recurring themes included frequency, types, causes and effects of interruptions, interruption elimination strategies and coping with interruptions. Four central themes were identified across studies: setting the scene – interruptions and distractions impacting care; reducing interruptions – current research responses; shifting focus – multi-tasking and prioritising and strategising care – managing interruptions.' (Hayes et al., 2015: 3066)

There are no hard and fast rules about the minimum number of studies that should be included in each theme; however, there should be sufficient that a reasonable in-depth discussion can be presented. Similarly the number of themes will depend to a degree on the word count available, as too many themes can reduce the depth of analysis and discussion, which may weaken the review. Usually about four themes is regarded as offering a good insight into the topic and a reasonable depth of the discussion within the individual themes.

Once the themes have been identified, it is important to ensure that the studies you include in that section relate to that theme. Quite often, novice reviewers can include studies not directly related to that subheading and find they have moved off on a tangent from the original theme. It is important, therefore, to constantly compare the findings being discussed with the title of that theme. If the literature under a particular subheading appears to be leading in multiple directions, it may be that the heading is too broad and may need to be refined.

As mentioned earlier, themes are based around the findings and outcomes of studies, so those studies whose findings appear to support each other should be compared and contrasted in relation to these outcomes. Literature reviews are not about presenting the findings of individual studies but presenting collective outcomes from multiple studies (Wakefield, 2014). Comparing and contrasting the methodologies, populations and samples can also be helpful as they can show the similarity or diversity that exists in the cohorts included in the studies. Sample size and adherence to methodological principles can also offer an insight into the robustness of the individual studies. It is important to remember that research should not be taken at face value and should be critically appraised so the reader can make an informed judgement.

As well as presenting studies that support each other, it is also important to present studies with alternative findings. Reviews should be about presenting both sides of the debate so that the reader is informed. Studies that have alternative findings are not necessarily inaccurate and, in fact, because they may have a larger sample size or perhaps due to the use of a more appropriate methodology, may be more accurate in their findings. It is, therefore, important that you critically review the methodologies used when comparing studies on both sides of the debate and perhaps offer a rationale as to why the findings appear to differ.

Differentiating Between Quantitative and Qualitative Research

When appraising research studies it is important to have an understanding of the research paradigms and the research methods that are associated with them. The approaches to research can be broadly classified as quantitative, which includes the positivist and the post-positivist paradigms, and qualitative research which includes the interpretivist/constructivist paradigm and the critical/transformative/participatory/advocacy paradigms (Cronin et al., 2015).

Modern quantitative research is strongly influenced by the post-positivist paradigm. This type of research is concerned with measurable objective outcomes. However, measurable outcomes in post-positivist research are only indicators of a probable result and not an indicator of proof. For example, when research indicates that there is a strong probability that cigarette smoking leads to lung cancer, it is not stating that it will, only that there is a good chance that it will. In order to demonstrate this type of outcome the ideal group to use would be the whole population but as this is virtually impossible, a representative sample from the population is the next best thing. Statistics can then be used to extrapolate how representative this result is or how probable the outcome is due to chance. So quantitative research is interested in using statistics to study large numbers of subjects in order to determine what the probable answer to the research question will be. There are a number of different research approaches associated with the post-positivist paradigm and some of these can be seen in Box 6.2.

In contrast to the post-positivist deductive approach to measurable outcomes, the paradigms associated with qualitative research focus more on the experiences and beliefs of the individual. Proponents of this approach claim that the individual's experience needs to be studied in a holistic way rather than selecting one or two variables to examine in isolation (Polit and Beck, 2014). Qualitative designs subscribe to the notion of subjective multiple realities that are constructed by individuals and are contextually framed. Data are not measured numerically and are usually collected through interviews, focus groups and observation. The findings from this type of research reflect the views of the individual and are not generalisable to the population. Some of the different approaches used in this type of research can be seen in Box 6.2.

Box 6.2   Paradigms and Associated Approaches

Post-positivist paradigm:

- Descriptive quantitative research.
- Comparative descriptive research.
- Correlational research.
- Quasi-experimental research.
- Experimental research.

Interpretivist/constructivist paradigm:

- Qualitative descriptive research.
- Phenomenology.
- Grounded theory.
- Ethnography.

Critical/transformative/participatory/advocacy paradigm:

- Critical theory.
- Feminist theory.
- Participatory action research.

Appraising Research

The purpose of appraising a research study is to identify the strengths and limitations that exist within that work. It is wrong to assume that because something appears in print, or because an author appears well qualified, that the findings will be accurate or that the study was undertaken in a robust manner. It can sometimes be daunting for the novice reviewer to be faced with critically appraising an article that has been published in a prestigious journal, or written by an individual or individuals who appear so much better qualified. However, even well-known medical journals have published and later retracted works when they were shown to be inaccurate. It is therefore important when reading research to do so with a critical eye and never take what is written at face value.

It is important at this point to differentiate between critically appraising an article and criticising it. Evaluating a study with the sole purpose of identifying limitations may be regarded as an attempt to denounce the study or admonish the author, and may be regarded as a subjective position. Alternatively a critical appraisal is an impersonal, objective review of the strengths and weaknesses of the study.

Appraisal is an evaluation of the strengths and limitations of a study – it is not an opportunity to criticise the author or the study.

Critical appraisal is also different from a critique. A critique of a study usually looks at all the steps in the research process undertaken by the researcher when performing a study and compares these to what is generally regarded as the accepted standard. This type of critique is usually comprehensive in nature and considers such factors as the organisation and presentation of the study, the literature review, methodological issues, findings and discussion (Polit and Beck, 2014). Critiques are often undertaken as academic assignments to encourage research students to critically apply their newly acquired knowledge of the research process in evaluating a single study. However, when critically appraising studies in a literature review, the analysis will not be in the form of comprehensive critiques, otherwise the review would simply be a series of critiques. Rather, the analysis identifies one or two important strengths and/or limitations that will allow the reader to make a judgement on that study. There are numerous tools available for critiquing research studies. Some of these instruments were developed to critique both quantitative and qualitative studies, while others were developed to critique either quantitative or qualitative research. Guidelines for undertaking a comprehensive critique of a quantitative and a qualitative study are included in the Appendix to give you the opportunity to explore the full spectrum of elements that can be considered when appraising the strengths and limitations of a study. When critically appraising a study as part of a literature review only one or two elements presented in the critiquing tool will be used. These elements should focus on the robustness of the study and identify and discuss its strengths and/or limitations. Other instruments that are available for appraising different types of research studies and systematic reviews are available at the following websites:

CASP (2013) www.casp-uk.net/#!casp-tools-checklists/c18f8

SIGN (2013) www.sign.ac.uk/methodology/checklists.html

The purpose of critical appraising studies, as previously stated, is to ensure that research studies that influence practice, or that are used to support concepts within a literature review, are methodologically robust and have quality evidence that is relevant (Johnson and Taylor, 2014). A guide to determining the relevance and critically appraising a research study can be found in Table 6.1.

Table 6.1 Guidelines for Critically Appraising a Research Study

Verify if the study is relevant to the review	Read the title and the abstract of the study.
Review the study in detail and consider its robustness	Explore the study and become familiar with the purpose and the methodology used. Identify and appraise how faithful the authors were to the steps in the research process.
Identify the strengths and limitations	Offer examples of strengths and limitations as appropriate. Support the implications of your appraisal with evidence from the literature.
Recommendations for future studies in this field	The author may have identified how this study might be improved, any gaps in the literature and suggestions for future studies.
Overall evaluation of the study	This is an objective indication of how you rate the study in the context of the robustness of the study and its contribution to the topic being studied.

Source: Adapted from Cronin et al., 2015

Relevance of the Study

When undertaking a search of the literature there are always a number of research studies and articles identified that are of little or no relevance to the current review of the literature. As there can be quite a lot of literature to examine and time is often a constraining factor, it is important to quickly determine which studies are relevant and which ones are unwanted. Some factors that may be considered when attempting to determine relevance are displayed in Table 6.2.

Table 6.2 Factors Influencing Relevance

Factors Influencing Relevance	
Title	From the report title you should be able to identify if the study is related to your topic of interest. This is often the first indicator whether a study may be relevant or not. If the study is clearly not relevant then it should be rejected at this point.
Abstract	If there are doubts after checking the title, the abstract should clarify the relevance of the study. You should be able to determine the purpose of the study, its methodology, main findings and recommendations from the abstract.
Author	The professional experiences and/or qualifications of the author can suggest a knowledge or expertise in this particular field of enquiry. This may be particularly relevant if the author is well known for research in this area.

On perusing the title of a research study or article you should have a reasonably clear idea of the purpose of the work. If the article is clearly not related to the topic being reviewed it should be rejected at this point. If a study is relevant to another aspect of your work, put it aside to review at another time. Reviewing works that are not relevant can lead you away from your current goal and can be time consuming. If the study appears to be relevant to your review, the abstract should then be examined. The abstract should give a summary of the purpose of the study, how it was undertaken and an overview of the key findings and recommendations which should allow you to determine whether the study is relevant or not (Rebar et al., 2011). The author's qualifications or professional experience may also be helpful in deciding whether a study is pertinent to the review. If an author is known to have a particular expertise in, and frequently write on the topic being reviewed, then works by that author may have relevance.

Determining the Robustness of the Study

Having decided that a study is relevant and will be included in the review the next step is to critically appraise the methodology of the study. There are philosophical differences between the purposes that underpin quantitative and qualitative research, so it is essential when evaluating the robustness of a study that you have a good understanding of the approach being used in that study and how the steps

Table 6.3   Steps in the Research Process

Steps in the Research Process	
Logical consistency	There should be a logical order in how the steps of the research approach were undertaken.
Purpose	The research problem/significance of the study should be clearly identified for the reader.
Review of the literature	An appropriate review of the literature should have been undertaken.
Theoretical framework	Ideally a theoretical or conceptual framework should be identified. If it was, it should be clearly described and it should be appropriate for this study.
Research question/ hypothesis	A research question/hypothesis should have been clearly identified.
Methodology / philosophical underpinning	A justification for the selecting of the philosophical approach/ research methodology should have been presented.
Research design and instruments	The research instrument should have been described and should be appropriate for this study.
Validity/reliability/rigour	The techniques used to ensure the robustness of the data gathering instrument/data gathered should have been described.
Sample	The target population should have been described. The method by which the sample was selected and the sample size should have been discussed. The selection method should be appropriate for the approach used.
Ethical considerations	All the ethical principles should have been considered and adhered to. Ethical approval should have been granted for the study.
Data analysis	The author(s) should have discussed how the data was analysed. The method of data analysis should be appropriate for the study.
Findings	The findings should be clearly and appropriately presented.
Discussion	The findings should be discussed with reference to the literature. The author(s) should have also identified any limitations of the study.
Conclusions/implications/ recommendations	The author(s) should identify how the findings of the study may be of interest professionally and the implications they may have for clinical practice. Recommendations for future research should ideally be presented.
References	All the texts, journal articles, websites and other media sources referred to in the study should be accurately referenced.

Source: Adapted from Cronin et al., 2015

in the research process are applied in that methodology. In a quantitative study, for instance, the literature review is used to determine what information is available on this topic, to refine the research problem and it may suggest approaches to further investigating this topic. To achieve these goals the literature review needs to be undertaken early in the study. On the other hand in some qualitative approaches such as grounded theory and phenomenology the literature review is undertaken after the data is gathered and analysed to reduce the risk that the researcher might be influenced by the literature. The purpose of a literature review in these qualitative approaches is to gather knowledge on the phenomenon of interest to support the themes that arise from the study data. An overview of the steps in the process has been included in Table 6.3 and a more comprehensive review of the steps in quantitative and qualitative research can be seen in tables A.1 and A.2 in the Appendix.

Identifying the Strengths and Limitations of the Study

Critically appraising a research study is not simply recognising the strengths or limitations of the research but also identifying for the reader how that strength or limitation can influence the outcomes of the study. When identifying the strengths, limitations and implications it crucial to remember that the appraisal is objective so therefore this analysis should be supported by evidence from the literature. An appraisal of a sample of a research study can be seen in Box 6.3.

Box 6.3   Critical Appraisal of a Research Study

Surveying the hidden attitudes of hospital nurses towards poverty (Wittenauer et al., 2015: 2186)

'We administered cross-sectional surveys to registered nurses with direct care responsibilities in a small community hospital located in a Midwestern state in the USA that serves a blend of rural and urban areas. The hospital employs about 400 full and part-time registered nurses in both direct and nondirect care positions.

Sample and procedures

After Institutional Review Board (IRB) approval, the study was announced through committees and councils representing nursing shared governance... Three-hundred and twenty-one surveys were distributed over a two-week period to nurses working with adults. Specifically, surveys were distributed via mailboxes to those working on in-patient hospital units (e.g. medical-surgical, critical care) and surgery, post-anaesthesia care and cardiology areas. Surveys included a consent letter that explained the study but did not require signing and returning. Surveys were returned anonymously via envelopes to closed boxes in a secure location on each unit. As an incentive for participation, nurses could choose to enter a lottery

(Continued)

(Continued)

to win one of two $25 gas gift cards. The response rate was 36 per cent (n = 117), a rate comparable to other hospital wide nurse studies at this same institution.

Instrument

Attitudes in this study were measured using the short form of the ATP scale developed by Yun and Weaver (2010). The ATP short form consists of 21 questions that assess three components of attitudes towards poverty, including personal deficiency (e.g. "Poor people are different from the rest of society"), stigma (e.g. "There is a lot of fraud among welfare recipients"), and structural perspective (e.g. "People are poor due to circumstances beyond their control"). The ATP short form instructs participants to respond to the items on a scale from 1–5, where 1 equals "strongly disagree" and 5 equals "strongly agree"....'

(Wittenauer et al., 2015: 2186)

Critical Appraisal

In Wittenauer et al.'s (2015) study the researchers do not identify a specific sampling method, although the participants appear to have been selected using consecutive sampling. Polit and Beck (2014) describe consecutive sampling as a non-probability sampling method in which all the available individuals who meet the inclusion criteria over a specific time frame are included in the study. While the sample invited to participate in this study is large, consisting of approximately 80 per cent of the accessible population, the participation rate was only 36 per cent which increases the risk of response bias (Polit and Beck, 2014). The participants in this study were all drawn from one community hospital. Grove et al. (2013) state that homogeneity can have the effect of limiting the results to the subjects in the study. Thus overall the findings of this study need to be read with caution if attempting to generalise the results.

There is no such thing as the perfect study, so all studies will have limitations. What is expected is that researchers recognise and acknowledge the limitations within their own work. Wittenauer et al. (2015) acknowledge these limitations when discussing their findings (Box 6.4).

Box 6.4   Limitations as Recognised by the Authors

Surveying the hidden attitudes of hospital nurses towards poverty (Wittenauer et al., 2015: 2188)

Discussion

'… Our findings may underestimate the degree of negative attitudes towards people who are poor for two reasons: since (1) social desirability is often a problem in attitude research (2) and implicit biases may be even stronger than explicit biases, as shown by research investigating implicit bias towards racial groups (Nosek et al., 2011)… Another limitation is the small homogenous group of nurses and the response rate. Our response rate (36%) was comparable to Kramer et al. (2009) who recommend a 40% response rate when studying the quality of nurse work environments in hospital clinical units…' (Wittenauer et al., 2015: 2188)

Recommendations for Future Studies

Having critically appraised a study and presented the implications of its strengths and limitations, the next step is to consider how these strengths might be enhanced and any limitations overcome. The author may have made suggestions for future studies or identified gaps in the literature. In the case of Wittenauer et al. (2015) they suggest 'Research with a larger, more diverse population of nurses is needed. Would an urban sample, for example, yield different findings?' (Wittenauer et al., 2015: 2189). Recommendations for future research or gaps in the literature may help the reviewer develop a research question especially where the review is part of a research study.

Overall Evaluation of the Study

Having critically appraised the study, and considered the implications that any strengths or weakness may have on the outcomes of the study, the next step is to evaluate the study. This is about determining if this study was undertaken in a sufficiently robust and trustworthy manner, and if its outcomes are significant enough to have an impact on professional knowledge and practice. While no single study should ever change practice, a study that is methodically robust can stimulate debate and ultimately influence knowledge and practice.

Critically Appraising Systematic Reviews

A systematic review is different to the conventional narrative literature review in that it is considered to be scientific research in its own right (Clarke, 2006). Similar to the traditional review of the literature, it identifies and selects research studies related to a topic of interest. However, it is the systematic manner in which studies are selected and managed that differentiates it from a narrative review. Systematic reviews are expected to be transparent and clearly describe, ideally in advance, the way in which studies will be searched, selected and evaluated (Bettany-Saltikov, 2012). Through the inclusion of all the studies related to a specific topic, the risk of bias is reduced as studies with divergent views are also presented. Both published and unpublished works should be included within a systematic review, as studies that may be important may not have been accepted for publication because their results were not deemed as statistically significant or the outcome was regarded as unfavourable. Reviewers in a systematic review are expected to systematically search for all studies, published and unpublished, in order to present the most accurate and unbiased overview of the research

(Bettany-Saltikov, 2012). Depending on the type of data gathered, the reviewer in a systematic review may present quantitative evidence as a narrative integration if statistical tests are inappropriate, or may statistically integrate the evidence using meta-analysis techniques (Polit and Beck, 2012). Qualitative data may be integrated using meta-synthesis (Polit and Beck, 2012). Systematic reviews are discussed in more detail in Chapter 3.

Questions Related to Integrity in Systematic Reviews

Instruments for appraising systematic reviews are now appearing more commonly in textbooks and journals. The principles that underpin these instruments are similar. Factors that can influence the robustness of a systematic review are presented in Table 6.4.

Table 6.4   Factors that Affect the Robustness of a Systematic Review

Factors that Influence the Robustness of a Systematic Review	
Research problem and research question	The research problem and question should be clearly identified. Any terminology, concepts or phenomena identified should be clearly defined by the reviewers. The implications of this review for the profession should be identified.
Search strategy and study screening	The search strategy used should be clearly identified. The databases and keywords that were used should be identified, as should the use of Boolean operators and combinations of keywords. The inclusion and exclusion criteria that were applied to the studies should be clearly stated and appropriately applied in a fair and consistent manner. An attempt should have been made to secure missing data from the original authors rather than simply excluding a study. Any studies that were excluded should be identified along with a rationale for the exclusion.
Quality appraisal	The reviewers should have appraised the quality of the studies selected. In doing so they may have used a recognised instrument or developed their own. The appraisal instrument should be appropriate for the task. It is preferable if at least two reviewers appraise the studies independently and compare results.
Combining and summarising the data	The reviewers should have clearly identified how the evidence gathered would be combined and summarised. The quality of the studies should be suitable for the analysis they used. **Meta-analysis:** The effects of heterogeneity should have been discussed. The reviewer should offer a rationale for the selection of a fixed or random effects model. **Meta-synthesis:** The reviewers should have discussed how the data was managed. There should have been sufficient data presented to support the reviewers' findings.
Conclusions	There should be a sufficient quantity of robust studies to adequately support the conclusion drawn. The reviewers should have identified and discussed the limitations of their review and the overall strength of the outcome. The reviewers should have identified the implications for clinical practice and made recommendations for further research.
References	All the studies and other works referred to in the review should be correctly referenced.

Research Problem and Research Question

In a systematic review the research problem is identified, and the research question is posed at the outset of the review. These should both be clearly stated so as to leave no ambiguity as to what is being investigated. Any terms or concepts that are used to describe or discuss the problem or question should be defined to further assist the reader in this regard. The reviewers should also identify why this review is being undertaken and why it is important to the profession.

Search Strategy and Study Screening

Systematic reviewers are expected to undertake an exhaustive, meticulous review of the literature, and how this is accomplished can offer a good insight into the robustness of the review. The reviewers should use as many alternative search strategies as possible when undertaking the search to ensure inclusivity. The databases and other data sources that were accessed should be clearly identified for the reader, as should the keywords and keyword combinations that were used. Strategies to access the grey literature should also be identified.

The inclusion and exclusion criteria need to be clearly identified at the beginning of the review and the reviewers should offer sound rationales for these criteria. Reasons for exclusion can include non-conformity with the selected study design or the age of a study. However, caution needs to be taken so that exclusion criteria do not exclude a seminal study simply because it is, for example, in a different language. Missing data should not be an exclusion criterion without the reviewers first attempting to locate this information.

Quality Appraisal

There are instruments available to assess the quality of studies for a systematic review, for example the CASP checklist for systematic reviews (CASP, 2013). However, Clarke (2006) recommends that reviewers should identify what they consider the key components of quality for their review and develop their own guidelines, and then evaluate and describe each study on that basis. Ideally, two or more reviewers should independently appraise the studies, using the agreed guidelines. The higher the degree of inter-rater agreement, the more reliable the appraisal is deemed to be (Whittaker and Williamson, 2011).

Combining and Summarising the Data

The reviewers need to clearly state how they plan to combine and present the data. The data may be presented using narrative integration (synthesis), meta-analysis or meta-synthesis (Polit and Beck, 2014). Narrative integration, which involves discussing the data and the studies rather than undertaking statistical analysis, is usually used when there are multiple disparities (heterogeneity) between the studies that preclude meta-analysis (Whittaker and Williamson, 2011). The rationale for using this approach should be clearly stated by the reviewers (Polit and Beck, 2014). In meta-analysis the general rule is that studies should be individually analysed and then the individual statistical results combined. Heterogeneity can be managed through using either a fixed or random effects model (see Chapter 7 for additional detail of these models). Both models have their strengths and limitations (Whittaker and Williamson, 2011), so a clear rationale for selecting either should be given.

Meta-synthesis is used to combine the data in qualitative systematic reviews. The results are either described or, more frequently, interpreted as the reviewers integrate and seek to identify new insights into, and greater understanding of, the phenomenon. In doing so the reviewers should identify how they compared and interpreted the data. Any interpretations made should also be clearly supported by the data. In some situations systematic reviews use a mixed methodology approach using both qualitative and quantitative studies. Analysis in such situations is possible but is more complex (Whittaker and Williamson, 2011).

Conclusions

The reviewers should identify and discuss their conclusions and any inconsistencies between studies in the review. They should also discuss the strengths and limitations of their review, for instance how closely they adhered to the criteria they set for screening and selecting studies. All studies have limitations, and studies in which the reviewers are aware of and identify their own weaknesses are more likely to be trustworthy. As with any research study, systematic reviews, in adding to the body of knowledge, often discover other areas that warrant further study or review, and the authors should identify these to the reader.

References

As in all studies, all included works should be correctly referenced for the benefit of the reader.

Critically Appraising Non-research Literature

While the majority of the literature presented and appraised within a review will be from research studies or systematic reviews, some supporting information may come from the theoretical, philosophical, practice or policy literature. This supporting information should also be critically appraised. A useful instrument for analysing practice and policy literature is the Appraisal of Guidelines for Research and Evaluation II (AGREE II) available at www.agreetrust.org.

Another helpful tool for critically analysing non-research literature is presented by Hek and Langton (2000). This instrument focuses on the perceived accuracy, trustworthiness and quality of the paper being reviewed. The use of this tool does require a reasonable knowledge of the subject area. Hek and Langton (2000: 51) acknowledge that the appraisal in their review was performed by 'subject knowledgeable' reviewers. An adaptation of Hek and Langton's (2000) instrument is displayed in Table 6.5.

Table 6.5 Appraising Non-research Literature

Factors that Influence the Robustness of Non-research Literature	
Purpose and relevance	The aim of this article should be clearly identified and should be congruent with the purpose of the review.
Credibility	The article should be presented in a clear and organised manner. It should be easy to read and understand, and grammatically correct. It should avoid excessive use of jargon and should appear credible at first glance.
Peer review	Preferably the article should have been published in a peer-reviewed journal.
Supporting evidence	The author ideally should have experience and/or qualifications that suggest a knowledge or expertise in this particular field of enquiry.
Accuracy and reliability	The information presented in the article should be accurate and congruous with the literature and what is known about the phenomenon. What the author suggests should be supported by what is known of the phenomenon.

Source: Adapted from Hek and Langton (2000)

Summary

The purpose of this chapter was to introduce the novice reviewer to the concept of critically appraising the literature. A literature review can consist of a large number of studies, and these need to be presented in an organised manner for the benefit of the reader. Studies with findings reflecting similar issues are thus identified and grouped together under themes so that the reader can consider the different perspectives and implications.

For the reader to make an informed judgement on the implications of a study, it needs to be presented in such a way that they can recognise how robust the findings of that study are. The reviewer has to be able to present the reader with both the findings and the critical appraisal of the study in a succinct but also in an objective manner. As a result it is not usually possible to present more than one or possibly two of the factors that influence the robustness of a study when critically appraising it. In critically appraising a study the reviewer can remain objective by using research texts or articles to support the appraisal. It is also important to remember that strengths are as important as limitations, and only seeking the latter could be regarded as criticising someone's work rather than evaluating it.

The next step after appraisal is synthesis – that is, the combining of data from a number of studies to create new insights or perspectives. Combining the literature is the focus of the next chapter.

❝ Key Points ❞

- Reading and critically appraising literature should go hand in hand.
- Appraisal is about identifying the strengths and/or limitations of a study or report; it is not about criticising the authors or their work.
- Appraisal should be undertaken in an objective manner and supported by appropriate texts and literature.
- There are a variety of different instruments available to help you appraise the different types of studies and literature.

COMBINING (SYNTHESISING) THE RESULTS OF THE ANALYSIS

❝ Learning Outcomes ❞

Having read this chapter you should be able to:

- explain how to summarise and present the findings of your analysis of the literature;
- describe the steps involved in combining (synthesising) the findings of your analysis of the literature;
- explain the main types of synthesis that can be undertaken;
- describe how an appropriate method of synthesis is chosen.

Introduction

Whatever type of literature review you are undertaking, at this point in the process you will have identified and collected your literature, undertaken an analysis (quality assessment) of that literature and identified and extracted appropriate data. The next step is to combine or pool the results, and this chapter explores the various means by which this might be done. As with many other parts of undertaking a literature review, how you will go about this is dictated by the type of review you are undertaking and the type of data (literature sources) you have included. The chapter focuses firstly on what is described as thematic analysis. This is because most undergraduates undertaking a literature review as a stand-alone academic assignment or as a thesis chapter undertake narrative reviews with which thematic analysis is most commonly associated. However, the chapter outlines other methods of combining data often used in systematic reviews so that you have an awareness and understanding of them and where and in what situations they are used.

Presenting and Summarising Results

Regardless of the type of literature review that is being conducted, the first step of the synthesis is to present your findings. This should include a detailed presentation of your search strategy, the results of your search, the process by which literature was included or excluded and a collation of information about each study.

All contemporary literature reviews require a detailed presentation of the search strategy you conducted. This can be presented in text or tabular form, although the latter aids clarity and readability. Aspects that might be included are: the databases searched, time and language delimiters, search terms with Boolean operators, the date the search was conducted, the number of hits, the number judged to be irrelevant and discarded following review of the title, and the number retained for full review (see Table 7.1).

Table 7.1   Example of Tabulation of Online Database Search

	Database and Time Limits	Language	Search Date	Search Terms	No. of Hits	No. Discarded (unrelated title)	No. Reviewed (title and abstract)	No. Reviewed (full text)
Online Databases	PubMed (Unlimited)	English	01.09.12	'pancreatitis'	425	344	81	24
				'pain'				
				'assessment' 'management'				
				'analgesia'				
	CINAHL (1990-present)	English	10.09.12	'pancreatitis'	209	160	49	19
				'pain'				
				'assessment' 'management'				
				'analgesia'				

Most contemporary literature reviews do not confine themselves to searching online databases, and other sources such as manual searches, textbooks, catalogues, grey literature and dictionaries (see Chapter 4) are valuable. The results of these searches should be presented also.

In systematic reviews it is a requirement that a collation of information about each study included in the review is presented. Increasingly, this standard is being applied to narrative reviews in order to counter criticisms about them being less systematic and explicit than other approaches (Mays et al., 2005). As a result, many now present tabular summaries (summary tables) of the research studies included in their review. However, because narrative reviews are often concerned with the current state of knowledge on a topic, literature other than primary studies (systematic reviews, literature reviews and non-research literature such as policy reports, theo-retical/philosophical papers) will be included also as they can be important for contextualising or situating the problem or focus of the review. Therefore, some narrative reviews may also present tables for these types of publications.

As part of the processes of undertaking a quality assessment of the included litera-ture and extraction of the findings you will probably have developed or used published templates to record the appraisal and document the detail of each publi-cation. It is these individual summaries that will now form the basis of your overall summary. If you have used a recognised scoring system for quality appraisal you are likely to have created an individual record for each study. For the extraction of find-ings you should have at least documented the source and full reference, the title of the article, the author, the purpose and methodology used in a research study and the findings and outcomes (see Tables 7.2 and 7.3).

How you decide on what should be included in your summary table is largely dependent on the type of literature you are presenting – that is, research or non-research.

Table 7.2   Summary Table – Example 1

Reference	Aim	Methods	Findings
Staggers and Blaz (2013)	To make recommendations for change processes involving the computerisation of handovers on medical and surgical units	Integrative literature review	1. Verbal handovers have important functions other than information transfer and need to be retained 2. Handover should be tailored to meet the contextual needs of nurses. Further research is required 3. A preference for bedside handovers was not supported
Ahmed et al. (2012)	To investigate the ability to improve compliance and quality of clinical handover through a standardised and structured template	Pre and post survey	1. Recommended a structured and standardised handover tool 2. Audit of handover practice demonstrated improvement after training had occurred
Bost et al. (2012)	To explore clinical handover between ambulance and ED staff and identification of strategies that improve information transfer	Ethnographic study that included participant observation, conversational interviews, examination of handover tools	1. Quality of handover related to personal expectations; prior experience; workload; working relationships 2. Issues included: lack of active listening; access to written information

Source: Anderson et al. (2014)

Table 7.3 Summary Table – Example 2

Reference and Country of Study	Research Design and Methods	Study Aims and Objectives	Definition of Carer Provided	Participants and Setting	Main Findings Relevant to the Review
Pinto et al. (2007) Brazil	Cross-sectional descriptive study Assessment tools: medical outcome survey – short form (SF-36) Caregiver Burden Scale	To determine the effect of COPD on the quality of life of carers	Yes – a person who provides most of the care required by the patient during the course of the disease and is most intimately aware of the patient's needs	42 patients who had COPD and their caregivers visiting a pulmonary outpatient department	Regression analysis showed caregiver/patient relationship quality, SF-36 caregiver mental component summary and SF-36 patient physical component summary are important predictors of caregiver burden
Seamark et al. (2004) UK	Semi-structured interviews analysed using interpretative phenomenological analysis	To explore the experiences of patients with severe COPD	Not provided	Sample of nine men and one woman with COPD and their carers	Loss of personal liberty and dignity; distress at seeing breathlessness; adaptive strategies to cope with the disease; appreciation of continuity of care and reassurance received from healthcare professionals

Source: Grant et al. (2012)

Other factors that you will need to consider are whether or not you are following a strict protocol, as in a systematic review, or if you are preparing a review for publication where reporting guidelines such as the Preferred Reporting Items for Systematic Reviews and Meta-Analyses (PRISMA) are being used (Moher et al., 2009).

In Chapter 3 on systematic reviews, two templates based on PICO and PEO for recording information were presented. However, your literature may not easily fit within these types of templates. Alternative examples of tabular summaries for primary (research) studies are outlined in Tables 7.2 and 7.3. The first, taken from Anderson et al. (2014) is an integrative review (see Chapter 2) of literature that supports implementing bedside clinical handover in nursing practice and identifies key issues associated with its poor implementation. The tabular summary presented in the publication identifies both research and non-research literature that was included in the review.

The literature review outlined in Table 7.3 was a narrative review of the impact of caring for those with chronic obstructive pulmonary disease (COPD) on carers' psychological well-being and consisted of 20 studies (13 quantitative, seven qualitative).

As can be seen from these examples, there are variations in the focus and detail provided. Whilst this may be due, in part, to publishing restrictions, it is evident that collating data in this way enhances the rigour of the review primarily because it enables the reader to discern the relationship between the reviewer's interpretation and the literature upon which it was based. It is recommended, however, that when you are preparing such a table for an academic assignment, as opposed to a journal publication, additional details are useful, such as the full reference and source.

When preparing a summary table for secondary sources such as systematic reviews, your template will have different headings from those used for primary research. Drawing on the evaluation tool presented in Chapter 6, Table 7.4 offers an example of the headings that could be used in a summary table of systematic reviews. An example of an alternative, based on the AMSTAR (assessment of multiple systematic reviews) instrument (Shea et al., 2007), is presented in Table 7.5. The objective of this review of systematic reviews was to identify effective training strategies for teaching communication skills to qualified physicians. Twelve systematic reviews on communication skills training programmes were included.

Table 7.4   Example 1 of Summary Table for Systematic Reviews

Reference	Research Question/ Purpose	Search Strategy, Inclusion/ Exclusion Criteria	Study Selection	Quality Assessment	Data Synthesis	Findings/ Results

Deciding if and how to present non-research literature can be complex because it can vary considerably. For example, if you were undertaking a literature review about social support in persons with chronic obstructive pulmonary disease (COPD), you are likely to have sourced literature related to theories of social support and you may also have accessed government reports, health policies and/or practice guidelines related to the care of those with COPD. While it is important that you do not assume that such publications are valid and they should be appraised in terms of their credibility and evidence, it may be that they will not ultimately be presented in a summary table. In fact many published reviews do not include summary tables for this type of literature.

Table 7.5 Example 2 of Summary Table for Systematic Reviews

Review	Type of Review	No. of studies	Quality of Studies Included	Type of Studies Included	Target Population	Patient Groups	Control Groups	Type of Outcome	Theoretical Background	Conclusions
Lane and Rollnick (2007)	Review	25	Not reported	RCTs	HCPs (Health Care Practitioners)	Sim patient	No training	Behavioural observation	Interactive training strategies	Outcomes were better in programmes that included skills practice than in purely didactic programmes. No significant differences were found between simulated patients and role play.
Fellowes et al. (2004)	Review	3	All studies met the criteria	RCTs	Specialists (oncology)	Real patients	No training	Objective assessments of patients' and nurses' behaviour with validated coding strategies	Lipkin model	Two programmes were effective; one was unclear.

Source: Berkhof et al. (2011)

Depending on the nature of your review, you may choose to present additional information in tabular or diagrammatic representations that aid understanding or enhance the clarity of the review. For example, you may want to extract details such as sample sizes, types of interventions or any scoring measures that were used, such as pain scales and quality of life measures (Table 7.6).

Table 7.6 Example of Additional Information that May be Presented

Reference	Number of Participants	Male	Female	Age Range
Taylor (1999)	52	30	22	18–64
Brown (2004)	112	45	67	25–70
Johnson (2010)	86	52	34	22–60

Once you have completed the presentation and summary of your results, how you progress to the next stage depends on the type of data that you have. For example, your review may contain a mixture of literature, as outlined above, or it may be confined to research studies. If it is the latter these can either be similar in design (for example, RCTs) or a mixture of designs (qualitative and quantitative data). Therefore, the most fundamental factor in what you do with your data is heterogeneity (difference), either at the level of the type of literature you have or at the level of the types of studies that are included.

Methods of Synthesis

A large number of methods of synthesis have emerged, some of which were referred to in Chapter 3. Many of these methods have been developed to manage the synthesis of particular types of data and can be crudely divided into those that address qualitative studies, quantitative studies, mixed research or mixed literature. The most prominent of these are outlined in Table 7.7, although this is not a finite or all-encompassing list. Whilst some of these are addressed later in the chapter, in order to enable you to become familiar with them, the main focus is on what is known as thematic analysis since this is the approach you are most likely to use when undertaking a narrative literature review.

Table 7.7 Methods for Synthesising Data

Synthesising mixed literature	Thematic analysis, narrative synthesis
Synthesising quantitative studies	Meta-analysis, narrative synthesis
Synthesising qualitative studies (meta-synthesis)	Meta-ethnography, meta-study, meta-narrative, qualitative meta-summary, thematic synthesis, critical interpretive synthesis and grounded theory

Thematic Analysis

As outlined earlier, thematic analysis is the most common method for summarising and synthesising findings in a narrative review, although it is considered more basic and less rigorous than other strategies. While there is always a level of interpretation of the findings from your included literature, the focus of thematic analysis is often on providing a summary rather than new insights or knowledge.

The reviewer identifies and brings together the main, recurring or most important themes in a body of literature (Mays et al., 2005). However, in many of the literature reviews presented in academic assignments or in published narrative reviews, one of the things that is rarely clear is how the reviewer arrived at the said themes. To some extent, this impacts on the overall rigour of the review. Outlined below is a process that is not unlike data analysis in qualitative research, which enhances and strengthens the integrity of your review.

As indicated above and as its name suggests, the overall aim of a thematic analysis is to identify themes from the literature. Therefore, it is important that analysis is undertaken in such a way that it is evident that the final themes have emerged clearly from the data (literature). In order to ensure this, the first step should be to engage in coding. Essentially, a code is a symbol or abbreviation used to classify words or phrases in the data. Simply put, a code labels and identifies the point being made in a particular piece of data. What constitutes data, and therefore what will be coded, will differ depending on the type of literature you have. For example, if you are coding a research study then your focus should be on the findings section. If you are coding non-research literature then the discussion section of the paper should be your focus. Although this may seem laborious, you should examine and code the findings or discussion section of each piece of literature. These initial codes may alter as the process progresses and as you become more familiar with and more proficient at identifying appropriate codes.

Once all the relevant sections have been coded, the next step is to develop themes, which involves grouping the codes. It is advisable to begin this process by grouping codes that are the same or very similar as they are likely to be the easiest to manage. Grouping of codes that are not obviously similar presents more of a challenge and therefore takes longer. What is important here is that you keep the original articles to hand to ensure that you are remaining faithful to the findings.

You then need to label or give a name to the theme(s). The theme name should be a reflection of the codes contained therein. However, naming the theme at this stage does not mean you cannot change the name at a later stage. This process should proceed until all codes are assigned to a theme. Table 7.8 provides an example of a process of analysis that included 49 qualitative reports and six concept analyses in a meta-synthesis of caring in nursing (Finfgeld-Connett, 2008). Although different terms were used – that is, sub-categories and categories – the principles of thematic analysis remain the same.

At the end of the process, you will have findings (codes and themes) that support each other but it is important to note that you are likely also to have some that are contradictory. These similarities or differences require further scrutiny,

Table 7.8 Example of Analysis in a Meta-synthesis of Caring in Nursing

Codes	Sub-categories	Categories
Skills	Nursing knowledge and skills (competence)	Professional maturity
Decision-making	Professional maturity	
Interpersonal skills		
Competence		
Knowledge base		
Experience		
Ability to cope		
Self-confidence		

Source: Finfgeld-Connett (2008)

and it is at this point that you return to your critical analyses to try to account for them. For example, the studies in your review are likely to have been conducted in different contexts or cultures, used varying research designs and/or had different sample sizes or composition. Examining these factors enables you to draw inferences about why results are different. It also offers you the basis for presenting an analytical rather than a descriptive account of the literature in your review because you will be able to discuss the strength of the evidence that supports any particular argument. There may also be contradictions between the findings of research studies and, for example, experts in the field. Whilst this is not unusual, you will be required to evaluate the evidence and draw conclusions as to the strength of each.

Aveyard (2014) suggests that in some situations you may not be able to account for differences in the results of studies or there may not be any real consensus. To a large degree, this 'finding' is as significant as if the literature achieved a consensus because it may point to a need for further study in the area. However, it may also mean that you are not able to provide an answer to your original review question. Documenting this process as you are undertaking it is a good idea and also helps you prepare for the writing of your review. The themes you have developed constitute your findings and will structure your subsequent discussion (see Chapter 8).

Narrative Synthesis

A short discussion of narrative synthesis is included here because of the potential for confusing it with the thematic analysis used in a narrative or traditional literature review. A narrative synthesis is similar to a thematic analysis in that it uses a narrative (words) as opposed to a statistical (numbers) approach to combine or pool findings from the literature. Where it differs is in its level of synthesis in that it attempts to generate 'new' knowledge or insights (Mays et al., 2005) by encompassing an analysis of the relationships within and between studies as well as providing an assessment of the strength of the evidence (CRD, 2009).

Popay et al. (2006) suggest that narrative synthesis can be used in three ways: before undertaking a statistical analysis (meta-analysis); instead of undertaking a statistical analysis where the studies are too different to allow for meta-analysis; and where the review questions include diverse research designs and research/non-research literature. To date, however, its use has been associated primarily with the synthesis of multiple studies in systematic reviews.

As part of a project for the Economic and Social Research Council (ESRC) Methods Programme, Popay et al. (2006) developed a framework for narrative synthesis (Box 7.1) that focuses largely on the effects of interventions and the factors that influence how these are implemented. However, the authors argue that the process is flexible and iterative (non-linear) and has the potential to be applied to a range of literature. The framework comprises four main elements (Box 7.1) within which they suggest 19 tools and techniques that can be used for undertaking a narrative synthesis. The reviewer chooses whichever tools or techniques are most appropriate for the data that is being handled. For example, when exploring relationships within and across qualitative studies techniques such as conceptual mapping and qualitative case descriptions could be applied, while moderator variables and subgroup analysis might be used for the findings of quantitative studies (Popay et al., 2006). Essentially, what this framework does is provide a systematic means of organising, describing and interpreting study findings for the purpose of explanation. While some of the tools and techniques are complex and beyond what would be expected for an academic assignment or literature review as part of a dissertation, there is potential to adapt or use some of them to enhance the transparency and credibility of your review process. The authors of the framework have published two examples of how its elements can be applied (Arai et al., 2009; Rodgers et al., 2009).

Box 7.1   The Four Main Elements of Narrative Synthesis (Adapted from Popay et al., 2006)

- Developing a theory of how the intervention works, why and for whom.
- Developing a preliminary synthesis:

  o   tabulations;
  o   groupings and clusters;
  o   textual descriptions;
  o   translating data;
  o   transforming data: constructing a common rubric;
  o   vote counting as a descriptive tool.

- Exploring relationships within and across studies:

  - conceptual triangulation;
  - reciprocal/refutational translation;
  - investigator and methodological triangulation;
  - moderator variables and subgroup analyses;
  - idea webbing/conceptual mapping;
  - qualitative case descriptions;
  - visual representation of relationship between study characteristics and results.

- Assessing if the synthesis is robust:

  - use of validity assessment;
  - best evidence synthesis;
  - checking the synthesis with authors of primary studies;
  - reflecting critically on the synthesis process.

Meta-analysis

As outlined in Chapter 3, meta-analysis is a process of statistical analysis of numerical data whereby the results from individual studies are pooled and re-analysed as one, bigger data set. In order to undertake a meta-analysis the research designs and methods of the included studies must be reasonably homogeneous (similar), e.g. randomised controlled trials/controlled trials, as must the populations, interventions, comparisons and outcomes (Booth et al., 2012). The outcome of a meta-analysis tells us about the strength of the evidence to support the effectiveness of an intervention, something which may not be evident from single studies. In addition, meta-analyses can also resolve controversy where there have been conflicting results or claims arising from them (CRD, 2009; Higgins and Green, 2011). However, caution must also be exercised as meta-analyses have the potential to be misleading. This may be where studies have biases or errors that render them of poor quality, and in the act of combining them they are given a level of credibility they should not have. Therefore, the review team must carefully consider biases within studies, variations across studies and any reporting biases during the review process (Higgins and Green, 2011).

Most meta-analyses are undertaken in two stages, the first being an analysis of the outcome and a calculation of summary statistics for each included study. In the second stage, the results of each study are pooled to give an overall summary effect (CRD, 2009). The calculated result is referred to as a 'single summary statistic' or 'effect measure' (Booth et al., 2010: 294). Simply stated, the effect measure is the observed relationship between an intervention and an outcome. Standard effect measures include: 'odds ratio', 'relative risk', 'risk difference', 'numbers needed to treat', 'standardised mean difference' and 'weighted mean difference' (Booth et al., 2010: 294). Odds ratio and relative risk are the most commonly used measures but they can only be used with dichotomous (binary) outcome data. Data are referred to as dichotomous or binary data when for every subject or participant there can only be one of two outcomes – for example, sick/well, pregnant/not pregnant. Brief definitions of odds ratio and relative risk are given in Box 7.2.

Box 7.2 Definitions of Effect Measures – Binary Data

Odds Ratio

The odds ratio is a relative measure of risk that assesses how likely it is that someone who is exposed to the factor being studied, e.g. smoking, will develop the named outcome (e.g. lung cancer) compared to someone who is not exposed. An odds ratio of 1 indicates no difference between the groups being compared.

Relative Risk

Relative risk compares different risk levels. Therefore, in a study where there is an intervention and a control group, the relative risk is the proportion of participants who experience an event in both groups. A relative risk of 1 indicates no difference between the groups being compared.

(Higgins and Green, 2011; Booth et al., 2010)

Effect measures for continuous data include the 'mean difference' (weighted mean difference) and the 'standardised mean difference' (Box 7.3). Continuous data is that which can have an infinite number of possible values. Weight, area and volume are true examples of continuous data but in meta-analysis the above effect measures are also applied to data such as that found in measurement scales (Higgins and Green, 2011).

Box 7.3 Definition of Effect Measures – Continuous Data

Mean Difference (Weighted Mean Difference)

The mean difference is a summary statistic that measures the absolute difference between the mean (average) value in two groups. It estimates the amount by which the intervention changes the outcome (has an effect) on average when compared with the control group (who did not receive the intervention).

Standardised Mean Difference

The standardised mean difference is a summary statistic that signifies the extent of the effect of the intervention relative to the variability (Standard Deviation) observed in an individual study. It is used when studies have measured the same outcome but have not done so in the same way. For example two studies could measure quality of life but may not have used the same measurement scale. This statistic enables the results of individual studies to be standardised to a uniform scale before being combined.

Note: As the name suggests summary statistics provide concise information about a set of observations (data) in a study. The most commonly used summary statistics include mean, mode, median, standard deviation, range. For more information on this, please see Chapter 10 on 'Gaining insight into data analysis' in Cronin et al. (2015).

As stated above, in the second stage of a meta-analysis the statistics from each individual study are 'pooled' to give an overall summary estimate (CRD, 2009). This is generally done by weighting each study estimate using what are known either as 'fixed-effect' or 'random-effect' models (Whiting, 2009). The reason for weighting the contribution of each study is that not all studies are the same in terms of how similar and precise they are and how much information they present. It is not possible therefore to simply take the effect size in each study and calculate the overall mean. What the fixed-effect or random-effect models offer is a way of determining how studies are weighted. However, because these models operate under different assumptions, the manner in which studies are weighted differs. For example, the fixed-effect model assumes one effect size and it only assigns weight by virtue of the amount of information contained within each study. Thus, studies that are larger and contain more information are given more weight than smaller studies. Conversely, and as its name suggests, the random-effect model does not assume one effect size but argues that the effect can vary across studies. This can be due to factors such as the population in the study, the manner in which the intervention was implemented or even the reliability of the methodology for measuring the effect. Therefore, in a random-effect model the weighting of studies is more balanced between larger and smaller studies.

Results from a meta-analysis are commonly presented using what is known as a forest plot (Figure 7.1). A forest plot presents the results of each study

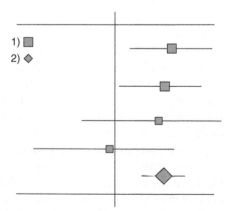

Figure 7.1   Example of a Forest Plot

(represented by a horizontal line and a box) within a review as well as the combined result of the meta-analysis (represented by a horizontal line and a diamond shape). An important part of a forest plot is that it can display what is known as the confidence interval. The confidence interval, represented by the width of the horizontal line, is the range in which we are reasonably confident that the true effect lies. The wider the confidence interval the greater the uncertainty about the effect size and therefore the less knowledge that is available to make a decision about the usefulness of the intervention. The vertical line represents 'no effect', which means that there is no difference or benefit to the intervention group when compared to the control group. The overall meta-analysis result is often represented as a diamond-shape.

This brief introduction to strategies used in meta-analysis highlights the complexity of the endeavour, and any attempt at such an undertaking will, almost certainly, require the assistance of a statistician. There are also software packages that are available to help with process, notably Review Manager (RevMan) which is used for preparing and maintaining Cochrane Reviews.

Meta-synthesis

Chapter 3 on systematic reviews introduced meta-synthesis as a term that encompasses the various methods that have been developed to address the pooling of findings from qualitative research. As with meta-analysis, developments in meta-synthesis can be associated with the recognition that the results of single studies may offer little in terms of having an impact on clinical practice and/or healthcare policy or research. According to Ring et al. (2010) in an era where healthcare strategy is focused on developing person-centred services, combining the results of findings from qualitative research studies facilitates knowledge accumulation of the needs and experiences of the patient or service user.

Methods of meta-synthesis are concerned for the most part with interpretation, whereas the focus in a meta-analysis is aggregation (adding together). Although the process by which this is done varies, most involve deconstruction (or breaking down) of the research findings from individual studies, and examination of the findings to discern the key features, following which they are combined in a transformed whole or new interpretation (Flemming, 2007; Finfgeld-Connett, 2010). Whilst numerous methods for synthesising qualitative research findings have emerged, this section will introduce meta-ethnography, meta-study and qualitative meta-summary as three distinct approaches.

Meta-ethnography (Noblit and Hare, 1988) is included because it is the most commonly cited and possibly leading method for synthesising qualitative healthcare research. Meta-study (Paterson et al., 2001) is a multi-faceted approach that has three analytic phases, which differentiates it from other methods. Both of these methods are oriented towards data synthesis and interpretation (Finfgeld-Connett, 2010). Qualitative meta-summary is an approach that looks to aggregate qualitative findings for the purpose of determining the frequency of each finding (Sandelowski and Barroso, 2007). Strictly speaking, because of its emphasis on aggregation and not interpretation it could be argued that it is not a form of meta-synthesis. Nonetheless, it is included here because it is a novel approach that was developed originally to address qualitative findings.

Meta-ethnography

Meta-ethnography was first proposed by Noblit and Hare (1988) in the field of education as an alternative to meta-analysis and has emerged as the leading method for synthesis of qualitative research (Ring et al., 2010). Noblit and Hare (1988) focused originally on studies that they described as ethnographic, although the contemporary use of the term has been extended to include a range of qualitative studies. The main purpose of a meta-ethnography is to create what is described as a new or third-order interpretation. First-order concepts are those identified by the participants in the original studies while second-order concepts are the interpretations made by the authors of these studies. Therefore, meta-ethnography is a synthesis of first- and second-order concepts to construct a new interpretation or theory about the phenomenon under study (Atkins et al., 2008). Whilst Noblit and Hare developed a whole method (Box 7.4) the emphasis here is on stages 4, 5 and 6 that are concerned with managing the data after it has been identified and extracted from the included studies.

Box 7.4   Meta-ethnography Method (Adapted from Noblit and Hare, 1988)

1. Getting started (determining the research question).
2. Deciding what is relevant to the initial interest (defining the focus, determining inclusion/exclusion criteria, identifying relevant studies, undertaking quality assessment).
3. Reading the studies.
4. Determining how the studies are related (creating a list of themes, concepts or metaphors, putting them side by side or close together (juxtaposing) and determining how they are related).
5. Translating studies into one another (comparing the concepts/metaphors).
6. Synthesising translations (trying to create a new, higher-order interpretation).
7. Expressing the synthesis (presenting the synthesis).

Before the studies are translated into one another in stage 5, it must first be determined how they are related. Therefore, in stage 4 of the meta-ethnography, the reviewers examine each study and construct a list of themes, concepts or metaphors that form the data for the synthesis. This is the process of deconstructing and decontextualising the study findings so that they can be reconstructed into a new interpretation. Deconstruction can be undertaken in a number of ways that are similar to those used in the analysis of primary qualitative studies. For example, some use a purely inductive process similar to that used in grounded theory where each study is recoded. These new codes are then examined across the studies as part of the synthesis and translation. Others begin with a list of codes already identified and against which they examine each study in isolation before progressing to synthesis. Yet others do little re-analysing of the raw data and instead focus on synthesising and translating the central concepts and metaphors identified by the author of the original study (France et al., 2014). Whatever approach is chosen, the important factor is that it is transparent, justified and in keeping with the overall aim of the review. Once the individual studies are recoded the identified concepts are then placed side by side usually in a grid or table that facilitates comparison and enhances transparency.

As part of analysis and synthesis, Noblit and Hare (1988) suggest three ways in which studies can be related and translated. Reciprocal synthesis involves a search for concepts and metaphors within and across studies that are similar and/or appear repeatedly. Refutational synthesis is a search for findings of studies that refute or are in opposition to each other. This type of synthesis is valuable because it may result in the identification of another category or understanding that had not been identified in the original studies (Walsh and Downe, 2005). The third strategy is known as 'line of argument' (LOA) synthesis where the similarities and dissimilarities are examined and integrated into a new interpretation that most completely represents the emerging concepts or patterns (Noblit and Hare, 1988).

All of these processes are inductive and can use strategies, such as constant comparative analysis that was originally developed for use in grounded theory but which now has wider application as a method of qualitative data analysis. In constant comparative analysis, one piece of data is taken and compared with all other pieces of data that are either similar or different and the outcome is theory or new knowledge. Table 7.9 presents an example of themes, second-order and third-order analyses from a synthesis of identity and coping experiences in chronic fatigue syndrome in which a meta-ethnographic approach was used (Larun and Malterud, 2007).

Table 7.9   Example of Synthesis: Identity and Coping Experiences in Chronic Fatigue Syndrome

Thematic Groups from Original Studies	Second-order Analyses	Third-order Analyses
Symptom experience and consequences for everyday life	An empty battery or a blown fuse; controlled and betrayed by their bodies; bodies that no longer held the capacity for social involvement.	Identity: legitimacy of their illness being questioned; previous sense of identity became more or less invalid.
Illness beliefs and causal attributions	A classical infection striking a fragile immune system; bodily collapse due to stress and overload; definitely not a psychosomatic disorder; weak character.	Strategies for coping: knowing more about the condition; keeping a distance to protect oneself; learning to know more about their limits.
Doctor–patient interaction: 'Are you really sick?'	Negotiated the nature of the disorder; confrontations with their doctors when biomedical markers were absent; guilt, blame, shame game.	
	Challenges when a professional authority should be managed under considerable scientific uncertainty.	
	The significance of getting a diagnosis.	

Source: Larun and Malterud (2007)

Some issues that require clarification have arisen around the process of synthesis in a meta-ethnography. For example, Atkins et al. (2008), in their meta-ethnography of adherence to tuberculosis treatment, identified that there was a lack of guidance in respect of how to relate and translate the concepts/metaphors from each study. Similarly, the process of synthesising translations is not clearly delineated. Decisions around these areas are complex, and considerable expertise in the areas of qualitative research analysis is necessary to undertake such an endeavour. As Campbell et al. (2011) suggest, meta-ethnography should be considered an advanced qualitative research method.

Meta-study

Paterson et al. (2001) developed a meta-synthesis method derived from a general approach developed within sociology and anthropology and termed meta-study (Thorne et al., 2002). Meta-study, as conceived by Paterson et al. (2001), aims to go beyond meta-ethnography because it examines the findings of each study (meta-data analysis), the method by which the study was conducted (meta-method) and the theory or theoretical influences underlying the study (meta-theory). This, they contend, is because research takes place in a social, historical and ideological context that affects how it is undertaken as well as shaping the results. For example, the theoretical perspective the researcher adopts has an influence on the choice of topics, the questions that are posed about those topics, the research designs that are chosen to answer those questions and the manner in which the findings are interpreted. Therefore, Paterson et al. (2001) argue, their method requires an examination of all components of the research process in order to develop a more complete interpretation and understanding of those factors that influenced the conduct and outcome of the research.

Paterson et al. (2001) separate analysis and synthesis and state that the three analytic strategies of meta-data analysis, meta-method and meta-theory must be undertaken before meta-synthesis can occur (Figure 7.2). This approach, they

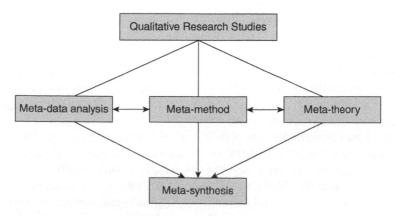

Figure 7.2   Components of Meta-study

Source: Adapted from Paterson et al. (2001)

argue, generates new and more complete understandings of the phenomenon under study (Paterson et al., 2001: 2). See Figure 7.2 for the components of meta-study.

Meta-data analysis is the analysis of the findings of individual studies by means of processing the 'processed data' (Zhao, 1991). Processed data are the results of the analysis undertaken by the researcher. In a primary study, the researcher interprets the raw data to identify key concepts or metaphors. In meta-data analysis, it is these that form the focus of the analysis. Meta-data analysis, then, involves reinterpretation of the actual findings from the original qualitative studies in light of those from other studies (Thorne et al., 2002). The analysis proceeds by critically comparing the central concepts in each study with those in the other studies in the review for the purpose of identifying similarities and differences. Analytic methods similar to those outlined in meta-ethnography can be adopted. For example, in a meta-study of early professional socialisation and career choice in nursing, S.L. Price (2009) adopted thematic analysis as her method of data analysis.

Meta-method is an examination of the methodologies of the studies in the review. Various aspects, such as design choice, sampling, data collection and analysis, are scrutinised to determine the rigour with which the study was conducted, and the process is similar to that of critical appraisal (Barnett-Page and Thomas, 2009). However, there is an additional requirement in meta-method as conceived by Paterson et al. (2001) to determine whether there was congruence between the research question and the methodology chosen to answer it. In other words, did the researcher choose the correct method to answer the question posed? In addition, the meta-synthesist should explore whether the chosen methodology impacted on how the outcomes or findings of the study were conceived (Thorne et al., 2002).

Meta-theory is the examination of the philosophical and theoretical perspectives and assumptions that directed the research studies in order to determine how they might have influenced interpretation of the data. For example, in their meta-study of fatigue in chronic illness, Paterson et al. (2003) identified that most of the studies that used a phenomenological methodology focused on the phenomenon of fatigue rather than fatigue as part of the whole experience of living with a chronic illness. As a result, the findings did not consider the important social, environmental and personal factors that affected how fatigue is experienced and managed.

Meta-synthesis is undertaken when the analytic phases of meta-data analysis, meta-method and meta-theory are complete. It involves bringing together the ideas that have been taken apart and constructing a new interpretation. However, Paterson et al. (2001) give little guidance on how the three components are integrated as they said they were unwilling to oversimplify the process. They state that the process is non-linear and dynamic and involves thinking, interpreting, creating, theorising and reflecting.

As with meta-ethnography, meta-study is an advanced method that Paterson et al. (2001) claim should only be undertaken by seasoned researchers. To undertake such an endeavour the researcher(s) must be completely familiar with the theories and research designs that are likely to be sampled. In addition, considerable time and resources are needed to undertake the three analytical processes and subsequent synthesis. Therefore, meta-study is generally beyond the remit of undergraduate study, although the principles of the tripartite analysis of data, method and theory could be adopted and applied to any literature review. Readers requiring additional information are referred to Paterson et al.'s (2001) original text where a comprehensive account of the method is provided.

Qualitative Meta-summary

Qualitative meta-summary is a 'quantitatively oriented aggregation of qualitative findings that are themselves topical or thematic summaries or surveys of data' (Sandelowski and Barroso, 2007: 151). What this means is that a meta-summary includes a quantitative process of identifying the frequency of individual findings. It works on the assumption that qualitative and quantitative data can be transformed into one another. It differs from meta-ethnography and meta-study in that the findings of the studies are accumulated and summarised (aggregated). Sandelowski and Barroso (2003; 2007) argue that in qualitative research some findings occur with sufficient frequency to form a pattern or theme. It is this frequency of occurrence that facilitates the quantitative transformation. They contend this gives more meaning to the extracted data and is a way of verifying the patterns and themes that emerge from the studies. Although originally developed to accommodate reports from qualitative descriptive surveys, meta-summary can also be used with the findings of quantitative descriptive studies or even syntheses of other studies (Sandelowski and Barroso, 2007; Sandelowski et al., 2007).

Box 7.5   Techniques of Qualitative Meta-summary (Adapted from Sandelowski and Barroso, 2007)

- Extracting findings.
- Editing findings.
- Grouping findings about the same topic.
- Abstracting and formatting findings.
- Calculating frequency and intensity effect sizes.

Qualitative meta-summary techniques are outlined in Box 7.5. The first step in the process is to extract findings from individual study reports or syntheses about the topic area of interest. It is important that the topic area in which the reviewer is interested is reasonably well defined. This will ensure that the appropriate findings are extracted in a consistent way. Once the findings have been extracted, Sandelowski and Barroso (2007) recommend that they are edited so that they can be understood by any reader. For example, this may involve editing the themes and patterns so that they form complete sentences that are easily understood. The third technique involves grouping findings that appear to be about the same topic. For example, if the reviewer was interested in exploring the self-management practices of those who live with type II diabetes, they may identify findings from several reports that refer to dietary practices. At this point of the process these findings would be grouped together. Once all the findings have been grouped, they are abstracted. This is a process of developing statements that succinctly capture the content of all the findings and reducing them to a smaller number.

The final stage of meta-summary is determining the frequency of a finding with the assumption that the higher the frequency the greater its validity (Barnett-Page and Thomas, 2009). This is done by firstly determining the frequency effect size – that is, calculating the percentage of reports containing a particular finding against the overall number of reports. For example, if 10 reports identified that those with type II diabetes had dietary knowledge deficits and the overall number of reports was 20, then the frequency size effect would be 50 per cent (10 ÷ 20). The second part of the process is about determining the intensity size effect. Simply stated, this is about calculating the contribution of the findings in each report to the overall number of findings. For example, if an individual study contained 12 findings and the total number was 48 then the intensity size effect is 25 per cent (12 ÷ 48). Sandelowski and Barroso (2007) claim that as a result of calculating the intensity effect sizes it will be possible to see how much the findings in each study contributed overall.

Meta-summary is considered a relatively new approach but Sandelowski and Barroso (2007) claim that the technique has the potential to enhance the validity of the findings of qualitative studies, particularly in respect of the findings that have a high frequency. However, this approach is also a complex one that requires significant skills in data analysis and aggregation. For additional detail on the techniques of meta-summary, look at Sandelowski and Barroso's (2007) text on synthesising qualitative research.

In summary, the three approaches to meta-synthesis presented here are but a small example of a range of methods that have been and are being developed and appearing in the literature. All are complex methods that require a high level of expertise and skill in the conduct and evaluation of qualitative research. Moreover, they are limited in their applicability because they concentrate on research studies of one type or another and do not facilitate the synthesis of non-research literature. You will find further detail on the range of methods being adopted for the synthesis of qualitative research in Barnett-Page and Thomas (2009), Ring et al. (2010) and Campbell et al. (2011).

Summary

This chapter has explored the various means by which the results of research studies can be combined and pooled. The first part of the chapter focused on the importance of presenting the results from your analysis of the literature. Examples of how the search strategy, search results, inclusion and exclusion criteria and a collation of information about each study could be presented were offered. Thematic analysis as a means of undertaking a synthesis of literature that includes research and non-research literature was presented because this is the approach you are more likely to use in narrative literature reviews that are undertaken for an academic assignment or as a chapter in a dissertation. Additional and more complex methods of synthesis, including narrative synthesis, meta-analysis and meta-synthesis were introduced and their various techniques were presented. Although the knowledge accumulated from synthesis using these methods is key in terms of the potential impact on clinical practice and/or healthcare policy or research, the methods are limited in their appropriateness for the undergraduate student undertaking a literature review. Primarily, they are confined to combining research studies of one type or another and, therefore, do not facilitate the synthesis of the wide range of studies you are likely to encounter in your reading. Moreover, they do not accommodate the synthesis of non-research literature that is likely to inform, situate and contextualise your review. Nonetheless, you should now have an appreciation of the requirements of each method of synthesis, the similarities and differences between them and when each might be used.

❝ Key Points ❞

- Synthesis is the part of the process of the literature review where results are combined and pooled.
- In all literature reviews the first step of synthesis should be to present the findings, including: the search strategy, the results of the search, inclusion and exclusion criteria and a collation of information about each study.
- Thematic analysis is most commonly undertaken in the synthesis of mixed literature (research and non-research).
- Synthesis methods that are used to combine or pool the results of reviews of research studies include, but are not limited to: narrative synthesis, meta-analysis, meta-synthesis (e.g. meta-ethnography, meta-study, meta-summary).
- Narrative synthesis was developed for use where statistical analysis is not possible because of the range of different research designs included in the review. Although it can be used with mixed literature, to date its use has been primarily associated with the synthesis of multiple studies in systematic reviews.
- Meta-analysis is a process of statistical analysis of numerical data. Results are pooled and re-analysed to determine with more accuracy whether or not an intervention is effective. Studies suitable for meta-analysis must be of a similar design, with the gold standard being RCTs.
- Meta-synthesis is adopted in this text as a term that encompasses the various methods that have been developed to address the synthesis of qualitative research. Examples are meta-ethnography, meta-study and qualitative meta-summary.
- Meta-ethnography was first proposed as an alternative to meta-analysis and has emerged as the leading method for synthesis of qualitative research. Its purpose is to construct a new interpretation or theory about the phenomenon under study.
- Meta-study is an approach to synthesis that has three analytic phases. It examines the findings of each study (meta-data analysis), the method by which the study was conducted (meta-method) and the theory or theoretical influences underlying the study (meta-theory). These three analytic strategies must be undertaken before

(Continued)

(Continued)

meta-synthesis can occur. The aim is to generate new and more complete understandings of the phenomenon under study.

- Qualitative meta-summary aggregates qualitative findings through a quantitative process for the purpose of determining the frequency of each finding in and across studies.
  It assumes that qualitative and quantitative data can be transformed into one another.
  It differs essentially from meta-ethnography and meta-study in that the findings are
  accumulated and summarised (aggregated).
- Synthesis methods are directed by the type of data (research and/or non-research
  literature) and the purpose of the review.

WRITING YOUR LITERATURE REVIEW

❝ Learning Outcomes ❞

Having read this chapter you should be able to:

- prepare your literature review for publication or as an academic assignment;
- recognise the importance of adhering to writing guidelines;
- understand the value of good grammar and syntax when writing your review.

Introduction

Having undertaken the steps of identifying a review topic, locating and gathering the appropriate literature, organising, appraising and combining the results of your literature search, it is now time to consider how you will present your work to others. In order for you to receive the appropriate recognition for your review and to add to the knowledge available on the topic you selected, it is essential that your outcomes are presented both accurately and unambiguously in a manner that demonstrates your knowledge of the subject to those who read your work, and also allows others to become acquainted with the information gathered. Consequently you will have to present your review in a written format. The structure and presentation of your work will to some degree be determined by the purpose of the review. If the review is being written as an academic assignment, for example, the structure will differ from a review being written for the purposes of publication in a journal (Fowler, 2016a). The purpose of an academic assignment is to demonstrate, to the marker, your knowledge of the process of undertaking a review and that through the literature you have developed an understanding of the topic being studied. In a professional journal readers are more discerning about what they read. If it does not meet their professional needs or attract their interest they may not give more than a cursory glance to your work. So published work needs to attract the reader and focus more on new knowledge and insights that are applicable to practice (Fowler, 2016a).

Writing Your Review

The first thing to consider when you begin to write your review is who you are writing for. If the work is an academic assignment then it is important to consider any guidelines that may need to be adhered to in relation to presentation, and how many marks are allocated to each section. In academic assignments the majority of marks are usually allocated for demonstrating the process of undertaking a literature search and writing a review of the literature, so the main focus of your work will be on these areas. If you are writing to publish you will need to review the publisher's guidelines in relation to word counts and how they expect the work to be presented. Fowler (2016a) suggests that publishers expect the largest portion of the article's content to be focused on the discussion of the information gleaned, and its application to practice. A literature review may also be a part of a research study. Grove et al. (2013) suggest that the usual way for this type of review to be structured is an introduction, followed by a discussion of the theoretical literature that supports the review, then the empirical literature is usually presented using themes and ending with a concise summary and conclusion. However, whatever the purpose of the review, it is expected that the review will be presented in a logical way and that all the necessary key elements are included. All the steps that informed your literature review need to be included as you write up your work although the depth of information may vary. It is important that you are logical as to their inclusion – that is, identifying your review topic comes before your search of the literature and so forth. Many of the factors you considered when critically analysing another author's works now apply to your own work. As you write you need to reflect on your own review in the same way you considered those you reviewed for study.

ACTIVITY 8.1

Identify a literature review that has recently been published and appraise it critically. If you were doing a literature review on this topic, would you select this review for inclusion? What are the strengths and limitations of the review?

Title and Abstract

The title and the abstract are often the first two points of contact between you and the reader. A reader may decide to ignore or read your work based on how you have formulated your title and the information you have included in your abstract. In presenting your title and abstract first impressions are important, so it is therefore critical to convey the essential features of your review to the reader in a manner that is interesting yet enlightening (Fowler, 2015a). As a general rule your title should ideally be about 10–15 words in length. If your title is too long there is a risk that it will be unwieldy and confusing to the reader. If it is too short then there is the risk that important information, which may have encouraged the reader to study your article further, may be omitted.

The abstract is a brief summary of your work and should contain enough information to give the reader an overall impression of what the review is about and how it was conducted. Abstracts vary in length but are usually about 150–200 words. An abstract should include some background on the problem/review topic, how the search was undertaken, including the keywords and databases used, the outcome of the review and any recommendations. Although both the title and abstract appear at the start of the review, they are usually written last.

Introduction

The purpose of the introduction is to put your literature in context and to offer the reader a concise background to the purpose of the review (Grove et al., 2013). You know why you have selected this topic and why it is important, and how it can potentially improve patient care and help the development of the profession; however, the reader does not necessarily know this and certainly does not understand it from your perspective.

Perhaps when caring for patients post-operatively you observed that some patients appeared to have a lot more pain than others, despite the fact that they had all undergone similar operations and had received similar post-operative analgesia. Having done a quick survey of the literature, which indicated that there may be other factors that potentially could exacerbate pain, you decided to undertake a review of the literature to identify these potential causes and also check if alternative treatments were available. When introducing your review it is therefore important to identify to the reader that the 'problem' is that 'some post-operative patients appear to have a lot more pain than others'. You can then present what was discovered on briefly examining the literature and cite supporting works that suggest that there may be other factors that can exacerbate a patient's experience of pain. Now you are in a position to state the purpose of your review.

The search strategy that you developed to identify the literature can either be presented now or at the beginning of the literature review section. You need to include the list of keywords and keyword combinations that were used in the search, the databases and other sources that were explored and any limits that were set on the search. You should also identify how many studies were initially identified in your search, and how many were excluded and why. Overall there should be enough detail that another reviewer could replicate your search and study selection (Bettany-Saltikov, 2012). Following the search strategy, the organisation and structure of the review should be identified. This should include any proposed subheadings that will be used to organise the literature review.

Although the introduction appears at the beginning of your review, it is usually only a draft outline until the review is complete. However, having a working draft of your introduction as you conduct your review can be useful because it identifies the purpose of your review and what you are aiming to achieve. It is, therefore, important to regularly return to your introduction to ensure that you are still focused on the purpose identified. As mentioned, the introduction is often finalised when the review is completed. At this stage the end of the review is in sight and the tendency can be to rush to get the introduction complete and wrap up this piece of work. However, the introduction is the first part of the actual literature review readers will encounter, and if you have convinced them to read further through a good title and abstract you want to continue to make a good impression. It is, therefore, worthwhile spending extra time on the introduction so as to encourage readers to continue reading your work.

The Review of the Literature

This section is where the literature related to the problem or topic of interest is presented, critically analysed, synthesised and discussed in relation to other literature. A literature review is an objective, academic piece of work and should therefore be presented in an organised and objective manner, without personal views or opinions being expressed by the reviewer. It often commences with a short discussion of the theoretical literature which may be used to identify a framework for the review before the empirical literature is presented. All of the significant research studies related to the topic being reviewed should be included in your review. These studies need to be critically analysed and the implications of the strengths or limitations should be discussed. As a review is objective, any analysis of the studies needs to be supported by reference to the relevant literature. It is important to remember that this is a literature review and not a series of critiques. The critical analysis of the study needs to be succinct but at the same time offer enough information for the reader to make a determination on quality of evidence being presented in the study (Polit and Beck, 2012). The reader needs to be able to appraise your outcomes and recommendations, and without a good insight into the quality of the studies being reviewed this can be difficult (Bettany-Saltikov, 2012). Not all studies included in your review need to be critically analysed, and in some instances studies that have similar findings, or support each other, may be synopsised together (see Box 8.1).

Box 8.1   Example of Studies Summarised Together

'However, for some women who disclose their HIV status, their family and friends are not always supportive (Brickley et al. 2009, Rouleau et al. 2012). In several qualitative studies from the USA, Canada, South Africa, the UK, Vietnam and India, women have described that after revealing their HIV status to family, friends or loved ones, they were devastated by their negative reactions (Anderson & Doyal 2004, Carr & Gramling 2004, Brickley et al. 2009, Ndirangu & Evans 2009, Rahangdale et al. 2010, Logie et al. 2011, Lekganyane & du Plessis 2012, Okoror et al. 2012, Rouleau et al. 2012 and Kako & Dubrosky 2013). These negative reactions include forcing them to stay away from children, stopping them from having any physical contact, separating eating utensils, ending relationships and not being allowed to stay with their family members (Anderson & Doyal 2004, Carr & Gramling 2004, Brickley et al. 2009, Ndirangu & Evans 2009, Rahangdale et al. 2010, Logie et al. 2011, Lekganyane & du Plessis 2012, Okoror et al. 2012, Rouleau et al. 2012 and Kako & Dubrosky 2013).'

(Ho and Holloway, 2016: 11)

To assist the reader, the literature is usually organised into subheadings or themes that reflect the content of the review. The information from the literature then needs to be analysed and synthesised, to identify new meanings and ideas that need to be discussed. If you are writing for publication then the focus of your writing should be more on discussing the information gained from syntheses of the literature. On the other hand, if your review is an academic assignment you may be expected to put a greater emphasis on critically analysing the methodology of the studies included (Fowler, 2016a). When writing your review, you should interpret and paraphrase the information gleaned from the studies being reviewed. Simply stringing together a series of passages or quotations from different studies without undertaking analyses or interpretation usually indicates a failure to internalise and comprehend the significance of the literature and is not an acceptable way to write a literature review.

When writing your review, you will find that some studies may be included in more than one subheading or theme. If you do include a study under a number of subheadings it only needs to be critically appraised once; it is not necessary to appraise the study again under subsequent headings. When presenting literature with similar themes, the characteristic that connects or differentiates these studies is the findings. It is, therefore, important to present the findings early when discussing a study. In doing this, it is also crucial to ensure that the studies and their findings match the theme of the subheading under which they are being included.

When reviewing the literature on a particular theme, you will notice that not all studies will have similar outcomes and some studies can be at complete variance with what may be perceived as the mainstream beliefs on this topic. It is important that these alternative findings are given recognition. This is not to say that you are conceding they are correct, only that you are acknowledging that they exist. When comparing different perspectives it can also be useful to compare methodologies. Differing results may be a result of sampling error, so it is important to critically appraise how the samples were selected and the size of the sample in the study.

It is important to remember, when writing your review, that post-positive quantitative research only infers from the findings of a study. This is because conclusions are drawn from a sample of the population and so if the methodology is sound the findings will probably reflect what would be found in the population (Polit and Beck, 2014). However, nothing is definitive so the result is always a probability. In naturalistic qualitative inquiry the outcomes are the views and perspectives of individuals so this paradigm does not claim generalisability to the population. Therefore you should avoid using terms or words that generalise or are definitive when describing the outcomes of a study. Statements to avoid include 'it is obvious that...' and 'it is evident...'. More appropriate statements would be 'it appears that...' and 'it seems...'. The latter statements indicate what appears to be, but also allows for the element of chance, which in some instances does play a role.

In summary, a literature review is more than simply a description of a number of studies on a particular topic. The literature needs to be analysed to determine the robustness of the studies included. The studies also need to be compared and contrasted to identify similarities and differences, which in turn may offer plausible rationales for any inconsistencies that may exist between studies (Polit and Beck, 2012).

Summary, Conclusion and Recommendations

The summary/conclusion is a succinct overview of the salient points within the literature review and includes the deductions and possible outcomes that the reviewer has established while analysing and synthesising the literature. Reviewers often commence this section by restating the review question or problem. This is followed by a short summary of what is known about the topic, areas where there is a dearth of information or deficit in the knowledge base, and the identification of inconsistencies in the literature. Arguments central to the review are presented in a concise manner and, finally, conclusions are identified. Again it is important that these conclusions correspond with the initial review problem. This section to a large degree summarises your review. No new studies or information should, therefore, be presented at this stage. If a piece of evidence is important enough to be included here, then it should have been in the main body of the review. This section of the review is where you, the reviewer, have an opportunity to objectively put forward your opinions. However, this is not a *carte blanche* to say whatever you want. Your comments need to be supported by the literature, be objectively presented, and relate to the analysis and synthesis you have done.

Having summarised your review and identified your conclusions the next step is to identify what you believe should happen next. These are your recommendations to the reader and the profession. The recommendations you make should reflect what you identified in your conclusion and include suggestions such as a change of practice, or whether the evidence is inconclusive or there are gaps in the literature that further research on this topic is required (Wakefield, 2014). Recommendations may be part of the summary/conclusion or a separate heading. This depends on the guidelines for writing the review.

References

At the end of your literature review there should be a full bibliographical reference list of all source material contained therein. All of the journal articles, books and other media that were cited in your review need to be included in your reference list. Common errors include complete omission of references from the reference list, incomplete references and incorrect publication dates. Failing to acknowledge another author's work can lead to claims of plagiarism, which is regarded as a serious offence (see Chapter 9 for more information on referencing and plagiarism).

Student Comment

'Referencing should be done as you go as it is a nightmare having to go back and add in when you have finished writing.'

(2nd year undergraduate mental health nursing student)

ACTIVITY 8.2

When you have finished writing your review, appraise it critically. If you were another author doing a literature review on this topic, would you select your review for inclusion? What are the strengths and limitations of your review?

Writing, Grammar and Syntax

A clear writing style with good grammar and syntax are important in all forms of written communication and even more so when undertaking an academic assignment or writing for publication. When composing your written review it is important to check if there are assignment or publishing guidelines that you need to adhere to. Ignoring the guidelines for either increases the likelihood of a poor academic mark or a letter of rejection from the publisher (Fowler, 2015b).

Guidelines can include, among other things, the word count for the work, the referencing system to be used, the layout of the work, and the use of personal pronouns. Different academic institutions and publishers all have their own conventions in relation to referencing and these can be quite different. It is important to know what is expected and to adhere to the conventions required (see Chapter 9 for referencing conventions). It is also important to check if there are academic conventions that you are expected to adhere to in regard to the use of personal pronouns. There is some debate within academic circles as to whether it is appropriate to use 'I' in a sentence or to refer to yourself in the third person as 'the author' or 'the reviewer'. The use of the third person, in some instances, is regarded as being more objective, but Aveyard (2014) adds that it can also be a source of confusion, leaving the reader unsure to whom the writer of the review is referring. It is a good idea, if you are using the third person to refer to yourself, to pick one title that you will use throughout your work. Constantly changing between 'this author', 'writer' or 'reviewer' can potentially cause confusion for the reader.

When writing your review you should endeavour to use a use a proper sentence structure, and to use the correct tense and spelling. A proper sentence starts with a capital letter and contains a subject, a verb and an object, and it ends with a full stop. When work is rushed, it is not unusual for full stops, capital letters and other parts of sentences to be omitted. The result is usually a lack of clarity as to what the writer is attempting to communicate. Sentences that are too long create a similar problem. Keep your sentences short and simple and focus on one concept. Sentences should ideally be no longer 14 to 16 words in length, unless you are good at punctuation. Otherwise there is a likelihood the reader will end up having to read the sentence a number of times to try to make sense of it. Ensure that your sentences have a logical flow and that they link with the preceding sentences. A paragraph is a series of linked sentences, so it should contain more than a single sentence. A common error is to hit the return key instead of the spacebar, and the result is a new paragraph. One-sentence paragraphs usually lack continuity and undermine the flow of your work. It is a good idea to link your themes/subheadings also. This can be done by finishing a theme with a sentence identifying the how the next subheading relates to the current one. Introduce the theme when starting a new section and ensure that the theme is maintained throughout (Bettany-Saltikov, 2012). By doing this you should have a logical flow within both your sentences and paragraphs and thus within your review.

Other considerations are spelling and grammar. Words that are pronounced similarly can be spelled differently, for example, their and there or led and lead. Also there can be a difference between UK English spelling and US English. Words such as haematology (hematology [US]), oesophagus (esophagus) and theatre (theater) are just some examples. Exposure to texts from different continents can easily lead to spelling errors so it is important to use the lexicon of the country in which you are studying. If you are using a spell check on your computer, make sure it is set to the relevant version of English. Ensure that sentences are complete and that words have not been omitted. It is important to include both the definite article (the) and the indefinite article (a) as appropriate. The proper use of punctuation can make reading a literature review so much simpler. Conversely, poor punctuation can totally change the meaning of a sentence and cause confusion for the reader. Computer spelling and grammar checks can be set to help with punctuation, but it is useful to know a little about it. There are texts available that are amusing yet helpful in coming to terms with English grammar and punctuation, such as *Eats, Shoots and Leaves* (Truss, 2003).

Consistency in the use of tenses is important. The majority of the main body of the literature review will be in the past tense as it will consist of the presentation and appraisal of studies that have already been undertaken. However, other sections, such as identifying the purpose, will be written in the present tense. It is important to use tenses appropriately and to maintain the same tense within a sentence and ideally within a paragraph. Jargon should be avoided, and if a particular slang term needs to be used it should be placed in inverted commas. 'Texting' language should not be used when writing your literature review. Indeed, any form of abbreviation should be used with caution, and only recognised abbreviations used. When using acronyms use the full form in the first instance with the abbreviated form beside it in brackets, for example Department of Health (DoH). After this the acronym DoH can be used. It is always a good idea to get someone to read your review before you submit the final work. During the course of writing the review you can become so familiar with what you have written that typing mistakes, such as omitted words or wrong tenses, can be missed. The feedback you receive offers critical insights into your work so do give your review to someone who will appraise it judiciously.

Undertaking and writing your review is a time-consuming endeavour and many students and novice reviewers underestimate how long it will take. It is important to give sufficient time to all aspects of the review as writing up your review is, in its own way, as important as identifying the review topic and searching the literature. It is through the writing you review that the efforts you made in undertaking the review will be highlighted, and this will become the evidence by which your literature review will be evaluated.

Student Comment

'Writing the review can be very time consuming.'

(2nd year undergraduate mental health nursing student)

Summary

Having done your review it is now necessary that you present your work. Your review will be evaluated on how well you completed the steps of the review, and discussed the decisions that were made in searching and selecting, and analysing and synthesising the literature. This written record will be the evidence on which your review will be judged, and it needs to be presented clearly, accurately and with attention to detail. In writing up your review it is important to follow a logical sequence, beginning with why you selected this topic for your review through to your summary and recommendations. Good grammar and sentence structure play an important part in demonstrating attention to detail. So create a good first impression.

Key Points

- Your literature review will be judged on the evidence supplied by you in the written presentation – so accuracy, clarity and attention to detail are very important.
- There should be a logical consistency to how your review is presented.
- Good grammar and proper sentence structure are important elements of good writing.
- Remember, first impressions count.

REFERENCING AND PLAGIARISM

❛ Learning Outcomes ❜

Having read this chapter you should be able to:

- understand the importance of referencing;
- reference literature in the body of your review;
- complete a reference list at the end of your review;
- discuss plagiarism and comprehend its implications;
- use good referencing techniques to avoid accidental plagiarism.

Introduction

Accurate referencing is a fundamental part of all forms of academic writing, writing for publication as well as writing a literature review. An individual reading a report needs to be able to identify the sources of literature the author is using to support any statements or comments being made. This allows the reader the opportunity to source the literature and verify the assertions being made and also do further reading on the topic (Grove et al., 2013). All sources of information used when writing, whether quoted or paraphrased, need to be acknowledged through referencing. Failure to acknowledge a source may be interpreted as claiming someone else's ideas as your own, which may be regarded as plagiarism. A defence often offered for plagiarism is ignorance; however, this is rarely an acceptable excuse as all writers are expected to understand what plagiarism entails and how to avoid it.

The aim of this chapter is to present some general guidance on referencing both in the text of your review and in the reference list at the end of your review. This chapter will also discuss aspects of plagiarism and how they might be avoided using good referencing techniques.

Referencing

All forms of original work and intellectual property are subject to the laws of copyright (Klimaszewski, 2012). This includes the written word, music and songs, and intellectual property such as artistic work and inventions. It is therefore important that the laws relating to copyright are adhered to. In academic writing this involves acknowledging the work of other authors whose words are quoted or paraphrased, or whose ideas are used to support an argument. Failure to correctly acknowledge the work of others is regarded as academic fraud or plagiarism. A synopsis of some of the reasons why referencing is important are included in Box 9.1.

Box 9.1   Reasons for Referencing

- References are used to calculate the number of citations and research impact.
- References uniquely identify each work presented within the review.
- References identify the literature used to support the assertions made in the review.
- References acknowledge the works of other authors and so avoid the risk of plagiarism.
- The number of references used demonstrates how widely you have read around this topic.
- References allow the reader to access the original works presented within the review.

As with other forms of academic writing, referencing is important when undertaking a literature review. Citation indices measure how frequently an article is cited in other published works and this is used to calculate the overall impact of an author's work. So incorrect referencing can give credit for a publication to the wrong author. Journals are also ranked by these indices. The more frequently articles from a particular journal are cited, the higher its impact factor. The impact of an article or where it is published can have an effect on how that work is viewed by an author's peers, and so it is important to give recognition to the original author.

When undertaking a review of the literature one method of demonstrating objectivity is to report both sides of a debate. It can be necessary at times to report claims that you, the reviewer, do not agree with. Omitting this information can undermine the integrity of the review; however, novice reviewers may feel reluctant to include this information for fear that it may be attributed to them. On the other hand, good referencing practices can clearly demonstrate that this is the view of the author being cited. Likewise, as a reviewer you should also strive to ensure that comments with which you agree are correctly attributed to that author. Acknowledging the work of others is also important to avoid the suspicion of plagiarism. It also allows the reader to see the depth of reading on the topic that has occurred. If a reviewer has only a limited number of references related to the topic being reviewed, a justification for this needs to be made.

Good referencing can uniquely identify the different pieces of work that have been used within your review. So even if an author has two studies published in the same year, the two studies should be clearly distinguished both in text and in the reference list (see Fowler 2015a, 2015b: Boxes 9.5 and 9.6). Referencing is a form of recognition and acknowledgement by the reviewer of an author's work.

Another reason for referencing the literature in your review is to demonstrate how widely you have read around a topic. It is important when undertaking a literature review to demonstrate that you are familiar with the topic, have read widely around it and that that the most significant works have been included in your review. Word limits may restrict the number of articles that you will be able to include in your review. However, it will always be a balancing act between being too broad (including too many articles and not analysing them adequately) and being too in-depth (offering a comprehensive analysis and synthesis on a limited number of articles). Academic assignment guidelines may address this by suggesting a minimum number of references, so it is important to read these guidelines carefully.

Finally, references allow the reader to access the original works that are included in your literature review. There are a number of reasons why readers may wish to do this, including to source articles for their own assignments or reviews, to gain a greater insight into a particular issue discussed within your review, to check the accuracy of interpretations made within your review, or simply to check if those references are accurate or exist. It is, therefore, important to ensure that the references in the text accurately match those in the reference list at the end of the review.

ACTIVITY 9.1

Consider the following scenarios:

You are rightly proud of yourself. After expending considerable time and energy undertaking a literature review and preparing it for publication you finally got it published. A few months later you find a large portion of your review used in another article without any acknowledgement that this is your work.

- How would you feel, particularly as it now appears that this author is claiming your work as his own?
- Alternatively, the reviewer did acknowledge the work, but cited another person as the author – not you. So now someone else is receiving academic recognition for your work. Would you be happy?

The process of referencing occurs in two parts. The first part is where the author's work is cited in the written text. It is important that this is accurate as it is the key to identifying the full bibliographical reference for this citation. The full bibliographical reference is the second part of the referencing process and is included in a reference list at the end of the review. The most popular system of referencing is the Harvard (author, date) system. This system uses the name of the author and the year of publication to identify the work in the text. An alternative is the Vancouver system which uses citation numbers.

Citing Authors in Text

There are two methods of presenting the work of other authors in your review. These are: directly quoting the original text, or paraphrasing the information you wish to convey. A direct quotation involves selecting a portion of the original work and presenting it word for word within your literature review. To differentiate a quotation from the rest of the text it is usually presented in inverted commas or as an indented block of text that is single-line spaced. Inverted commas are usually used for short quotations, whereas block quotations are usually used for a longer quotation. Block quotations may be used with or without inverted commas depending on local guidelines and publishers' preferences. The page number of the book or article where the quotation originally appears should also be included in the in-text reference along with the author and the year of publication. Examples of both types of quotation can be seen in Box 9.2.

Box 9.2   Quotations

Use of Inverted Commas

Price (2014: 46) defines plagiarism as '... the representation of others' words in a piece of coursework or academic assignment as one's own, without clear reference to the source ...' He also adds that this includes failure to use inverted commas when quoting directly (Price, 2014).

Use of Block Quotation

In relation to plagiarism, Price (2014) states that

> '...plagiarism refers to the representation of others' words in a piece of coursework or academic assignment as one's own, without clear reference to the source and/or failure to present the words of others as a quotation (in inverted commas).' (Price, 2014: 46)

Quotations should appear word for word, exactly as they appeared in the original text with grammatical or spelling errors included. If an error is identified, the word *sic* (from the Latin '*sic erat scriptum*' – thus it was written) is usually placed in square brackets after the error – for example, 'I know you herd [sic] what I said.' Quotations can be a powerful tool in academic writing, but only if used correctly. Over-use of quotations detracts from their effect and can leave the reader wondering if there is any originality in the review. Quotations are best used sparingly and to emphasise rather than explain a point. When using a quotation, there should be a continuity between the quotation and where it is fitting into the text as can be seen in Box 9.2. All too frequently, students and novice writers include a quotation that is outside the natural flow of the sentence. This is sometimes because the quoted sentence does not fit, in its complete state, within the reviewer's sentence. One way of overcoming this is to omit part of the quotation. This is usually indicated by the inclusion of an ellipsis (...) to indicate something has been omitted. However, in doing this, the reviewer must ensure they are not changing the meaning of what was written. An example of the use of ellipses can be seen in Box 9.3. In this example text has been omitted from the start of the sentence, mid-sentence and at the end. However the intended meaning within the sentence is maintained.

Box 9.3   Using Ellipses

Price (2014: 46) states that '...plagiarism refers to the representation of others' words ... as one's own, without clear reference to the source ...'

Paraphrasing is the most common method used to present the work of another author. It involves rephrasing another author's words but keeping the original meaning of the work. The original author must be given recognition by including the author's name and year of publication. This can be added either as part of the sentence or at the end of the paraphrase. It is not usually necessary to include a page number in the text when paraphrasing; however, it is not incorrect to do so. An example of both of these methods of paraphrasing can be seen in Box 9.4.

Box 9.4   Paraphrasing

Example 1

Price (2014) states that using other authors' work without giving the appropriate recognition is regarded as plagiarism.

Example 2

The use of another author's words or ideas without the appropriate acknowledgement to indicate that this work is either paraphrased or quoted is regarded as plagiarism (Price, 2014).

Student Comment

'You don't fully understand a study until you can put it into your own words.'

(4th year undergraduate general nursing student)

Citing in the Reference List

Readers will naturally move from the citation in the text to the bibliographical reference list at the end of the review if they are accessing articles. The reference list should offer enough information to the reader so that they can easily access that study in the appropriate journals database. The reference requirements for academic and journal submissions do vary, so it is necessary to be familiar with what is required; for example, most academic institutions require a full list of authors for an article, whereas journals may accept the use of et al. if there is a long list of authors. Referencing using the more common citation conventions is discussed later in this chapter.

When comparing the text references to those in the reference list, there are sometimes discrepancies. Common inconsistencies include:

- the date of publication of a reference in the text and the corresponding date in the reference list do not match;
- the in-text reference is for a single author, but there are multiple authors for that work in the reference list;
- 'et al.' is included with the author's name in the text, but it is a single author in the reference list;
- the in-text reference is not included in the reference list.

In the first three cases the reader does not know if the difference between the in-text reference and the reference list is due to lack of attention to detail by the reviewer, if a different article is being referred to, or which reference, if either, is correct. In the latter case the reader has no reference to access. Poor referencing undermines the integrity of your review and can lead to a lower mark being received for your work. It is, therefore, worth investing time to ensure that references are accurate and complete.

Plagiarism

Plagiarism is regarded in academia as a form of fraud, and in publication circles as a potential breach of copyright law. It usually involves presenting the work of another author without due recognition or acknowledgement; and thus the work appears to be that of the current writer rather than the original author (Price, 2014). Zafron (2012) states that students are often not fully aware of writing conventions and incorrectly believe they are correctly citing sources. Another issue is the electronic access granted by modern technology. Horrom (2012) adds that it has become too easy to just copy and paste large chunks of information from sources such as the Internet or journals. If students do not clearly identify the work as being taken directly from another author, or do not keep good notes as to who the original author was, they may mistakenly assume it is their own work and inadvertently plagiarise (Price, 2014). Plagiarism can be intentional or unintentional; however, from an academic perspective, both are regarded as serious offences and strong sanctions can be imposed on anyone who is deemed to have plagiarised. Claiming ignorance is usually not accepted as a defence as all students are expected to be familiar with what constitutes plagiarism. Student and novice reviewers may often fail to completely appreciate the extent of what plagiarism encompasses. Turnitin (2012) have identified a 'Plagiarism Spectrum' which contains a number of different types of plagiarism. These can be viewed at http://turnitin.com/assets/en_us/media/plagiarism_spectrum.php.

Plagiarism does not only apply to another author's work. Using work that you have previously submitted or published yourself and presenting it as new original work is known as self-plagiarisation and is also a form of academic fraud (Horrom, 2012). It is also regarded as plagiarism to attempt to get the same piece of work published in more than one journal. Generally, third-level institutions will not accept work that was previously submitted on another course or for another assignment. Finally, if you do wish to use elements of your own published work in a review you must acknowledge the original work by citing yourself as the author.

With the increase in technology and wide access to obscure journals and books on the Internet, it may seem that plagiarism would be difficult to identify. However, differences in writing styles and in how ideas are presented from one part of a literature review to another will draw the attention of an experienced reader. Technological tools such as Turnitin and SafeAssign can also help to identify similarities between works that have been submitted as assignments in different institutions or have been previously published. So it is a good idea to check the degree of similarity in your work before submission.

Avoiding Plagiarism

Plagiarism often occurs when students unknowingly or unwittingly fail to acknowledge another author's contribution. However, a study by Walker (2010) suggests that a small number of students knowingly indulge in plagiarism. Walker (2010) identified three most common types of plagiarism:

- *Verbatim:* This is transcribing literally another writer's work without any acknowledgement of the original author.
- *Sham paraphrasing*: This is transcribing another author's work, word for word, without indenting or using quotation marks. The material is cited as if the writer had paraphrased the original work rather than directly copying it.
- *Purloining*: In this case the writer submits, as their own, work that has either extensively or entirely been done by another individual. There is usually some attempt to paraphrase but no recognition is given to the original authors.

To avoid plagiarism, it is essential to know what plagiarism is and what it entails. Most third-level institutions have clear guidelines for students as to what is regarded as plagiarism and it is expected that students will make themselves familiar with this information. Here are some things you can do to reduce the risk of plagiarism:

- When taking notes differentiate between what you paraphrase and direct quotations. Always put quotations in inverted commas. The latter is particularly important if you are cutting and pasting.
- Accurately record the reference for paraphrased and quoted information and link this information so you know the source. For quotations you also need the number of the page from which the quotation was drawn.
- Carefully check your review before submission and ensure that the correct form of citation is applied to the work of other authors.
- Check each in-text citation to ensure that it is accurate and corresponds with the reference in the reference list.

Correctly citing other authors and ensuring the references are correct demands both time and patience and should not be rushed. Tools like Turnitin and SafeAssign can also be used to identify the degree of similarity that exists between your review and other published/submitted work. However, these tools will not identify missing or inaccurate references or citations.

Student Comment

'I find it easier to add a reference to my reference list as soon as I use it in my review so I don't forget about it.'

(4th year undergraduate general nursing student)

Referencing/Citation Conventions

There are a number of different referencing/citation conventions, and the decision as to which convention to use is often determined by professional, institutional or publisher preference. An example of each of the two main types of conventions will be presented here, namely the author–date system and the number-based system. The overview presented here gives the more common variations of these conventions, so in all cases it is advised that you check and use the recommended guidelines for your course or assignment. An important consideration, no matter which system you are using, is consistency. It is important to keep the same format for all journals, books and other material you cite throughout your work and include in your references.

A references list (which may be titled simply 'References') occurs at the end of your literature review and is a list of all the citations that you presented in your review. A 'bibliography' is a reading list – a catalogue of the books and articles you read to inform yourself about the subject, but which might not all be cited in your review. It, also, is situated at the end of a review. In some instances, the terms 'references' and 'bibliography' are used interchangeably; however, technically there is a difference between these two lists. Depending on your guidelines you may not have to include a bibliography, but you will have to include a set of references.

Harvard

The Harvard referencing system is one of the most commonly used conventions within academic circles. It is a broad designation encompassing styles that use the author–date system of referencing in-text and in the reference list (University of Queensland Library, 2016). The basic principles are common to all Harvard referencing systems; however, there are also some minor variations which mainly occur in areas such as the use of punctuation. It is, therefore, important to be familiar with how punctuation is applied within the system you are using. In the Harvard system the bibliographical references at the end are known as a reference list and are presented in alphabetical order starting with the author's surname. Full bibliographical references, including the names of all the authors, must be included. In the text, if an article or a book has more than two authors 'et al.' is placed after the first author to identify that there are other authors. Examples of a reference list for books and journals, and of in-text referencing are presented in Box 9.5.

Box 9.5   Example of Harvard References

In-text

Price (2014) states that …

'Paraphrasing involves the student using the main points from another author and putting them into her own words. This is not always as easy as it appears' (Price, 2014).

Reference List

Fowler, J. (2015a) 'From staff nurse to nurse consultant: writing for publication part 6: writing the abstract', *British Journal of Nursing*, 24 (22): 1170.

Fowler, J. (2015b) 'From staff nurse to nurse consultant: writing for publication part 3: following the journal guidelines', *British Journal of Nursing*, 24 (19): 978.

Grove, S., Burns, N. and Gray, J. (2013) *The Practice of Nursing Research: Appraisal, Synthesis and Generation of Evidence* 7th ed. St Louis: Elsevier Saunders.

Price, B. (2014) 'Avoiding plagiarism: guidance for nursing students', *Nursing Standard*, 28 (26): 45–51.

Rebar, C.R., Gersch, C.J., MacNee, C.L. and McCabe, S. (2011) *Understanding Nursing Research*. 3rd ed. Philadelphia: Wolters Kluwer/Lippincott Williams & Wilkins.

Walker, J. (2010) 'Measuring plagiarism: researching what students do, not what they say they do', *Studies in Higher Education*, 35 (1): 41–59.

Zafron, M.L. (2012) 'Good intentions: providing students with skills to avoid accidental plagiarism', *Medical Reference Services Quarterly,* 31 (2): 225–229.

Vancouver

The Vancouver referencing system is, like the Harvard system, a broad designation that encompasses all systems that use a number-based, in-text referencing system

(University of Queensland Library, 2016). This system uses a number in the text instead of an author and date. The first reference is numbered (1) and so on, and the reference section is presented in numerical order with (1) being the first reference. Each time that a reference is used the allocated citation number appears at that point in the text. In the reference list the date appears at the end of the reference in books and after the journal title for an article. The title of the journal appears in the Medline abbreviated form and is followed by a full stop. Examples of Vancouver references for books and journals, and in-text referencing are presented in Box 9.6.

Box 9.6   Example of Vancouver References

In-text

Price (4) states that …

Paraphrasing involves the student using the main points from another author and putting them into her own words. This is not always as easy as it appears (4).

References

1. Zafron ML. Good intentions: providing students with skills to avoid accidental plagiarism. Med Ref Serv Q. 2012; 31(2): 225–9.
2. Fowler, J. From staff nurse to nurse consultant: writing for publication part 3: following the journal guidelines. Br J Nurs. 2015; 24(19): 978.
3. Grove S, Burns N, Gray J. The practice of nursing research: appraisal, synthesis and generation of evidence. 7th ed. St Louis: Elsevier Saunders; 2013.
4. Price, B. Avoiding plagiarism: guidance for nursing students. Nurs Stand. 2014; 28(26): 45–51.
5. Walker J. Measuring plagiarism: researching what students do, not what they say they do. Stud High Educ. 2010; 35(1): 41–59.
6. Fowler, J. From staff nurse to nurse consultant: writing for publication part 6: writing the abstract. Br J Nurs. 2015; 24(22): 1170.
7. Rebar CR, Gersch CJ, MacNee CL, McCabe S. Understanding nursing research. 3rd ed. Philadelphia: Wolters Kluwer/Lippincott Williams & Wilkins; 2011.

There are other referencing conventions and styles, such as the use of footnotes. However, these are generally specific requirements within courses or disciplines and as such will not be discussed here.

Summary

The aim of this chapter was to highlight the importance of good referencing. Good referencing can help support a writer's assertions, can offer the reader the opportunity to delve further into the topic, and acknowledges the work of other authors. The use of a good referencing technique reduces the likelihood that a writer will accidentally fail to acknowledge another author's work and risk being accused of plagiarism. There are a number of different conventions that offer guidance regarding how to present references. However, it is important to follow the conventions that are identified for your assignment or in your college handbook. If no conventions are recommended then remember to be consistent within the style that you select.

❝ Key Points ❞

- Accurate referencing is an essential part of writing a literature review.
- Failure to reference another author's work may be regarded as plagiarism, a form of academic fraud.
- To avoid plagiarism, ensure all media information that is quoted or paraphrased within your review is accurately referenced, both in the text and in the reference section at the end.
- When referencing, be consistent and follow the conventions that are recommended for your literature review or course.

Further Information

Anglia Ruskin University: Harvard system
http://libweb.anglia.ac.uk/referencing/harvard.htm

University of Cambridge: Referencing convention guidelines and tutorials
www.admin.cam.ac.uk/univ/plagiarism/students/referencing/conventions.html

University of Leicester: Avoiding plagiarism
www2.le.ac.uk/offices/careers/ld/resources/study/avoiding-plagiarism

University of Leicester: Referencing and bibliographies
www2.le.ac.uk/offices/careers/ld/resources/writing/writing-resources/ref-bib/

University of Leicester: Vancouver (numbered) system
www2.le.ac.uk/library/help/citing/vancouver-numbered-system/vancouver-numbered-system

University of Queensland: Referencing styles
https://www.library.uq.edu.au/research-tools-techniques/referencing-style-guides#harvard

WHAT COMES NEXT?

❝ Learning Outcomes ❞

Having read this chapter you should be able to:

- identify possible avenues for the dissemination of the findings of your literature review;
- outline the issues involved in submitting a literature review for publication in a journal;
- explain how a literature review can be submitted for a verbal presentation or poster at a conference, seminar or workshop.

Introduction

The final chapter of this book is a brief outline of what you might do when you have finished your literature review. As has been indicated throughout this book, there are many reasons for undertaking a literature review and, to a large degree, this will determine what you do next. In the chapter on systematic reviews it was suggested that a plan for disseminating the findings is developed at the protocol stage, with the intention of ensuring that the outcomes reach the intended audience, be they practitioners, end-users, policy-makers, organisations or commissioners of research. Inherent in this is the belief that without dissemination the findings of your review are rendered valueless. This does not only apply to systematic reviews. Reviews that form part of a dissertation or have been written for the primary purpose of an academic assignment have the potential to be published in one form or another. This chapter focuses on some avenues for dissemination of these types of literature review. For detailed consideration of the dissemination of the results of systematic reviews you should look at publications by CRD (2009), Bettany-Saltikov (2012), Gough et al. (2012) or access the websites of organisations such as the Cochrane Collaboration, the National Institute for Health Research Dissemination Centre and the Joanna Briggs Institute.

For most of us who have undertaken a narrative review as part of an academic assignment, the goal is to successfully complete the assessment and we give little consideration to doing anything else with it. Similarly, although we prepare a plan for dissemination of research findings when we conduct a study as part of an academic award, we do not often consider publishing the literature review chapter. Yet a well-conducted literature review may produce findings that are of interest to your discipline and it is worth considering how you might share them.

Much of the published literature that addresses dissemination tends to focus on means of sharing the results of research studies or systematic reviews. However, some of these can also be used and applied to various types of literature review. Broadly, these can include a written report that is published as an article in an academic or professional journal, a verbal report or poster at a conference, seminar or workshop, or even a journal club (Gerrish and Lacey, 2010). In addition, a well written literature review can be submitted to an academic awards programme such as the international, pan-discipline, undergraduate awards (www.undergraduateawards.com/about-us/) where your work is not only recognised for its academic excellence but also has the potential to facilitate wide dissemination of your findings.

Writing an Article for a Journal

Writing an article for publication in a journal has been the most widely used means of dissemination and it is likely to reach the widest audience, both nationally and internationally. This is because many journals are now available online or through open access, and accessibility has been greatly enhanced. However, for a novice, preparing an article for submission to a journal can be an overwhelming prospect and many may consider their work is not of a publishable standard. Nonetheless, those who do make the effort have the potential, at the very least, to raise awareness or provoke discussion about the topic in question that may identify, for example, implications for future practice, education and research in the area.

For a person new to publication, it is suggested that co-authoring with another who has published previously is beneficial. Although the choice of co-author is a personal one, it is worth considering the person who originally suggested the work could be published. It is a good idea at the beginning of the process that you establish how you will work together and the role and contribution each will make to the overall preparation and submission. Journal articles now require a declaration that each author contributed to the preparation of the article. It is not sufficient that a person's name is included simply because they were a tutor or supervisor. Moreover, as the work belongs to you, first authorship should remain with you.

Choosing a journal for publication is an important step and requires careful consideration. It is probably worth discussing with your co-author the message you wish to convey and to what readership. Glasper and Peate (2013) suggest that an article can be written for a number of purposes, one of which is a critical review of the literature. Moreover, if your review findings indicate that ways of looking at a topic need to be challenged or reconsidered then publishing an article is a good means to disseminate these conclusions. In terms of readership, some journals have a more academic, advanced practitioner or postgraduate readership whilst others are directed more towards practising professionals with a particular emphasis on clinical issues. It is important that you determine at the outset how your proposed article would fit with the overall ethos of the journal. The overwhelming majority have dedicated websites that can tell you about the journal, its focus and the types of article it publishes.

One thing you should be able to discern from the journal website is where it is published, which will give you a sense of its international reach. While it is not suggested that journals do not publish international work, the focus of some topics might have a more national than international appeal and are therefore more suited for publication in the jurisdiction in which the journal is published. An example of this is Foran and Brennan's (2015) literature review of the prevention and early detection of cervical cancer in the UK, published in the UK-based *British Journal of Nursing*. This review highlights the fact that an absence of clear information still exists about prevention and early detection of cervical cancer in the UK, a gap in UK policy regarding women under the age for screening (25) but above the age for vaccination and that barriers to change exist for nurses and healthcare professionals. While this problem is likely to exist in other healthcare jurisdictions, the problem, solutions and outcomes of the review are contextualised to the UK, which reduces its applicability to other settings. Therefore, if Foran and Brennan wished to publish the review in the North American-based *American Journal of Public Health*, the focus of the review would have had to be constructed to suit a more international readership.

Another issue that can be determined from accessing journal websites is the type of journal article that the editorial board seeks to publish. This is extremely important in terms of successfully publishing your work. Whilst most journals accommodate the publication of literature reviews, some have specific criteria for publication that may be beyond what was achieved in a traditional or narrative review. For example, some journals indicate a preference for various types of protocol-driven reviews such as qualitative, quantitative and mixed-method systematic reviews, systematic methodological, economic and policy reviews, realist and integrative reviews. Conversely, others may not specify the type of literature review they accept. This means that if you have conducted a thorough and comprehensive traditional or narrative review on a particular aspect of nursing it will be considered for publication. These differences in publication criteria largely reflect the variation in the intended purpose of different journals and the readership to which they are directed. Therefore, it is essential that you familiarise yourself with the author guidelines as it will ultimately reduce the chances of your work being rejected. A further strategy in the process of determining the journal to which you wish to submit is to read back issues. Reading previously published literature review articles will not only assist with identifying the types of reviews that are published but may help you to understand more fully the submission guidelines for structuring the manuscript.

Once you have decided on which journal to pursue, you should access the author guidelines on the journal website. Although you may have structured your original review differently, it is crucial that you follow these guidelines closely. Failure to do so delays the review process at best and at worst can result in a rejection of your article. A key part of revising and preparing your literature review for submission is ensuring that you seek feedback on your drafts. A more experienced co-author can be very helpful at this stage by providing feedback and suggestions about how the article can be developed. Even if you have chosen to publish alone, it is still advisable to seek feedback from peers or colleagues who can provide advice on how to improve the paper. Before you submit your article you should ensure that you have met the manuscript preparation criteria specified by the journal, such as font size, formatting, submitting figures and tables and use of the preferred referencing system. Particular attention should be paid to ensuring that you have included all the references you have cited.

The majority of journals now require electronic submission through a manuscript tracking system. This has the advantage of giving instant feedback on the submission process and allows you to track the progress of your article by providing you with a unique code. Although completing the submission process can take some time, most allow you to save what you have done and return to it later. Manuscript tracking systems also permit you to review the document before final submission. Once completed, it is usual to receive a confirmation email.

The journal's website should provide you with information regarding the review process. Many journals undertake what is known as an editorial review before sending the manuscript to independent reviewers. The purpose of this is to make an initial assessment of the suitability of the article. This process also facilitates prompt feedback to the author. In the event of a paper being rejected it enables earlier submission to an alternative journal. If it is deemed an appropriate publication it is subjected to a blind peer review by at least two reviewers. You may be asked, as part of the submission process, to suggest a possible reviewer but in other instances journals retain a list of reviewers who have expertise in a particular area. Reviewers are asked to appraise submissions against specified criteria that are usually associated with the relevance of the topic to the discipline and the readership. In terms of rigour, reviewers are asked to provide feedback on the comprehensiveness of the review and its potential contribution to practice and/or knowledge. Other aspects that are considered are writing style and the clarity with which the content of the review is presented. This process can take some time, ranging from weeks to months.

Once the review process has been completed, the author receives the reviewer feedback and an editorial decision regarding publication. A paper may be accepted but with requests for revision that can range from minor to major. In this situation, the author is usually given a time limit for resubmission with amendments. Although revisions can necessitate substantial additional work it is worth completing them and attending to the reviewers' comments as you will then have the satisfaction of having your paper published. If major revisions are required, the paper may be sent for a second review.

It may also happen that your paper is rejected. Despite the fact that most people who publish will have experienced this, the first time it happens is quite disappointing and frustrating. Although it feels like a comment on the quality of your work, it may be that the topic is not consistent with the current focus of the journal. It is important, therefore, to attend carefully to the reviewers' comments as they often suggest how the paper might be developed for publication in an alternative journal.

Once revisions have been completed and approved, you will receive notification of the acceptance of your paper. Prior to publication, you will receive proofs of the article to check. You may be asked also for clarification and/or to correct any mistakes or omissions. It is very important that you check the proofs carefully as editorial changes may have been made to the original paper. At this stage, you should make sure that you are satisfied that any changes that have been made do not distort the intended message. If you are dissatisfied with the changes, you must inform the editor.

From the first submission of an article to publication can take many months, which to some extent is dictated by the review and revision processes. However, many journals now publish online ahead of paper publication and this has shortened the process.

Preparing a Verbal Presentation

Presenting a paper is another method of disseminating the findings of your literature review, and the process is considerably quicker than publishing a journal article. Papers can be presented in a number of settings, such as conferences, seminars, workshops and journal clubs.

The principles for choosing where you wish to present are very similar to those for deciding on an appropriate journal for an article. Primarily, you should focus on the purpose of your presentation and the audience to whom you wish to disseminate the findings of your literature review.

Presenting a paper at a conference is a popular means of sharing findings. There are numerous local, national and international conferences held every year and choosing the most appropriate one at which to present can be a daunting task. It is, therefore, advisable to consult with an experienced colleague to help you make the decision about which conference to target. Academics, senior practitioners or managers may be more familiar with potentially suitable conferences. Moreover, most conferences focus on a theme such as practice, education, research or management and it is important that your paper addresses this.

When the idea for presenting at a conference is first suggested you may feel anxious or nervous about presenting your work in a public setting. This is particularly the case when it is your first time, and it may influence your decision about whether to present locally, nationally or internationally. Many health service providers host annual conferences and you may feel more comfortable presenting locally to a familiar audience. Alternatively, some universities host student conferences that provide the opportunity to showcase students' work within a less perturbing environment. A further option is to consider seminars or workshops, which often focus on areas of specialist practice.

Regardless of which setting you ultimately choose, it is likely that you will be required to submit an abstract for review to the organisers. An abstract is essentially a summary of the paper you wish to present and it is the only means by which the selection panel can decide whether or not to accept your submission. Therefore, the golden rule for preparing an abstract is to follow the conference/seminar/workshop guidelines very closely. It is also crucial that your abstract title gives a very clear indication of what your presentation is about; as Fowler (2016b) suggests, titles that are too short or too long should be avoided. In addition, the abstract may subsequently appear in a book of abstracts that enables conference delegates to decide which presentations they wish to attend. Therefore, it is important that it is clear, succinct and accurate. Following review by the selection panel you will be informed if your abstract has been accepted. It is at this time that you can begin to plan how you will deliver your paper. For most, the presentation time is between 15 and 20 minutes with an additional 5 to 10 minutes for a question-and-answer session. Your paper is likely to be part of what are known as concurrent sessions where a group of presentations around a generally similar topic area are presented together. Adherence to the time allocated is, therefore, fundamental to the smooth running of the session and should be a key factor when preparing your presentation.

Keeping to a strict time allocation is a difficult task. Many speakers want to present as much of their material they can. For the most part, however, this will not be possible and you should begin your preparation by deciding on the key message you wish to convey. This could be a particularly interesting or controversial finding from your review. Do not be tempted to try to cram all the available information into the time allocated as this may lead to a rushed presentation that fails to capture the attention of your audience.

Most contemporary presentations are prepared using PowerPoint or similar. For a presentation of less than 30 minutes, there should be a maximum of 15 slides (equivalent to one every two minutes). Key points should be displayed on each slide with no more than six per slide. Overcrowded slides mean the font sizes are too small and they are difficult to read. It is recommended that for ease of reading and accessibility font sizes should be 20 or above. In addition, when there is too much information on a slide you can lose the audience as they are focusing on trying to read your slides rather than listening to what you are saying. If you have prepared well you should be sufficiently familiar with the material to be able to address each of the points with the aid of prompt cards or notes.

Other features that should be used with caution are vivid colour schemes, animated text and complex animations and transitions. While these can look impressive on a computer, when transferred to a projector they can be difficult to read and, if overused, can detract from the essential message. Help with preparing presentations may be available locally from the university or health service provider but assistance can also be found on the Internet.

Rehearsing is fundamental to ensuring that your final presentation is as polished as it can be. It also gives you the opportunity to ensure you are keeping to the allocated time. While a minute or two over time may not appear important, strict scheduling of sessions means that timing is important for the overall smooth running of the conference. Many conference organisers have timekeepers who may stop the presentation if you go over your allocated time and this can be frustrating for you and your audience. Moreover, going over your allocated time means there is less time for questions from interested attendees.

Presenting to peers or colleagues is a good idea as you will be able to receive constructive feedback within a safe environment. It will also allow you to practise and seek comments on your delivery. It is very likely that you will be nervous when you are presenting and this can affect how you communicate verbally and non-verbally. With practice you can moderate both the clarity and the speed with which you speak, as well as rehearse how to assume a good posture and maintain eye-contact with your audience.

Many conference organisers require that the presentation is submitted before the conference begins. This allows presentations to be loaded onto the appropriate computer before the conference starts with the aim of facilitating the transition from one presentation to the next. However, you should ensure that you have a backup copy on a flash drive in the event of a technological problem. When you arrive at the conference you should visit the venue for your presentation and ensure you are familiar with the audiovisual equipment.

Preparing a Poster Presentation

An alternative means of presenting at a conference, seminar or workshop is through a poster presentation. Developing posters is a skill that many undergraduates develop during their educational programmes as they often form part of a module assessment. Thus, when presented with the opportunity to develop a poster for presentation, students may feel less fearful. Moreover, poster presentations at conferences are often located together in a given area where conference attendees can examine them at their leisure. This facilitates a mode of communication that is less formal and more relaxed.

The same criteria apply when submitting an abstract for a poster presentation as for an oral presentation. The selection panel will review the submission and inform you when it is accepted. The time needed to prepare a poster should not be under-estimated and it is important to begin preparations once you have received the acceptance notification. Since you will not be able to include all the information from your review on the poster you will have to decide on the key message. Following this, the poster will have to be designed and possibly edited on more than one occasion before it is finally produced.

Seeking assistance with designing and producing a poster is recommended. Some universities and health service providers may be able to help with the design, following which you may be able to send it to a printer for a relatively small cost. The alternative is to design and produce the poster with the assistance of a professional graphic designer, although this can make the process expensive.

The conference organisers will have specified the size of the poster and it is important that you adhere to this so that it will fit the poster display units. General principles regarding the use of colour, typefaces and text are similar to those for an oral presentation using PowerPoint. Posters that are too busy, with strong colours, too much text and too many photographs or images can be difficult to read and detract from the overall message. Background and foreground colours should be chosen with care so that the text stands out clearly. Limiting the colours to two or three that complement each other is recommended. Typefaces should be limited to one or two and used consistently. Text should be presented concisely but preferably in blocks that can be read easily.

Despite the need to exercise caution about colour, typeface, text and content, your poster should still be sufficiently visually appealing to attract attention. Having a clearly visible title is important as conference attendees are likely to be viewing posters during breaks in conference proceedings. Therefore, they will have limited time and you need to grab their attention. Used judiciously, graphics, figures and photographs will add to the visual impact of the poster.

Whatever the setting in which you are presenting your poster, it is expected that you will be available to answer any questions viewers may have. You should, therefore, be present at the poster at times when you know there are people likely to be viewing it. An unattended poster will receive less attention and removes the opportunity for you to showcase your work.

Summary

This chapter has provided a brief outline of some of the avenues you might pursue to disseminate or share the findings of a literature review that forms part of a dissertation or which has been submitted as an academic assignment. These include submitting to a journal for publication or presenting a paper or poster at a conference, seminar or workshop.

❛ Key Points ❜

- A literature review may produce findings that are of interest to your discipline.
- Literature reviews that form part of a dissertation or have been written for an academic assignment have the potential to be published.
- Disseminating the findings of a literature review through publication in a journal or an oral presentation or poster at a conference, seminar or workshop has the potential to raise awareness, provoke discussion and identify implications for future practice, education and research in the area.

APPENDIX

CRITIQUING QUANTITATIVE AND QUALITATIVE RESEARCH

Critiquing Quantitative Research

There are numerous instruments available for critiquing quantitative research. Most research textbooks offer their own instruments, while many others are to be found in research journals. However, while these instruments are based on the same principles and ask similar questions, some questions are more important than others, especially in relation to evaluating a study for a literature review. When critically analysing a study in a literature review the questions that are most likely to be of importance are those that focus on the integrity or robustness of the study (Ryan-Wenger, 1992; Coughlan et al., 2007). However, for the sake of completeness, those questions that focus on the credibility of the study will also be included. When using an instrument to critique a study it is best to read through the study once or twice and become familiar with the content before beginning the critique.

Questions Related to Credibility in Quantitative Research

Credibility or believability questions (Ryan-Wenger, 1992; Coughlan et al., 2007) are usually presented first in a critiquing tool. These questions focus on aspects such as the title of the work, the abstract, the author's qualifications, and writing style. These questions can be useful when critiquing a study as they can offer the reviewer some insight as to how well the study may have been conducted. A common error that is made by students or novices to the art of critiquing is to state that a study is 'weak' or has limitations based on credibility variables. These questions do not look at the robustness of the study, so while these questions may lead to a first impression, judgements should be reserved until the questions related to the integrity of the study are appraised.

When considering the questions in these critiquing tools, you should regard them as stimulating inquiry. So rather than simply responding with a yes or no, you should reflect on the potential implications of the researcher's action and whether this appears to strengthen or limit the credibility or the integrity of the study, depending on which factors and questions are being reviewed (see Table A.1). Remember to support your critique with evidence from the literature.

Table A.1   Credibility and Integrity Factors in a Quantitative Research Study

Credibility/Believability: Influencing Factors and Related Questions	
Title	Does the report title identify what the study is about in a clear and unambiguous way?
Abstract	Is an outline of the study clearly present? Does it include the research problem, sampling method and size, methodology, findings and recommendations?
Author	Do the author's experiences and/or qualifications suggest knowledge or expertise in this particular field of enquiry?
Writing style	Is the report on the study presented in a clear and organised manner? Is it easy to read and understand, grammatically correct and does it avoid excessive use of jargon?

Integrity/Robustness: Influencing Factors and Related Questions	
Logical consistency	Is the study presented in a logical order following the steps of the research process?
Research problem/ purpose	Is the purpose of the study or the research problem clearly defined?
Review of the literature	Is the literature review presented in an organised manner, demonstrating development of themes from previous research? Does the review offer a balanced overview of the research problem/topic of interest? Is there evidence of critical analysis of the works presented? Is the literature mainly from primary sources and is it mainly empirical or theoretical in nature?
Theoretical framework	Has a conceptual framework been identified? If yes, is it clearly described and is it an appropriate framework for this study?
Aims, objectives, research questions, hypotheses	Have the aims or objectives, research questions and hypotheses been presented in a clear and concise manner? Do they reflect the purpose of the study/research problem and the information gleaned from the literature review?
Research design and instruments	Has the research methodology and the rationale for selecting it been discussed? Has the research instrument been described? Is it appropriate for this study? How was it developed? Were reliability and validity testing performed? Were the results of these discussed? Was a pilot study performed?
Operational definitions	Have all the terms, theories and concepts that may influence the study been defined and clearly described to the reader?
Sample	Was the target population described? Was the method of sample selection described? Was a probability or non-probability sampling technique used? Was the sample size adequate? Were inclusion/ exclusion criteria identified?
Ethical considerations	Were participants given enough information to make an informed choice in regard to participating in the study? Was confidentiality/ anonymity guaranteed by the researcher? Were the participants protected from harm? Was ethical approval granted for this study?
Findings/data analysis	Were the data obtained and statistical analysis undertaken appropriate for the study? How many of the sample participated in the study? Were the data tables/charts accurate? Was the statistical significance of the findings identified?

Integrity/Robustness: Influencing Factors and Related Questions	
Discussion	Were the findings discussed with reference to the literature review? If there was a hypothesis, was it supported or rejected? Did the author(s) discuss the strengths and limitations of the study? Were recommendations for future studies identified?
References	Were all the texts, journal articles, websites and other media sources referred to in the study accurately referenced?

Source: Adapted from Coughlan et al. (2007)

Title

A good title should give a reasonable insight into the purpose and type of study being undertaken. The PRISMA guidelines (Liberati et al., 2009), for example, recommend that a systematic review or meta-analysis should be identified as such in the title. A question frequently asked is, how long should a report title be? Titles should be long enough to give the reader sufficient information as to what the study is about but short enough to avoid confusion (Parahoo, 2014). A general rule of thumb is that they should be between 10 and 15 words in length.

Abstract

Abstracts are expected to be concise but offer enough information for the reader to determine if this study is of interest. The abstract should identify the purpose of the study, and offer an overview of the research method, sample, the main findings, conclusions and recommendations. They are usually about 150–200 words in length, but there are variations between journals, and in some journals abstracts may not be clearly identified or presented.

Author

The expertise and qualifications of the author(s) can be good indicators of the knowledge and skills that are being brought to the study. A background and familiarity with the topic under investigation increases the likelihood that the questions will be relevant and reflect the reality of the situation. However, novice researchers with little background in an area can still do very good research, and experienced researchers can do poor research. So never assume that because the researcher is well qualified that the study will not have limitations.

Writing Style

A research report should be written in a clear and concise style. It should be easily understood and grammatically correct, avoiding the unnecessary use of jargon. It is usually expected that quantitative reports are written in the third person, which is deemed to increase objectivity.

Questions Related to Integrity in Quantitative Research

The focus of these questions is to determine how robust the study appears to be, and how thoroughly the steps in the research process were adhered to. It is within this section of a critique that the strengths or limitations of a study can be determined.

Logical Consistency

A research study should be presented in a coherent manner that indicates that the researcher(s) followed the steps in the research process. The steps should be clearly defined, with logical development as the study progresses from the research problem through the literature review and onwards (Cronin et al., 2015).

Research Problem/Purpose

The research problem or purpose of the study is usually identified early in the work and offers the reader a broad idea of what is to be investigated. It often represents a general area of interest that may need to be further refined.

Review of the Literature

In a research study the function of a literature review is to explore and refine the research problem. Any gaps in the literature, related to the research problem, should be identified. There should be evidence that an appropriate depth and breadth of reading related to the topic, was undertaken. While the majority of studies presented should be of recent origin, it is important that influential seminal works are also included. Seminal research can help put the study into context, so it is expected that authors will include some older studies as well as contemporary literature within the review. Studies should ideally be contemporary at the time of publication, but this will depend on the amount of literature available that is related to the research problem. The source and the nature of literature presented are two other important considerations. The literature should come from the primary source, with secondary sourced literature being used only in exceptional circumstances. Furthermore, the literature in a review should be mainly empirical in nature rather than from anecdotal or opinion articles that are not research based.

In the introduction to the literature review it is expected that the keywords used and databases sourced in the literature search will be identified. The author then usually identifies the themes that emerged from the literature as a means of signposting how the literature will be presented. The literature presented should be critically analysed and the strengths and limitations of studies included should be identified for the reader.

Theoretical Framework

A theoretical or conceptual framework is a means of organising a study. While the terms are often used interchangeably, Polit and Beck (2012) state that where the study is constructed around a theory, the framework is theoretical; and where the study is structured around a concept, the framework is regarded as conceptual. The purpose of these frameworks is to identify the concepts/theories being studied and the relationships between them. It must be stated that while not all researchers are explicit in identifying a theoretical framework, every study has a framework (Polit and Beck, 2012). Experimental and correlational studies tend to have theoretical frameworks that are better developed, with a greater likelihood of an implicit framework being found in descriptive studies. Ideally, the theoretical framework should be explicitly stated.

Aims, Objectives, Research Questions, Hypotheses

Aims, objectives, research questions and hypotheses should reflect what was found in the literature review and form a link with the original research problem or purpose. They are usually more developed than the research problem and identify the variables of interest, their possible interrelationships and the target population (Polit and Beck, 2012). Their use varies in different types of quantitative studies. In descriptive studies, aims, objectives or research questions can be used to express the focus of the research; however, in some instances, the researcher will only refer to the purpose of the study. In correlational studies, where the existence of a relationship between variables is the focus of the research, research questions and/or hypotheses (a hypothesis is the research question expressed as a statement) may be presented. In experimental, quasi-experimental studies and randomised controlled trials (RCTs) hypotheses are used to identify the variables that are being explored.

Research Design and Instruments

The terms 'research method', 'research design' and 'methodology' are often used interchangeably (Parahoo, 2014). What they describe is the blueprint for the study. The research design should identify how the study will be performed, the method of data gathering and the type of analysis that will be performed on the data gathered.

The researcher is expected to clearly describe the research method that has been selected and to discuss why this approach was selected. The research method selected should be compatible with the purpose of the study. The next consideration is the data-gathering instrument. Again, this needs to be appropriate for what the researcher is attempting to achieve. Depending on what the researcher is investigating, there may be research instruments available that can be purchased or used with the developer's permission. However, it may also be necessary for a researcher to develop a new instrument or to adapt a pre-existing instrument.

An important feature of any research instrument is its validity, which is its ability to measure what it is supposed to measure. Another is the consistency with which it measures these variables, how reliable it is. It is, therefore, important that the researcher tests both the validity and the reliability of the instrument that is being used. An exception is sometimes made for established instruments that have been shown to have strong validity and reliability with a variety of populations. In these cases the test results in relation to validity and reliability, from appropriate previous studies, should be presented. However, if the researcher has any doubts, has adapted the instrument in any way or is using it on a novel population, validity and reliability testing should be undertaken.

A pilot study can be described as field-testing an instrument to determine how well it works with a smaller sample of the population. Items that are unclear or ambiguous, which were not noticed earlier, can be identified and rectified at this stage before the main study is undertaken. Difficulties with sample selection and sample participation can also be diagnosed and corrected at this stage. The researcher should identify if a pilot study was undertaken, the numbers involved and the participation rate, and any changes that were made as a result of this field test. Those who participate in the pilot study are not usually included in the main study, nor are the results of the pilot study normally included in the findings of the main study.

Operational Definitions

It is quite common in a study to find terms or concepts whose meanings can vary considerably between one jurisdiction and another and thus alter the reader's perception of the research. It is, therefore, necessary for the researcher to ensure that all concepts and terms mentioned within the study are clearly defined so that the reader understands what exactly is being referred to.

Sampling

In quantitative research, studies should attempt to select samples that are representative of the population so as to increase the probability of generalising the findings. In order to increase the chance of a representative sample two things are required from a sampling perspective: a probability (random) sample and an adequate sample size. Probability samples require a sampling frame which can be difficult to acquire, so researchers sometimes use non-probability samples, such as convenience sampling. Non-probability samples are less likely to be representative and this should be acknowledged as a limitation by the researcher if this type of sampling is used. Sample size is important because there is always a risk that a minority group within the population might dominate the sample and skew the results – a sampling error. The larger the sample size the less likely this is to happen and the more likely the sample will be representative, but only if the sample is selected using a probability method.

The researcher should clearly define who the population for the study were, what method of sampling was used and how it was undertaken, and what the sample size was. Inclusion and exclusion criteria should also be made explicit and, if necessary, justified.

Ethical Considerations

There are four fundamental ethical principles, and four moral rules which are closely linked to these principles, which should be adhered to in all research. These are: autonomy, beneficence, non-maleficence and justice; and veracity, fidelity, confidentiality and privacy (Beauchamp and Childress, 2013). It is expected that the researcher will identify, within the study, how these principles and rules were adhered to and what processes were put in place to protect the participants. Autonomy implies that the participant has had the opportunity to make an informed decision as to whether or not to participate within the study. This decision should be made free from any coercion or promise of reward. The principle of beneficence implies that the participant and society will benefit from the outcomes of the study. Non-maleficence implies that the research will cause no harm, either physical or psychological, to the participant. While the latter two principles may appear to be similar, they are more like the two sides of the same coin with a different focus. Justice implies that all individuals and groups within the study are equal, and no group or individual will be privileged or disadvantaged because of their position within society. The four moral codes are closely linked to the principle of autonomy and imply the researcher will be honest, loyal and trustworthy in dealing with participants, and respect the confidentiality and privacy of subjects whether or not they participate in the study.

Ethical approval is another important issue that should be considered here. The researcher should state whether ethical approval was sought and identify the approving bodies. Hospitals and similar institutions generally have ethical committees to whom research proposals must be submitted before permission to undertake the research will be granted. In the case of third-level students, permission is usually also required from the educational institution before research can be undertaken.

Findings/Data Analysis

In this section, data are analysed and should be presented to the reader in a clear and concise manner. The researcher usually starts by identifying how many of the sample participated in the study, which can be an important factor in determining how generalisable the results may be (Polit and Beck, 2014). It is generally accepted that a participation rate of at least 50 per cent is needed to reduce the risk of response bias.

Quantitative data are analysed using statistical tests and these are usually under-taken using a statistical program such as Statistical Package for the Social Sciences (SPSS). In general, quantitative descriptive research uses descriptive statistics to present findings, whereas correlational, quasi-experimental and experimental stud-ies use both descriptive and inferential statistics. Descriptive statistics simply describe the numerical findings of the study. Inferential statistics are about drawing inferences or deductions from the results. The latter can be used to demonstrate if relationships exist, or if there are differences between variables, and the degree to which these relationships/differences are a result of a chance occurrence or are potentially real – this is known as the level of significance. The lowest acceptable level of significance is usually $p \leq 0.05$. This means that the probability (p) or odds of this result occurring by chance are 5 or less in 100.

The researcher should identify what types of statistical tests were used in the study and the results should be presented to the reader. Tables, graphs and charts can be used to enhance the clarity of the findings and should be compatible with the results.

Discussion

The purpose of the discussion is to contextualise the results for the reader by linking them to the literature presented in the review. The section usually commences with the researcher restating the purpose, research question or hypothesis. If the study had a hypothesis, the researcher should state if it was supported or rejected by the findings. He/she should also identify if the research question was answered or whether the purpose was achieved. In the discussion the researcher presents, with reference to the literature, an interpretation of what the results might mean. The implications for clinical practice should also be explored. It is also within this sec-tion that the researcher will usually acknowledge the strengths and limitations of the study, especially in relation to the significance of the findings and their generalisabil-ity to the target population. The study report usually concludes with a summary of the research undertaken, and the current state of knowledge in relation to the topic of interest. This is usually followed by recommendations for improving the current study or for future related research.

References

The author should ensure that there is an accurate reference list of all the books, articles and other media sources referred to in the study. This can be a useful resource for clarifying information or for future studies in the area.

Critiquing Qualitative Research

Qualitative research is more than simply a different way of studying a phenomenon of interest. It differs from quantitative research in a number of fundamental areas such as:

- *the nature of knowledge*: it accepts that knowledge is subjective rather than objective;
- *holism*: a phenomenon is more than the sum of its parts and cannot be reduced to a number of variables in order to study it;
- *generalisability*: qualitative research is interested in exploring the individual's experience rather than attempting to generalise to the sample population (Grove et al., 2013).

Therefore it is sensible to use a tool specifically designed for critiquing qualitative research when analysing studies in this paradigm. There is a wide range of critiquing tools available for critiquing qualitative research. Most textbooks will usually offer a critiquing tool specifically aimed at qualitative research and again the principles underpinning these tools are similar. As in the previous critiquing tool, the factors related to the integrity of the study are most likely to offer important insights. Factors and questions related to the credibility and integrity of a qualitative research study are presented in Table A.2.

Table A.2   Credibility and Integrity Factors in a Qualitative Research Study

Credibility/Believability: Influencing Factors and Related Questions	
Title	Does the report title identify what the study is about in a clear and unambiguous way?
Abstract	Is an outline of the study clearly present? Does it include the research problem, sampling method and size, methodology, and findings and recommendations?
Author	Do the author's experience and/or qualifications suggest knowledge or expertise in this particular field of enquiry?
Writing style	Is the report on the study presented in a clear and organised manner? Is it easily read and understood and grammatically correct, and does it avoid excessive use of jargon?
Integrity/Robustness: Influencing Factors and Related Questions	
Logical consistency	Is the study presented in a logical order following the steps of the research process?
Statement of the phenomenon of interest	Is the phenomenon of interest clearly identified? Does the research question reflect the phenomenon of interest?
Purpose/significance of the study	Are the purpose of the study and the research problem clearly defined?
Review of the literature	Has a review of the relevant literature been undertaken? Does it reflect the philosophical underpinnings related to the qualitative method selected? Were the purposes of the review achieved?
Theoretical framework	Has a conceptual framework been identified? If yes, is it clearly described and is it an appropriate framework for this study?

(Continued)

Table A.2   *(Continued)*

Integrity/Robustness: Influencing Factors and Related Questions

Method and philosophical underpinning	Was the research method identified? Why was this approach chosen? Did the researcher explain the philosophical underpinnings of the method selected?
Sample	Was the method by which the sample was selected discussed? Was the selection method suitable for the approach used? Did the sample have the appropriate experience to inform the research?
Ethical considerations	Were participants given enough information to make an informed choice in regard to participating in the study? Was confidentiality guaranteed by the researcher? Were the participants protected from harm? Was ethical approval granted for this study?
Data collection and analysis	Were the methods for gathering data and data analysis discussed? Were these methods congruent with the research approach selected? Was data saturation achieved?
Rigour	How was the trustworthiness of the study assured? Did the researcher discuss elements such as credibility, auditability, transferability and confirmability?
Findings and discussion	Were the findings presented clearly? Were the participant quotations used appropriately to support the themes? Was the report placed in context with what was already known regarding the phenomenon? Was the research question answered or the original purpose of the study addressed?
Conclusions, implications and recommendations	Will the findings of this study be of interest to the profession? Were the implications for clinical practice identified? Were recommendations made as to how future research might develop the findings of this study?
References	Were all the texts, journal articles, websites and other media sources referred to in the study accurately referenced?

Source: Adapted from Ryan et al. (2007)

Questions Related to Credibility and Integrity in Qualitative Research

The factors influencing, and the questions related to, the credibility of a qualitative article are similar to those discussed earlier in this appendix for quantitative research. The factors and questions related to integrity, however, differ substantially, demonstrating the differences in approach between these two paradigms. Again, it is within the integrity section that the strengths and limitations of a qualitative study can be recognised. It is important to remember that the qualitative paradigm consists of a number of different research approaches, each with their own, often distinct, philosophy, processes of managing and analysing data, and their own discrete terminology (Cronin et al., 2015). For example, within phenomenology there are a number of philosophical variations that lead to characteristic methods of managing and analysing data. Husserlian phenomenologists distance themselves from the phenomenon by 'bracketing' their views, beliefs and understandings so as to prevent these influencing their description of the participants' experience. This is in contrast to Heideggerian phenomenologists who do not believe bracketing is possible, but also use this pre-existing knowledge to help them interpret the participants' experiences. Ethnographic researchers use a different approach to data gathering, spending large amounts of time living or working in close proximity to their subjects, as well as observing or questioning them, in order to gain insights into their culture and way of life. An example of this can be seen in the movie *Avatar*, which also demonstrates one of the potential difficulties – 'going native' (Polit and Beck, 2012), when researchers completely lose their scholarly identity in favour of group membership. Grounded theory, on the other hand, uses participants' perspectives to develop and verify a hypothesis and so develop a theory grounded in the research. However, despite these differences, there are many similarities within these approaches and there are common factors that can be critically analysed.

Logical Consistency

A research study should be presented in a coherent manner that indicates that the researcher(s) followed the steps in the research process. The steps should be clearly defined, with logical development as the study progresses from the research problem through the literature review and onwards (Cronin et al., 2015).

Statement of the Phenomenon of Interest

A phenomenon is an abstract experience, for example pain or anxiety. The experience of a phenomenon can be shaped by numerous different factors and so an experience could be interpreted quite differently by two individuals or even by the same individual under different conditions. The phenomenon to be studied should be explicitly identified and this should be reflected in the research question.

Purpose/Significance of the Study

The researcher should clearly identify what they hope to achieve by undertaking this study and why this is important, and how the study will add to the body of information that already exists. The researcher should also offer a rationale for selecting a qualitative methodology to investigate this phenomenon.

Review of the Literature

The function of the literature review in qualitative research is to identify and present what is already known regarding the phenomenon of interest. This in turn will be used to support the themes that emerge from the data. In some qualitative approaches the literature review is not undertaken until after the data are gathered. Two such approaches are grounded theory and phenomenology. In grounded theory, data gathering and analysis should be undertaken without being prejudiced by pre-existing influences. The purpose is to generate theory from the data gathered, so for this reason the review of the literature is undertaken after data gathering is complete and with reference to the analysed data (Polit and Beck, 2012). In phenomenology, the lived experience of the participants is the central focus of the research. Again, the researcher attempts to avoid external influences until the participants' experiences have been described or interpreted, at which stage the literature is used to support the resultant themes (Grove et al., 2013). Ethnographic studies often use a combination of a short overview of literature at the outset of the study to contextualise the cultural issue to be investigated, and a more in-depth review later in the study to support the data analysis (Polit and Beck, 2012).

Whether the review is undertaken at the beginning of the study or after data analysis, the researcher should identify how the review was undertaken. If the literature review is done at the beginning of the study, it should be similar in nature to a quantitative review offering a comprehensive and balanced synopsis of the studies previously undertaken, conceptual or theoretical frameworks, and themes used to form a background to the study.

Theoretical Framework

Theoretical frameworks can be useful in some descriptive or exploratory qualitative studies for setting boundaries or identifying why certain aspects of a phenomenon where selected for investigation. However, in other qualitative methodologies, such as grounded theory, ethnography or phenomenology, where the purpose is to develop theory, an existing theoretical framework is not used.

Method and Philosophical Underpinning

The researcher should indicate why the qualitative paradigm and the particular methodological approach were chosen. The philosophical underpinnings of the approach should also be presented. The latter are important as they are the framework that identifies how the research process should proceed, for example how participants should be selected, how data should be gathered, how analysis should be undertaken and how findings are presented. Different qualitative methodologies have different philosophies, which are often not compatible with each other, so mixing and matching (method slurring) between the different approaches is not generally recommended. For instance if a researcher claims to be using grounded theory and presents the findings by identifying themes rather than a substantive theory then he/she is not being true to the underpinning philosophy (Polit and Beck, 2014). However, Nepal (2010) and Morse (2009) argue that there are exceptions to the use of mixed qualitative methods, for instance when the research question cannot be fully addressed unless two qualitative methods are used. However, these methods should be clearly identified from the outset of the study, and a rationale should be included as to why this mixed method approach is justified (Nepal, 2010; Morse, 2009). It is important, therefore, that there is congruence between the philosophy and the way the research is undertaken.

Sample

When selecting a sample for a qualitative study, the researcher should attempt to ensure that the participants have experience of the phenomenon being investigated. This type of sampling, known as purposive or purposeful sampling, ensures a breadth and depth of data on the phenomenon of interest. In grounded theory, as themes emerge the researcher may select participants with experience related to those themes. This type of selection is known as theoretical sampling. Convenience samples are also used in some qualitative studies.

Samples used in qualitative research are non-probability as there is no desire to select a representative sample. Instead, the researcher seeks to generate an in-depth knowledge of the phenomenon that reflects the participants' experiences. Samples are also usually small in size. The researcher's hope is to achieve data saturation – that is, a point where the inclusion of further participants will not lead to any new data. This should be the true determinant of a qualitative sample size; however, it is rarely more than aspirational especially in small research studies.

Ethical Considerations

The ethical principles and moral codes that apply in qualitative research are similar to those in quantitative studies, as is the process of ethical approval for the research. Some areas, however, need further consideration within qualitative studies. Data gathering in the qualitative paradigm often involves in-depth interviews during which participants can often inadvertently reveal information that they had not planned to discuss, or the interview may raise topics that trigger uncomfortable or forgotten experiences. As a result, participants my not feel happy or comfortable continuing with the interview. Process consent is a method of continuously negotiating with participants to determine whether they are happy to continue or wish to discontinue the interview. The principle of non-maleficence also has a role here, as the unresolved grief or other issues that may have arisen during the interview can have a negative emotional effect on the participant. In anticipation of such an event the researcher should have some form of psychological support available for participants.

Confidentiality is another ethical issue that needs consideration. The most common methods of data gathering used in qualitative research are interview and observation, and as a result participants are known to the researcher and therefore cannot be anonymous. Also, when presenting raw data to support the themes that emerge, the researcher needs to ensure the information presented will not expose the participant to being identified.

Data Collection and Analysis

There are a number of different methods of data collection available to researchers undertaking a qualitative study, the most common of which are interview (semi-structured and unstructured), focus groups and participant observation. The method of data collection, however, should be compatible with the methodology selected and the researcher should justify why that method was selected.

In qualitative research, data collection and analysis occur concurrently. Depending on the methodology adopted, there are specific steps that the researcher is expected to undertake when analysing the data. In some instances there are instruments available to aid this process; however, the instrument should be compatible with the given philosophy. To this end, there needs to be sufficient information available for the reader to determine if the final outcome of analysis is based on the data gathered in the study.

Rigour

The researcher is expected to demonstrate to the reader that steps have been taken to ensure the trustworthiness of the analytical process. The main criteria used to evaluate rigour are credibility, dependability, transferability and confirmability (Morse, 2015). Credibility attempts to establish how accurate the researcher is when representing the participants' experiences. One method of demonstrating credibility is by asking participants to review the results of the study to see if they are consistent with their experiences. Alternatively, Koch (2006) recommends that the researcher maintains a field journal – a record of interactions, reactions and content – that can be reflected upon when analysing the data and used to justify analysis. Dependability, also known as auditability, is said to exist when there is sufficient information presented for the reader to recognise and follow the decision trail. The decision trail discusses how decisions in relation to the theoretical, methodological and analytical choices were made (Koch, 2006). Transferability, also known as applicability or fittingness, is based on the degree to which the study's findings fit into other situations that are outside the context of the study. It is said to be present when readers can apply the study's results to their own experiences or when the findings are applicable to others not involved in the study. Finally, confirmability is about offering a clear demonstration of how interpretations were made and conclusions were drawn. Koch (2006) claims that confirmability can be deemed to have been achieved if the researcher can demonstrate credibility, dependability and transferability.

Findings/Discussion

There are a number of different ways in which the findings of a qualitative research study can be presented depending on the approach selected. Nonetheless, the findings should be presented clearly and supported with extracts from the data gathered. The findings should be discussed with regard to what is known about the topic, and depending on the methodological approach a further review of the literature may have been undertaken to achieve this. The findings should also be related back to the purpose of the study or research question, and the discussion should indicate if these have been satisfactorily addressed within the study.

Conclusions/Implications/Recommendations

The results of a study should add to the existing body of knowledge on that topic. It is expected that the researcher will conclude by identifying how this study is likely to do this and what implications these findings may have for clinical practice. The researcher should also state how the findings might be further developed and/or identify other related areas that arose during the study and need further investigation.

References

As in quantitative research all works referred to in the study should be accurately referenced.

GLOSSARY

Binary (dichotomous) data: Data in which there are only two categories – e.g. alive/dead, sick/well.

Citation: This is acknowledgement of another author's ideas or work by referring to or citing them as the source.

Concept: An abstract idea about a particular phenomenon.

Concept analysis: A method by which concepts that are of interest to any discipline are examined in order to clarify their characteristics, thereby achieving a better understanding of the meaning of that concept.

Conceptual framework: Concepts of similar meaning that provide a means for understanding a particular phenomenon and may be used to guide the analysis phase of a study.

Confidence interval: The range in which we are reasonably confident the population parameter lies, e.g. the mean of the population from which we have drawn our sample.

Continuous data: Data that can have an infinite number of possible values, e.g. weight, area, volume.

Critical appraisal/analysis: An assessment/evaluation of the quality of a research report. It differs from a critique in that only the significant strengths/limitations of the study are presented.

Critique: A critical examination of all aspects of a research report that identifies both the strengths and the limitations of a study.

Data: Information gleaned from any source.

Descriptive synthesis: The collation and presentation of information about each study included in a review. This is often presented as a summary table of key aspects. A descriptive synthesis of literature other than primary studies can also be collated and presented.

Dissemination: Most dictionary definitions refer to dissemination as 'scattering', 'spreading' or 'dispersing'. In the context of healthcare research and knowledge it is a planned process associated usually with informing others about the results of research studies. However, dissemination is not confined to the findings of research studies.

Effect measure: The observed relationship between an intervention and an outcome.

Ethnography: A qualitative research approach that has its origins in anthropology and studies group culture as a means of understanding behaviour.

Evidence-based medicine/evidence-based practice: Integrating the best available research evidence with clinical expertise and the individual patient's values and preferences in order to make decisions about that patient's care.

Fixed-effect model: A means of 'weighting' the contribution of a study to the overall summary estimate in a meta-analysis. Fixed-effect assumes one effect size with the result that studies that are larger and contain more information are given greater weighting than smaller studies.

Forest plot: A graphic display of the information from individual studies in a meta-analysis. It illustrates the amount of variation between studies and the overall result. It also displays the 'confidence interval' (see above) of each result.

Grounded theory: A qualitative research approach that attempts to generate a theory based on the data gathered from participants in a study.

Hierarchies of evidence: Some evidence is valued more highly than other evidence, based primarily on the type of research used to generate it. Randomised controlled trials (RCTs) are considered the 'gold standard', with qualitative studies rated as the least rigorous and reliable. This hierarchy is now seen as controversial.

Integrative literature review: Summarises and draws conclusions on past research on a given topic. Research is interpreted in its broadest sense and literature that is sourced can include primary research, and theoretical and conceptual literature.

Literature review: An identification, analysis, assessment and interpretation of a body of knowledge on a given topic/subject.

Literature search: Searching for and identifying appropriate literature to address a given research/review question.

Mean difference (weighted mean difference): The mean difference or 'difference in means' measures the absolute difference between the means in two groups. The difference represents the amount by which an intervention changes the outcome on average when compared with the control group.

Meta-analysis: A process of statistical analysis of numerical data where the findings of individual studies are pooled and re-analysed as one, bigger data set. The research designs and methods of the included studies must be reasonably homogeneous (similar) with the gold standard being RCTs. The outcome of such an exercise is to increase the power and the accuracy of the effect of an intervention.

Meta-ethnography: A synthesis of first- and second-order concepts to construct a new interpretation or theory about the phenomenon under study. First-order concepts are those identified by the participants in an individual study. Second-order concepts are the original researcher's interpretation of the first-order concepts. The main purpose of a meta-ethnography is to create a new or third-order interpretation.

Meta-study: An approach to the synthesis of qualitative research studies that has three analytic phases: meta-data analysis, meta-method and meta-theory. These three analytic strategies must be undertaken before meta-synthesis can occur. The aim is to generate new and more complete understandings of the phenomenon under study.

Meta-synthesis: A process whereby the findings from individual qualitative research studies are deconstructed (broken down), examined and reconstructed into a new interpretation.

Narrative/traditional/descriptive literature review: A literature review conducted to identify, analyse, assess and interpret a body of knowledge on a topic. The results of the review are presented narratively, usually in the form of themes.

Narrative synthesis: Similar to a thematic analysis in that it uses narrative to synthesise evidence. However, it differs in that it attempts to generate new knowledge or insights. The narrative involves an analysis of the relationships within and between studies and assesses the strength of the evidence.

Naturalistic: Associated with qualitative research, upholding the notion of multiple subjective realities that are constructed by individuals and are context bound.

Non-probability sampling: A sample that is probably not representative of the population of interest. Purposive and convenience sampling are examples of non-probability sampling.

Odds ratio: Assesses how likely it is that someone who is exposed to the factor under study will develop an outcome compared to someone who is not exposed. An odds ratio of 1 indicates no difference between the groups being compared.

Paraphrasing: Presenting another author's work or ideas in your own words. The original author must be acknowledged as the source.

Phenomenology: A philosophical movement that has had significant influence in the conduct of qualitative research. Phenomenology is concerned with the study of the lived experience.

Plagiarism: Taking another author's work and claiming it as your own. It most frequently occurs when writers fail to acknowledge another author's work that they have quoted or paraphrased.

Population: In research, a population consists of all the individuals who could potentially participate in the research and to whom the results apply.

Positivism: Is a paradigm (way of looking at the world) that is associated with the traditional method of scientific enquiry and quantitative research methods. Features of positivism include beliefs that an objective reality exists and can be measured. Positivism has largely been replaced with post-positivism, which is a more moderate extension of its philosophy.

Probability sampling: A quantitative sampling method in which all members of the population have an equal chance (greater than zero) of being selected. Random sampling methods are examples.

Purpose/aim: A clear statement that broadly identifies, both to the reader and the researcher, what is to be achieved. It is usually identified early in the work and acts as a signpost for the reader.

Purposive sampling: A form of non-probability sampling where participants are invited to participate in a research study on the basis that they have experience of the phenomenon under investigation. Used primarily in qualitative research.

Qualitative meta-summary: A process of aggregating qualitative research findings through a quantitative process for the purpose of determining the frequency of each finding in and across studies.

Qualitative research: Research involving the subjective experiences and perceptions of participants. Data are not analysed statistically.

Quantitative research: Research that involves quantifying and measuring data statistically.

Quotation: Taking a segment of another author's work and presenting it word for word as it originally appeared. The quotation is presented in inverted commas or is indented in the text, and the original author is acknowledged by the reviewer.

Random-effect model: Another means of 'weighting' the contribution of a study to the overall summary statistic in a meta-analysis. Random-effect assumes that factors in the study such as the population in the study, implementation or measurement of the intervention result in variation in effect sizes across studies. This results in greater balance between larger and smaller studies.

Randomised controlled trial (RCT): An experiment that is designed to test the effectiveness of an intervention. In an RCT participants are randomly allocated to one of two groups. One group receives the intervention and the other does not. The results are compared between the two groups.

Realist literature review: Developed originally for complex social interventions to examine how context influences the relationship between an intervention and its outcome. It focuses on discovering what works, how it works, for whom it works, the extent to which it works and under what conditions.

References: A list of all the authors and their works referred to or quoted within a review, study or any written work.

Relative risk: Compares risk levels. In a study with two groups (one control and one intervention) the relative risk is the proportion of people in *both* groups who would experience the event. For example, the risk of developing lung cancer is much higher among smokers than non-smokers. Relative risk calculates this proportion. A relative risk of 1 indicates no difference between the groups being compared.

Research problem: An issue or question that needs further evidence to help resolve it. The problem can relate to practice or other issues, such as patients' knowledge or behaviour. In some situations the research problem may be identified by reviewing some of the literature associated with the research topic and identifying where there are gaps. Alternatively, a clinical or practice problem can sometimes help to identify a research topic.

Research question: A brief statement formulated as a question. There can be more than one presented in a study. It usually has a narrow focus and is frequently presented after the literature review. In a systematic review, however, a focused research question is needed to perform the review as, in essence, this type of review is a research study in its own right.

Research topic/phenomenon of interest: A broad area of interest, also called a concept, which forms the basis for a research study or literature review. In qualitative research it is sometimes identified as the phenomenon of interest.

Response rate: The number of people who participate in a study.

Response bias: Where a low response rate in a study results in outcomes that are not a true reflection of those of the population from which the sample was drawn.

Sampling error: An error in statistical analysis resulting from the fact that the sample is not representative of the population from which it was drawn.

Scoping literature review: A non-protocol-driven literature review scopes the literature for a number of reasons that can include: mapping research activity in a given area; determining the feasibility of undertaking a full systematic review; summarising and disseminating research to interested groups; identifying gaps in the research; developing methodological/theoretical ideas for future research; justifying future research; and clarifying conceptual understanding. It differs from other types of review in that it does not formally appraise the quality of the research or make recommendations.

Search strategy: A plan that is defined in advance for searching for information on the topic of interest.

Standard deviation: A statistical measure of the dispersion or spread of data from the mean (average). Most data in a sample is what is known as 'normally distributed', which means that the results are close or reasonably close to the average. Standard deviation measures how tightly the results are spread around the average. The standard deviation is useful for determining how diverse the results are for a given study.

Standardised mean difference: Used as a summary statistic when a number of studies have measured the same outcome but have done so in different ways. Because different measures are used, the findings have to be standardised before they can be pooled. This is done by examining the size of the effect of the intervention in each study against the variability. Variability is referred to as the 'standard deviation' (see above).

Systematic review: A process that uses an explicit and transparent methodology to re-analyse and synthesise evidence from previously conducted research studies on a given topic. Systematic reviews are generally classed as 'research on research' or secondary research because they do not collect new data but use the findings from previous research.

Thematic analysis: A process whereby findings are summarised and synthesised and presented as a narrative using identified themes. The focus is primarily on providing a summary rather than new insight. Findings are generally preserved in their original form.

Theme: A unit of meaning that occurs regularly in data.

Theoretical sampling: A form of purposive sampling used in grounded theory, with participants selected on the basis of emerging study data.

Variable: Something that can change between different situations or different individuals, e.g. body temperature.

Theory: Assumptions and knowledge pertaining to a topic.

Theoretical framework: Underlying theory pertaining to a specific topic that serves to contextualise a literature review.

REFERENCES

Ahmed, J., Mehmood, S., Rehman, S., Ilyas, C. and Khan, L.U.R. (2012) 'Impact of a structured template and staff training on compliance and quality of clinical handover', *International Journal of Surgery*, 10: 571–4.

Anderson, S., Allen, P., Peckham, S. and Goodwin, N. (2008) 'Asking the right questions: scoping studies in the commissioning of research on the organisation and delivery of health services', *Health Research Policy and Systems*, 6 (7), available at: www.health-policy-systems.com/content/6/1/7 (accessed: 19 May 2016).

Anderson, J., Malone, L., Shanahan, K. and Manning, J. (2014) 'Nursing bedside clinical handover – an integrated review of issues and tools', *Journal of Clinical Nursing*, 24: 662–71.

Arai, L., Britten, N., Popay, J., Roberts, H., Petticrew, M., Rodgers, M. and Sowden, A. (2009) 'Testing methodological developments in the conduct of narrative synthesis: a demonstration review of research on the implementation of smoke alarm interventions', *Evidence and Policy*, 3 (3): 361–83.

Arksey, H. and O'Malley, L. (2005) 'Scoping studies: towards a methodological framework, *International Journal of Social Research Methodology*, 8 (1): 19–32.

Armstrong, R., Hall, B.J., Doyle, J. and Waters, E. (2011) Cochrane Update 'Scoping the scope of a Cochrane Review', *Journal of Public Health*, 33 (1): 147–150.

Atkins, S., Lewin, S., Smith, H., Engel, M., Fretheim, A. and Volmink, J. (2008) 'Conducting a meta-ethnography of qualitative literature: lessons learnt', *BMC Medical Research Methodology*, 8 (21), available at: http://biomedcentral.com/1471-2288/8/21 (accessed: 19 May 2016).

Avdic, A. and Eklund, A. (2010) 'Searching the reference databases: what students experience and what teachers believe that students experience', *Journal of Librarianship and Information Science*, 42: 224–35.

Aveyard, H. (2010) *Doing a Literature Review in Health and Social Care: A Practical Guide*. 2nd edn. Maidenhead: McGraw-Hill/Open University Press.

Aveyard, H. (2014) *Doing a Literature Review in Health and Social Care: A Practical Guide*. 3rd edn. Maidenhead: Open University Press.

Baker, J. D. (2016) 'The purpose, process and methods of writing a literature review', *AORN*, 103 (3): 265–9.

Barnett-Page, E. and Thomas, J. (2009) 'Methods for the synthesis of qualitative research: a critical review', *BMC Medical Research Methodology*, 9 (59), available at: www.biomedcentral.com/1471-2288/9/59 (accessed: 19 May 2016).

Beauchamp, T.L. and Childress, J.F. (2013) *Principles of Biomedical Ethics*. 7th edn. Oxford: Oxford University Press.

Berkhof, M., van Rijssen, H.J., Schellart, A.J.M., Anema, J.R. and van der Beek, A.J. (2011) 'Effective training strategies for teaching communication skills to physicians: an overview of systematic reviews', *Patient Education and Counseling*, 84: 152–62.

Bettany-Saltikov, J. (2012) *How to Do a Systematic Literature Review in Nursing. A Step-by-Step Guide*. Maidenhead: Open University Press.

Bissonnette, J. (2008) 'Adherence: a concept analysis', *Journal of Advanced Nursing*, 63 (6): 634–43.

Bondas, T. and Hall, E.O.C. (2007) 'A decade of metasynthesis research in health sciences: a meta-method study', *International Journal of Qualitative Studies on Health and Well-being*, 2: 101–13.

Booth, A., Papaioannou, D. and Sutton, A. (2012) *Systematic Approaches to a Successful Literature Review*. Los Angeles, CA: Sage.

Booth, A., Rees, A. and Beecroft, C. (2010) 'Systematic reviews and evidence synthesis', in K. Gerrish and A. Lacey (eds) *The Research Process in Nursing*. 6th edn. Oxford: Wiley-Blackwell. pp. 284–302.

Bost, N., Crilly, J., Patterson, E. and Chaboyer, W. (2012) 'Clinical handover of patients arriving by ambulance to a hospital emergency department: a qualitative study', *International Emergency Nursing*, 20: 133–41.

Broome, M.E. (2000) 'Integrative literature reviews for the development of concepts', in B.L. Rodgers and K.A. Knafl (eds) *Concept Development in Nursing: Foundations, Techniques and Applications*. 2nd edn. Philadelphia, PA: Saunders. pp. 231–50.

Brunton, G., Wiggins, M. and Oakley, A. (2011) *Becoming a Mother: A Research Synthesis of Women's Views on the Experience of First-time Motherhood*. London: EPPI Centre, Social Science Research Unit, Institute of Education, University of London.

Brunton, G., Caird, J., Sutcliffe, K., Rees, R., Stokes, G., Oliver, S., Stansfield, C., Llewellyn, A., Simmonds, M. and Thomas, J. (2015) *Depression, Anxiety, Pain and Quality of Life in People Living With Chronic Hepatitis C: A Systematic Review and Meta-Analysis*. London: EPPI-Centre, Social Science Research Unit, UCL Institute of Education, University College London.

Brusco, J.M. (2010) 'Effectively conducting an advanced literature search', *AORN*, 92 (3): 264–71.

Camak, D.J. (2015) 'Addressing the burden of stroke caregivers: a literature review', *Journal of Clinical Nursing*, 24 (17–18): 2376–82.

Campbell, R., Pound, P., Morgan, M., Daker-White, G., Britten, N., Pill, R., Yardley, L., Pope, C. and Donovan, J. (2011) 'Evaluating meta-ethnography: systematic analysis and synthesis of qualitative research', *Health Technology Assessment*, 15 (43): ISSN 1366–5278.

Catling-Paull, C., Johnston, R., Ryan, C., Foureur, M.J. and Homer, C.S.E. (2011) 'Clinical interventions that increase the uptake and success of vaginal birth after caesarean section: a systematic review', *Journal of Advanced Nursing*, 67 (8): 1646–61.

Centre for Reviews and Dissemination (CRD) (2009) *Systematic Reviews: CRD's Guidance for Undertaking Reviews in Health Care*. York: CRD, University of York.

Chapman, A.L., Morgant, L.C. and Gartlehner, G. (2010) 'Semi-automating the manual literature search for systematic reviews increases efficiency', *Health Information & Libraries Journal*, 27 (1): 22–7.

Clarke, M. (2006) 'Systematic review and meta-analysis of quantitative research: overview of methods' (Part 1, Chapter 1), in C. Webb and B. Roe (eds) *Reviewing Research Evidence for Nursing Practice: Systematic Reviews*. Oxford: Blackwell Publishing. pp. 3–8.

Colquhoun, H.L., Levac, D., O'Brien, K.K., Straus, S., Tricco, A.C., Perrier, L., Kastner, M. and Moher, D. (2014) 'Scoping reviews: time for clarity in definition, methods and reporting', *Journal of Clinical Epidemiology*, 67: 1291–4.

Coughlan, M., Cronin, P. and Ryan, F. (2007) 'Step-by-step guide to critiquing research. Part 1: quantitative research', *British Journal of Nursing*, 16 (11): 658–63.

Critical Appraisal Skills Programme (CASP) (2013) Appraisal tools. Available at: www.casp-uk.net/#!casp-tools-checklists/c18f8 (accessed: 19 May 2016).

Cronin, P. and Rawlings-Anderson, K. (2004) *Knowledge for Contemporary Nursing Practice*. Edinburgh: Mosby.

Cronin, P., Coughlan, M. and Smith, V. (2015). *Understanding Nursing and Healthcare Research*. London: Sage.

Cronin, P., Ryan, F. and Coughlan, M. (2010) 'Concept analysis in healthcare research', *International Journal of Therapy and Rehabilitation*, 17 (2): 62–8.

Davis, K., Drey, N. and Gould, D. (2009) 'What are scoping studies? A review of the nursing literature', *International Journal of Nursing Studies*. 46: 1386–400.

Day, J. and Higgins, I. (2015) 'Adult family member experiences during an older loved one's delirium: a narrative literature review', *Journal of Clinical Nursing*, 24: 1447–56.

Ely, C. and Scott, I. (2007) *Essential Study Skills for Nursing*. Edinburgh: Mosby.

Engberg, S. (2008) 'Systematic reviews and meta-analysis', *Journal of Wound Ostomy Continence Nursing*, 35 (3): 258–65.

Evans, D. (2003) 'Hierarchy of evidence: a framework for ranking evidence evaluating healthcare interventions', *Journal of Clinical Nursing*, 12: 77–84.

Evidence for Policy and Practice Information and Co-ordinating Centre (EPPI Centre) (2010) *EPPI-Centre Methods for Conducting Systematic Reviews*. London: EPPI-Centre, Social Science Research Unit, Institute of Education, University of London, available at: http://eppi. ioe.ac.uk/cms/LinkClick.aspx?fileticket=hQBu8y4uVwI%3D (accessed: 19 May 2016).

Fellowes, D., Wilkinson, S. and Moore, P. (2004) 'Communication skills training for health care professionals working with cancer patients, their families and/or carers', *Cochrane Database Systematic Reviews 2004*: CD003751.

Finfgeld-Connett, D.L. (2008) 'Meta-synthesis of caring in nursing', *Journal of Clinical Nursing*, 17: 196–204.

Finfgeld-Connett, D.L. (2010) 'Generalizability and transferability of meta-synthesis research findings', *Journal of Advanced Nursing*, 66 (2): 246–54.

Finlayson, K. and Dixon, A. (2008) 'Qualitative meta-synthesis: a guide for the novice', *Nurse Researcher*, 15 (2): 59–71.

Flemming, K. (2007) 'Synthesis of qualitative research and evidence-based nursing', *British Journal of Nursing*, 16 (10): 616–20.

Foran, C. and Brennan, A. (2015) 'Prevention and early detection of cervical cancer in the UK', *British Journal of Nursing (Oncology Supplement)*, 24 (10): S22–S29.

Fowler, J. (2015a) 'From staff nurse to nurse consultant: writing for publication part 6: writing the abstract', *British Journal of Nursing*, 24 (22): 1170.

Fowler, J. (2015b) 'From staff nurse to nurse consultant: writing for publication part 3: following the journal guidelines', *British Journal of Nursing*, 24 (19): 978.

Fowler, J. (2016a) 'From staff nurse to nurse consultant: writing for publication part 7: structure and presentation', *British Journal of Nursing*, 25 (1): 66.

Fowler, J. (2016b) 'Writing for publication part 11: writing conference abstracts', *British Journal of Nursing*, 25 (5): 278.

France, E.F., Ring, N., Thomas, R., Noyes, J., Maxwell, M. and Jepson, R. (2014) 'A methodological systematic review of what's wrong with meta-ethnography reporting', *BMC Medical Research Methodology*, 14 (119), available at: http://bmcmedresmethodol. biomedcentral.com/articles/10.1186/1471-2288-14-119 (accessed: 19 May 2016).

Gerrish, K. and Lacey, A. (2010) 'Disseminating research findings', in K. Gerrish and A. Lacey (eds) *The Research Process in Nursing*. 6th edn. Oxford: Wiley-Blackwell. pp. 475–87.

Glasper, E.A. and Peate, I. (2013) 'Writing for publication: science and healthcare journals', *British Journal of Nursing*, 22 (16): 964–8.

Gonçalves-Bradley, D.C., Lannin, N.A., Clemson, L.M., Cameron, I.D. and Shepperd, S. (2016) 'Discharge planning from hospital', *Cochrane Database of Systematic Reviews* 2016, Issue 1. Art. No.: CD000313. DOI: 10.1002/14651858.CD000313.pub5.

Gough, D., Oliver, S. and Thomas, J. (2012) *An Introduction to Systematic Reviews*. London: Sage.

Grant, M., Cavanagh, A. and Yorke, J. (2012) 'The impact of caring for those with chronic obstructive pulmonary disease (COPD) on carers' psychological well-being: a narrative review', *International Journal of Nursing Studies*. DOI: 10.1016/j.ijnurstu.2012.02.010.

Greenhalgh, T., Wong, G., Westhorp, G. and Pawson, R. (2011) 'Protocol – realist and meta-narrative evidence synthesis: evolving standards (RAMESES)', *BioMed Central Medical Research Methodology*. 11: 115, available at: www.biomedcentral.com/1471-2288/11/115 (accessed: 19 May 2016).

Grove, S., Burns, N. and Gray, J. (2013). *The Practice of Nursing Research: Appraisal, Synthesis and Generation of Evidence*. St Louis, MO: Elsevier Saunders.

Guyatt, G., Cook, D. and Haynes, B. (2004) 'Evidence based medicine has come a long way', *British Medical Journal*, 329: 390–1.

Hamer, S. and Collinson, G. (2005) *Achieving Evidence-based Practice. A Handbook for Practitioners*. 2nd edn. Edinburgh: Baillière Tindall.

Hamm, M.P., Chisholm, A., Shulhan, J., Milne, A., Scott, S.D., Given, L.M. and Hartling, L. (2013a) 'Social media use among patients and caregivers: a scoping review', *BMJ Open*. 3:e002819. DOI: 10.1136/bmjopen-2013-002819.

Hamm, M.P., Chisholm, A., Shulhan, J., Milne, A., Scott, S.D., Klassen, T.P. and Hartling, L. (2013b) 'Social media use by healthcare professionals and trainees: a scoping review', *Academic Medicine*, 88 (9): 1376–83.

Harrison, S.L., Apps, L., Singh, S.J., Steiner, M.C., Morgan, M.D.L. and Robertson, N. (2014) '"Consumed by breathing" – a critical interpretive meta-synthesis of the qualitative literature', *Chronic Illness*, 10 (1): 31–49.

Hayes, C., Jackson, D., Davidson, M. and Power, T. (2015) 'Medication errors in hospital: a literature review of disruptions to nursing practice during medication administration', *Journal of Clinical Nursing*, 24 (21–22): 3063–76.

Hek, G. and Langton, H. (2000) 'Systematically searching and reviewing literature', *Nurse Researcher*, 7 (3): 40–57.

Higgins, J.P.T. and Green, S. (eds) (2011) *Cochrane Handbook for Systematic Reviews of Interventions Version 5.1*. The Cochrane Collaboration, available at: http://handbook. cochrane.org/ (accessed: 19 May 2016).

Ho, S. and Holloway, A. (2016) 'The impact of HIV-related stigma on the lives of HIV-positive women: an integrated literature review', *Journal of Clinical Nursing*, 25 (1–2): 8–19.

Hole, J., Hirsch, M., Ball, E. and Meads, C. (2015) 'Music as an aid for postoperative recovery in adults: a systematic review and meta-analysis', *The Lancet*, 386 (10004): 1659–71, available at: http://www.thelancet.com/journals/lancet/article/PIIS0140-6736%2815%2960169-6/abstract (accessed: 19 May 2016).

Holly, C. and Poletick, E.B. (2014) 'A systematic review on the transfer of information during nurse transitions in care', *Journal of Clinical Nursing*, 23 (17–18): 2387–96.

Horrom, T.A. (2012) 'The perils of copy and paste: plagiarism in scientific publishing', *Journal of Rehabilitation Research & Development*, 49 (8): vii–xii.

Johnston, B., Larkin, P., Connolly, M., Barry, C., Narayanasamy, M., Östlund, U. and McIlfatrick, S. (2015) 'Dignity-conserving care in palliative care settings: an integrative review', *Journal of Clinical Nursing*, 24: 1743–72.

Johnson, N. and Taylor, R. (2014) 'Using research and evidence in practice', in R. Taylor (ed.) *The Essentials of Nursing and Healthcare Research*. London: Sage. pp. 265–88.

Klimaszewski, A.D. (2012) 'Preventing plagiarism', *Oncology Nursing Forum*, 39 (6): 525–7.

Koch, T. (2006) 'Establishing rigour in qualitative research: the decision trail', *Journal of Advanced Nursing*, 53 (1): 91–103.

Kübler-Ross, E. (1969) *On Death and Dying*. New York: Macmillan.

Lahlafi, A. (2007) 'Conducting a literature review: how to carry out bibliographical database searches', *British Journal of Cardiac Nursing*, 2 (12): 566–9.

Lane, C. and Rollnick, S. (2007) 'The use of simulated patients and role-play in communication skills training: a review of the literature to August 2005', *Patient Education and Counseling*, 67: 13–20.

Larun, L. and Malterud, K. (2007) 'Identity and coping experiences in Chronic Fatigue Syndrome: a synthesis of qualitative studies', *Patient Education and Counseling*, 69: 20–8.

Levac, D., Colquhoun, H. and O'Brien, K.K. (2010) 'Scoping studies: advancing the methodology', *Implementation Science*, 5: 69. DOI: 10.1186/1748-5908-5-69.

Liberati, A., Altman, D.G., Tetzlaff, J., Mulrow, C., Gøtzsche, P.C., Loannidis, J.P.A, Clarke, M., Devereaux, P.J., Kleijnen, J. and Moher, D. (2009) 'The PRISMA Statement for reporting systematic reviews and meta-analyses of studies that evaluate health care interventions: explanation and elaboration', *PLoS Medicine*, 6 (7): 1–28.

Lindahl, B. and Lindblad, B.M. (2011) 'Family members' experiences of everyday life when a child is dependent on a ventilator: a metasynthesis study', *Journal of Family Nursing*, 17: 241–69.

Marshall, J., Goldbart, J., Pickstone, C. and Roulstone, S. (2011) 'Application of systematic reviews in speech-and-language therapy', *International Journal of Language and Communication Disorders*, 46 (3): 261–72.

Maxwell, J.A. (2006) 'Literature reviews of, and for, educational research: a commentary on Boote and Beile's "Scholars Before Researchers"', *Educational Researcher*, 35 (9): 28–31.

Mays, N., Pope, C. and Popay, J. (2005) 'Systematically reviewing qualitative and quantitative evidence to inform management and policy-making in the health field', *Journal of Health Services Research and Policy*, 10 (Suppl. 1): 6–20.

McCabe, M. (2009) 'Fatigue in children with long-term conditions: an evolutionary concept analysis', *Journal of Advanced Nursing*, 65 (8): 1735–45.

McGinn, T., Taylor, B., McColgan, M. and McQuilkan, J. (2014) 'Social work literature searching: current issues with databases and online search engines', *Research on Social Work Practice*, 21 September: 1–12.

Moher, D., Liberati, A., Tetzlaff, J., Altman, D.G. and The PRISMA Group (2009) 'Preferred reporting items for systematic reviews and meta-analyses: the PRISMA Statement', *PLoS Med.* 6 (6), available at: http://journals.plos.org/plosmedicine/article?id=10.1371/journal.pmed.1000097 (accessed: 19 May 2016).

Morse, J.M. (2009) 'Mixing qualitative methods', *Qualitative Health Research*, 19 (11): 1523–4.

Morse, J.M. (2015) 'Critical analysis of strategies for determining rigor in qualitative research', *Qualitative Health Research*, 25 (9): 1212–22.

Muir Gray, J.A. (2001) *Evidence-based Health Care*. Edinburgh: Churchill Livingstone.

Murphy, S.M., Irving, C.B., Adams, C.E. and Waqar, M. (2015) 'Crisis intervention for people with severe mental illnesses', *Cochrane Database of Systematic Reviews* 2015, Issue 12. Art. No.: CD001087. DOI: 10.1002/14651858.CD001087.pub5.

Nepal, V.P. (2010) 'On mixing qualitative methods', *Qualitative Health Research*, 20 (2): 281.

Noblit, G.W. and Hare, R.D. (1988) *Meta-ethnography: Synthesising Qualitative Studies*. London: Sage.

Noyes, J. and Lewin, S. (2011) 'Chapter 5: Extracting qualitative evidence', in J. Noyes, A. Booth, K. Hannes, A. Harden, J. Harris, S. Lewin and C. Lockwood (eds) *Supplementary Guidance for Inclusion of Qualitative Research in Cochrane Systematic Reviews of Interventions*. Version 1 (updated August 2011). Cochrane Collaboration Qualitative Methods Group, available at: http://cqrmg.cochrane.org/supplemental-handbook-guidance (accessed: 19 May 2016).

Parahoo, K. (2014) *Nursing Research, Principles, Process and Issues*. 3rd edn. London: Palgrave.

Paterson, B., Canam, C., Joachim, G. and Thorne, S. (2003) 'Embedded assumptions in qualitative studies of fatigue', *Western Journal of Nursing Research*, 25 (2): 119–33.

Paterson, B., Dubouloz, C.J., Chevrier, J., Ashe, B., King, J. and Moldoveanu, M. (2009) 'Conducting qualitative metasynthesis research: insights from a metasynthesis project', *International Journal of Qualitative Methods*, 8 (3): 22–33.

Paterson, B., Thorne, S., Canam, C. and Jillings, C. (2001) *Meta-Study of Qualitative Health Research. A Practical Guide to Meta-Analysis and Meta-Synthesis*. Thousand Oaks, CA: Sage.

Pawson, R., Greenhalgh, T., Harvey, G. and Walshe, K. (2005) 'Realist review – a new method of systematic review designed for complex policy interventions', *Journal of Health Services Research and Policy.* 10 (Suppl. 1): 21–34.

Pinto, R.A., Holanda, M.A., Medeiros, M.M.C., Mota, R.M.S. and Pereira, E.D.B. (2007) 'Assessment of the burden of caregiving for patients with chronic obstructive pulmonary disease', *Respiratory Medicine*, 101 (11): 2402–8.

Polit, D.F. and Beck, C.T. (2012) *Nursing Research: Generating and Assessing Evidence for Nursing Practice*. 9th edn. Philadelphia, PA: Wolters Kluwer Health/Lippincott Williams & Wilkins.

Polit, D.F. and Beck C.T. (2014) *Essentials of Nursing Research: Appraising Evidence for Nursing Practice*. 8th edn. Philadelphia, PA: Wolters Kluwer/Lippincott Williams & Wilkins.

Popay, J., Roberts, H., Sowden, A., Petticrew, M., Arai, L. and Rodgers, M. (2006) *Guidance on the Conduct of Narrative Synthesis in Systematic Reviews. Final report*. Swindon: ESRC Methods Programme.

Price, B. (2009) 'Guidance on conducting a literature search and reviewing mixed literature', *Nursing Standard*, 23 (24): 43–9.

Price, B. (2014) 'Avoiding plagiarism: guidance for nursing students', *Nursing Standard*, 28 (26): 45–51.

Price, S.L. (2009) 'Becoming a nurse: a meta-study of early professional socialization and career choice in nursing', *Journal of Advanced Nursing*, 65 (1): 11–19.

Quinlan, E., Robertson, S., Millar, N. and Robertson-Boersma, D. (2014) 'Interventions to reduce bullying in health care organisations; a scoping review', *Health Services Management*, 27(1–2): 33–44.

Rebar, C.R., Gersch, C.J., MacNee, C.L. and McCabe, S. (2011) *Understanding Nursing Research*. 3rd edn. Philadelphia, PA: Wolters Kluwer Health/Lippincott Williams & Wilkins.

Rees, R., Caird, J., Dickson, K., Vigurs, C. and Thomas, J. (2013) *The Views Of Young People in the UK about Obesity, Body Size, Shape and Weight: A Systematic Review*. London: EPPI-Centre, Social Science Research Unit, Institute of Education, University of London.

Ridley, D. (2008) *The Literature Review: A Step-by-Step Guide for Students*. Los Angeles, CA: Sage.

Ring, N., Ritchie, K., Mandava, L. and Jepson, R. (2010) 'A guide to synthesising qualitative research for researchers undertaking health technology assessments and systematic reviews', *NHS Quality Improvement Scotland*, available at: www.nhshealthquality.org/nhsqis/8837.html (accessed: 19 May 2016).

Rivas, C., Ramsay, J., Sadowski, L., Davidson, L.L., Dunne, D., Eldridge, S., Hegarty, K., Taft, A. and Feder, G. (2015) 'Advocacy interventions to reduce or eliminate violence and promote the physical and psychosocial well-being of women who experience intimate partner abuse', *Cochrane Database of Systematic Reviews*. Issue 12. Art. No.: CD005043.

Rodgers, B.L. (2000) 'Concept analysis: an evolutionary view', in B.L. Rodgers and K.A. Knafl (2000) *Concept Development in Nursing: Foundations, Techniques and Applications*. 2nd edn. Philadelphia, PA: Saunders. pp. 77–102.

Rodgers, M., Sowden, A., Petticrew, M., Arai, L., Roberts, H., Britten, N. and Popay, J. (2009) 'Testing methodological guidance on the conduct of narrative synthesis in systematic reviews', *Evaluation*, 15 (1): 47–71.

Ryan, F., Coughlan, M. and Cronin, P. (2007) 'Step-by-step guide to critiquing research. Part 2: qualitative research', *British Journal of Nursing*, 16 (12): 738–44.

Ryan-Wenger, N. (1992) 'Guidelines for critique of a research report', *Heart and Lung*, 21 (4): 394–401.

Sackett, D.L., Rosenberg, W.M.C., Muir Gray, J.A., Haynes, R.B. and Scott Richardson, W. (1996) 'Evidence based medicine: what it is and what it isn't', *British Medical Journal*, 312 (7023): 71.

Sandelowski, M. (2008) 'Justifying qualitative research (Editorial)', *Research in Nursing and Health*, 31: 193–5.

Sandelowski, M. and Barroso, J. (2003) 'Creating metasummaries of qualitative findings', *Nursing Research*, 52 (4): 226–33.

Sandelowski, M. and Barroso, J. (2007) *Handbook for Synthesizing Qualitative Research*. New York: Springer.

Sandelowski, M., Barroso, J. and Voils, C.I. (2007) 'Using qualitative metasummary to synthesize qualitative and quantitative descriptive findings', *Research in Nursing and Health*, 30: 99–111.

Schöpfel, J. (2010) 'Towards a Prague definition of grey literature', *Twelfth International Conference on Grey Literature: Transparency in Grey Literature. Grey Tech Approaches to High Tech Issues*. Prague. 6–7 December: 11–26.

Scottish Intercollegiate Guidelines Network (SIGN) (2013) *Methodology Checklist 1: Systematic Reviews and Meta-analysis*, available at: www.sign.ac.uk/methodology/checklists.html (accessed: 19 May 2016).

Seamark, D.A., Blake, S.D., Seamark, C.J. and Halpin, D.M. (2004) 'Living with severe chronic obstructive pulmonary disease (COPD): perceptions of patients and their carers. An interpretative phenomenological analysis', *Palliative Medicine*, 18 (7): 619–25.

Shea, B.J., Grimshaw, J.M., Wells, G.A., Boers, M., Andersson, N., Hamel, C., Porter, A.C., Tugwell, P., Moher, D. and Bouter, L.M. (2007) 'Development of AMSTAR: a measurement tool to assess the methodological quality of systematic reviews', *BioMed Central Medical Research Methodology*. 7 (10), available at: www.biomedcentral.com/1471-2288/7/10 (accessed 19 May 2016).

Singata, M., Tranmer. J. and Gyte, G.M.L. (2013) 'Restricting oral fluid and food intake during labour', *Cochrane Database of Systematic Reviews*. Issue 8. Art. No.: CD003930.

Smith, C.M. and Baker, B. (2007) 'Technology in nursing scholarship', *International Journal of Mental Health Nursing*, 16: 156–160.

Spilsbury, K., Hewitt, C. and Bowman, C. (2011) 'The relationship between nurse staffing and quality of care in nursing homes: a systematic review', *International Journal of Nursing Studies*, 48: 732–50.

Staggers, N. and Blaz, J.W. (2013) 'Research on nursing handoffs for medical and surgical settings: an integrative review', *Journal of Advanced Nursing*, 69: 247–62.

Stroup, D.F., Berlin, J.A., Morton, S.C., Olkin, I., Williamson, G.D., Rennie, D., Moher, D., Becker, B.J., Sipe, T.A. and Thacker, S.B. (2000) 'Meta-analysis of observational studies in epidemiology: a proposal for reporting. Meta-analysis of Observational Studies in Epidemiology (MOOSE) group', *JAMA*, 283 (15): 2008–12.

Thorne, S., Paterson, B., Acorn, S., Canam, C., Joachim, G. and Jillings, C. (2002) 'Chronic illness experience: insights from a metastudy', *Qualitative Research*, 12 (4): 437–52.

Tong, A., Sainsbury, P. and Craig, J. (2007) 'Consolidated criteria for reporting qualitative research (COREQ): 32-item checklist for interviews and focus groups', *International Journal for Quality in Health Care*, 19 (6): 349–57.

Tong, A., Flemming, K., McInnes, E., Oliver, S. and Craig, J. (2012) 'Enhancing transparency in reporting the synthesis of qualitative research: ENTREQ', *BMC Medical Research Methodology*. 12 (181), available at: www.biomedcentral.com/1471-2288/12/181 (accessed: 19 May 2016).

Torraco, R.J. (2005) 'Writing integrative literature reviews: guidelines and examples', *Human Resource Development Review*, 4 (3): 356–67.

Truss, L. (2003) *Eats, Shoots & Leaves: the Zero Tolerance Approach to Punctuation*. London: Profile Books.

Turnitin (2012) *The Plagiarism Spectrum: Tagging 10 Types of Unoriginal Work*, available at: http://turnitin.com/assets/en_us/media/plagiarism_spectrum.php (accessed: 19 May 2016).

University of Queensland Library (2016) *Referencing Style Guides*, available at: https://www.library.uq.edu.au/research-tools-techniques/referencing-style-guides#harvard (accessed: 19 May 2016).

Wakefield, A. (2014) 'Searching and critiquing the research literature', *Nursing Standard*, 28 (39): 49–57.

Walker, J. (2010) 'Measuring plagiarism: researching what students do, not what they say they do', *Studies in Higher Education*, 35 (1): 41–59.

Walker, L. and Avant, K. (2011) *Strategies for Theory Construction in Nursing*. 5th edn. Norwalk, CT: Appleton & Lange.

Walsh, D. and Downe, S. (2005) 'Meta-synthesis method for qualitative research: a literature review', *Journal of Advanced Nursing*, 50 (2): 204–11.

Walshe, C. and Luker, K. (2010) 'District nurses' role in palliative care provision: a realist review', *International Journal of Nursing Studies*, 47 (9): 1167–83.

Whiting, L.S. (2009) 'Systematic review protocols: an introduction', *Nurse Researcher*, 17 (1): 34–43.

Whittaker, A. and Williamson, G.R. (2011) *Succeeding in Research Project Plans and Literature Reviews for Nursing Students*. Exeter: Learning Matters.

Whittemore, R. and Knafl, K. (2005) 'The integrative review: updated methodology', *Journal of Advanced Nursing*, 52 (5): 546–53.

Williams, A. and Manias, E. (2008) 'A structured literature review of pain assessment and management of patients with kidney disease', *Journal of Clinical Nursing*, 17: 69–81.

Wittenauer, J., Ludwick, R., Baughman., K. and Fishbein, R. (2015) 'Surveying the hidden attitudes of hospital nurses towards poverty', *Journal of Clinical Nursing*, 24 (15–16): 2184–91.

Yesufu-Udechuku, A., Harrison, B., Mayo-Wilson, E., Young, N., Woodhams, P., Shiers, D., Kuipers, E. and Kendall, T. (2015) 'Interventions to improve the experience of caring for people with severe mental illness: systematic review and meta-analysis', *British Journal of Psychiatry*, 206 (4): 268–74, available at: http://bjp.rcpsych.org/content/206/4/268.long (accessed: 19 May 2016).

Zafron, M.L. (2012) 'Good intentions: providing students with skills to avoid accidental plagiarism', *Medical Reference Services Quarterly*, 31 (2): 225–9.

Zhang, W., Barriball, K.L. and While, A.E. (2014) 'Nurses' attitudes towards medical devices in healthcare delivery: a systematic review', *Journal of Clinical Nursing*, 23 (19–20): 2725–39.

Zhao, S. (1991) 'Metatheory, metamethod, meta-data-analysis: what, why, and how?', *Sociological Perspectives*, 34 (3): 377–90.

INDEX